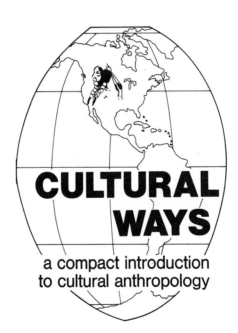

CULTURAL WAYS

a compact introduction
to cultural anthropology

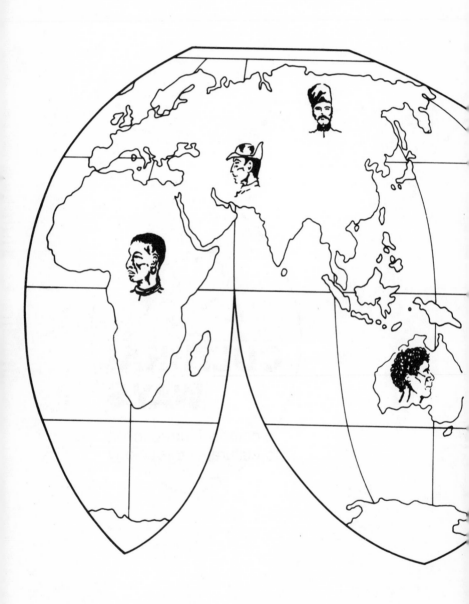

ALLYN AND BACON, INC. • BOSTON, MASS.

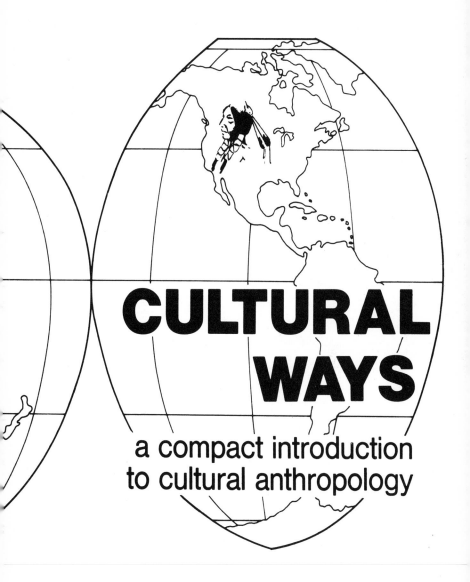

CULTURAL
WAYS

a compact introduction
to cultural anthropology

ROBERT B. TAYLOR
KANSAS STATE UNIVERSITY

PREFACE

Perhaps the main value of anthropology is the superior understanding of human nature to be derived from the investigation of the variety and total range of socially standardized responses to the circumstances of human living. It is a corrective to the culture-bound approach, which views things from the narrow perspective of one's native cultural background. In each aspect of human culture this introduction seeks to provide an appreciation of the range and variety of ways in which anthropologists have found human groups behaving and thinking. This approach, I suppose, is the one used by most authors of general works for students. Implicitly or explicitly, most anthropologists hope that people will learn from anthropology that there is more than one way to skin a cat and that there are means of which they may never have heard or may never have understood fully which work pretty well. Probably, many anthropologists also hope that such knowledge, in the long run, will result in improved human relations around the world.

This work introduces the basic concepts of cultural anthropology with minimum use of illustration or in-depth exploration. Illustrative material has been incorporated only when it was felt necessary to clarify a point; when it seemed desirable to forcibly emphasize a fundamental idea; or to provide relief from continuous explication of abstract concepts. This was done to achieve brevity, which, in turn, is to provide time for the exploration of primary and descriptive sources which will deepen the student's understanding and appreciation of the concepts. The basic rationale includes both the notion that concepts must be explicitly presented and the principle that they can be most effectively absorbed by exposure to ethnographic and other original anthropological writings. *Cultural Ways* emphasizes the former as a foundation for the latter.

Such a brief statement should prove useful in semester introductions to cultural anthropology and in those portions of general anthropology courses having to do with ethnology and the culture concept. The first version of *Cultural Ways* was used for several years as basic preparation for the study of six cultures from different parts of the world. The students were asked to relate the descriptive material to the concepts they had learned during the first weeks of the course. The book also can be used in conjunction with the several widely-used collections of anthropology readings. Whichever materials are used, I hope that the concepts are presented with sufficient substance and clarity to make the book useful either for formal courses or for independent study.

In a work as brief as this, trying to do justice to physical anthropology and archaeology in addition to ethnology often results in thinness. Therefore, although thoroughly convinced of the importance of the biological and the prehistoric in anthropology, I have limited my task pretty much to introducing ethnological concepts. Within this limitation I have attempted to achieve balance and reasonable coverage. Only in this way can the material constitute an adequate foundation for further study.

It is impossible in a work dealing with elementary concepts to give credit for the origins of all of my ideas; nor will I try. Surely most anthropologists are unable to remember when and where they first became familiar with many of the field's basic notions and findings. I only know that I have learned, not only from teachers of anthropology and from anthropological literature, but also from thoughtful, articulate students who have sharpened my understandings by questioning them and driving me to a more careful exploration of them. The present revision has been aided in large part by the reactions of students who have used the original version in duplicated form. Perhaps it is to them that I owe my greatest thanks. I am also especially grateful for the help given me by Paul G. Hiebert, James O. Morgan, and Patricia J. O'Brien, who evaluated portions of the manuscript and suggested improvements.

R.B.T.

CONTENTS

THE NATURE OF ANTHROPOLOGY

Anthropology is one of the most diverse of the academic disciplines. In fact, the anthropologist is willing to probe any area which shows promise of contributing to the solution of his problems. He may be interested, for example, in how blood types are inherited, techniques of disciplining children, the position of the opening in the base of the skull, or the socio-psychological functions of witchcraft.

Such diversity creates difficulties. For one thing, there is the apparent danger that specialists in the various branches of anthropology will lose touch with one another and the field will disintegrate. Moreover, there is the difficulty suffered by every anthropologist of becoming and remaining familiar with a wide variety of concepts, methods, and findings. Anthropologists, nevertheless, value this diversity and exert no little effort to maintain unity. In the United States, particularly, it is necessary to take training in all major subdivisions of anthropology to secure a doctoral degree; and several of the major journals publish articles from all areas of the field. Anthropologists intermittently discuss the problem of maintaining the unity of their discipline against the disintegrative pull of its diversity.

THE DEVELOPMENT OF ANTHROPOLOGY

A brief look at the development of anthropology can help one understand the reasons for this diversity and why anthropologists value it.

During the decades before the field began to be regarded as a single discipline, men from a variety of professions were pursuing the several lines of investigation which since have become firmly ensconced within anthropology. Many thinkers were interested in the notion of biological evolution, which was suggested, in part, by the similarities of men to the apes and other manlike primates. Others, interested in the strange physical appearance of exotic groups, were busy classifying them into races and trying to account for their existence. Note that both of these inquiries are concerned mainly with man's biological side. On the cultural side, amateur archaeologists were much intrigued by the evidence for the existence of prehistoric cultures, found in the form of crudely worked tools in association with the bones of extinct mammals. There also was much investigation and discussion of the odd "manners and customs" of the so-called savages or primitives.

It was during the second half of the nineteenth century that these interests—biological evolution, race, prehistoric cultures, and primitive cultures—came to be recognized as the concerns of a single discipline. Though no specific date or event marks this union, the convergent tendencies of the anthropological interests are illustrated by Paul Broca's definition of anthropology on the occasion of the founding of the Anthropological Society of Paris in 1859. He mentioned the investigation of man's biological characteristics as well as his intellectual and social traits, which easily includes the various interests in process of merging under the banner of anthropology. In subsequent statements Broca noted a diversity of endeavors by the members of the Anthropological Society. His report on the period 1865-1867, for example, mentions linguistics, ethnology, archaeology, races, craniometry, and music (1868: 379). Broca's hopes that anthropology would become a truly general study have been well realized, though on the European continent it remains necessary to use the words *prehistory, linguistics, ethnology,* and *anthropology* to cover the entire field.

At least three factors seem to have contributed to the convergence of the various interests. One is the obvious fact that all have to do with man. Of more specific significance is the strong evolutionary implication of each. Scholars were much impressed with the similarities between men and animals; and it was suspected by many that the primitive races and cultures were similar to those of the earlier stages of evolution through which the ancestors of European peoples had passed. Official acceptance of the antiquity of human cultures came in 1859, when the British Association for the Advancement of Science officially approved the long-rejected evidence for prehistoric human tools (Daniel, 1950: 60). It was also in 1859 that the publication of Charles Darwin's *Origin of Species* gave teeth to the long attractive notion of evolution by providing the first reasonable explanation of how biological change might take place, namely, natural selection. Developments of this sort gave further impetus to the utilization of evolutionary notions in both biological and social thought. This evolutionary orientation is still apparent in anthropology's concern with man's biological origins and the study of cultures of the prehistoric past; and, after several decades of unpopularity, evolutionism in the investigation of socio-cultural matters has enjoyed a revival in modified form (Sahlins and Service, 1960: 2ff.). A third factor contributing to the convergence of the several lines of investigation is the simple fact that all dealt with peoples and problems until then neglected by the other sciences of man. Biologists, historians, psychologists, and others largely had ignored those peoples without systems of writing, namely, the world's prehistoric and primitive races and cultures.

SUBDIVISIONS AND SPECIALTIES OF ANTHROPOLOGY

In spite of additions and modifications, an examination of modern anthropology reveals that the previously indicated areas of interest continue to be significant. Two of them, human evolution and race, have to do mainly with man's inherited biological characteristics and are included under *physical anthropology*, one of the two main divisions of this diverse subject. The other main division, *cultural anthropology*, has to do with those human traits learned by people as members of groups and embraces the study of both prehistoric cultures and primitive cultures. The primary distinction between the two divisions is that the former concentrates on the study of genetically transmitted characteristics while the latter is concerned with socially learned traits. A more careful look will reveal the place of these major divisions of interest in modern anthropology.

Human palaeontology is a branch of physical anthropology which seeks to learn about man's origins and evolution through the study of the fossil remains of prehistoric man and near man. *Racial anthropology* concerns itself with biogenetically inherited differences—anatomical, physiological and, provided they exist, psychological—among groups in different parts of the world. *Human genetics* was originally the almost exclusive possession of zoology, but the last generation has witnessed the establishment of a branch within anthropology. The anthropological arm of genetics is closely linked to *racial anthropology*, since the question of how biologically different populations originated and are maintained involves genetic processes. A few anthropologists are concerned with *comparative primatology*, the study of the similarities and differences among the primates, namely, the tree shrews, lemurs and lorises, tarsiers, monkeys, apes, and men. From these comparisons they hope to learn more about man's nature and development. In addition to these major subdivisions, two other specialties should be mentioned. Some physical anthropologists manifest an interest in *constitutional anthropology*, which studies different body builds and their possible relationships to temperament, disease, or other factors. Still others specialize in studying patterns of *human growth*.

Physical anthropology recently has undergone a noteworthy shift. Until World War II much of physical anthropology was concerned with the description and measurement of external biological features as the basis for classifying and comparing human types in different times and places. The new emphasis is on the study of the conditions and processes of change in the genetic makeup of human groups. Consequently, there is less preoccupation with external traits and a much stronger orientation toward the use of any concepts and techniques which will reveal the dynamic mechanisms by which man has come to be what he is biologically. This is why genetics has become so important in the field; and it is the basis for increasing suggestions that the new physical anthropology would better be referred to as *biological anthropology*. It is also important to note that the new physical anthropology is more than ever concerned with understanding man's biology within the context of socially acquired behavior, this in accord with anthropology's traditional emphasis on relating the biological and the cultural to one another in its attempts to understand human nature.

One of the major branches of cultural anthropology is *prehistoric archaeology*, which seeks to learn about extinct ways of life through the excavation and interpretation of their material remains. Usually, the study of literate civilizations of the past, such as ancient Rome or ancient Egypt, is left to classical archaeologists and is not considered a significant endeavor within anthropology.

Another major field of cultural anthropology is *ethnology*, which may be defined as the descriptive and comparative study of the world's cultures, usually nonliterate or other exotic cultures, for the purpose of formulating generalizations about human nature. Ethnology includes the study of techniques, economic organization, kinship, associations, government, law, religion, art, folklore, and other aspects of human culture, any of which may be treated as an area of specialization within cultural anthropology. Ethnologists who emphasize those aspects of culture which most extensively involve relations within and among groups, such as family, kinship organization, law, and political and economic relations, are often referred to as *social anthropologists*. Social anthropologists tend to be less interested in technology, the arts, folklore, religion, language, and cultural history than other cultural anthropologists. The term *ethnography* is applied to the descriptive field work aspect of ethnology and, also, to the written description of a culture which the ethnographer constructs from his field data.

Archaeology and ethnology may be thought of as the two major subdivisions of cultural anthropology. It is well to mention three other important specialties, however, which reasonably can be considered as parts of ethnology but which commonly are granted separate status. This is particularly true of *linguistic anthropology*, which, because language is commonly thought of as occupying a special place among the parts of culture, is usually treated as a major branch of cultural anthropology in its own right.

Another subdivision of cultural anthropology which tends to be given separate status is the study of *culture and personality*, the investigation of the relationships between the personalities of individuals and the ways of life in which they participate. Specialists in this area are particularly interested in how a child's personality is shaped to a pattern provided by the already existing customs, especially as they are impressed through child rearing practices.

Cultural·dynamics, the study of the processes of cultural stability and change, is not always set apart as a branch of cultural anthropology, but its concern with processes and the number of anthropologists who specialize in change studies justify its separation from other aspects of ethnology.

Applied anthropology involves research and consultation for the purpose of collecting and making available to administrators data useful for the solution of practical problems. The knowledge gained by physical anthropology has been applied extensively in the designing of equipment and clothing, the identification of human remains, and in a variety of other problem areas. Cultural anthropology has been used particularly as an aid in the administration of culturally dependent peoples, as in those Pacific Island areas governed by the United States as a trust from the United Nations. The United States Peace Corps and some missionary groups also have used anthropology in preparing their personnel to work successfully in culturally alien places. As long ago as 1961 it was reported that some thirteen per cent of anthropologists were working in the field of mental health (Mead, 1961: 478). Anthropologists, in fact, seem to have made their methods and findings available to almost every applied field concerned with human behavior.

THE UNIQUENESS OF ANTHROPOLOGY

The foregoing recital of anthropological specialties indicates the great variety of problems within the field. It is precisely this variety which makes anthropology different from its sister disciplines and, so anthropologists think, yields some advantages for their approach to understanding human nature. Two major emphases differentiate anthropology from other sciences which study man.

The first is that man must be studied as both a biological and a cultural being. The anthropologist is concerned to avoid exclusively biological or exclusively cultural explanations for human behavior, for he has found that the two sets of factors are intertwined in such a way that both kinds of explanation must be employed. The anthropologist refuses to assume without further investigation, for example, that Negroes are naturally more rhythmic or musical than whites, for it is known that the capacity for rhythm and music may develop or fail to develop as a result of experience. As far as behavioral and psychological differences among the biological groupings called races are concerned, the anthropologist is careful to avoid the popular notion that they are genetically transmitted, because he has learned that racially different groups often are subjected to divergent learning experiences which account for the differences. One of the central emphases of anthropology, then, is its abiding interest in the interrelationships between what man has inherited genetically and what he has learned as the result of cultural experiences. This may be referred to as the biocultural approach (Titiev, 1963: 18).

The second major emphasis differentiating anthropology from other disciplines is its *comparative* orientation. Anthropologists make a special effort to avoid basing their conclusions about man's nature on studies of Euroamerican races and cultures only; they also study races and cultures other than our own and compare data from the widest possible variety in making their generalizations.

In cultural anthropology this comparative emphasis takes the form of what is often called the *cross-cultural approach*. This means that the anthropologist utilizes data not just from civilized cultures of historic times but also from exotic cultures in every corner of the globe and from extinct cultures investigated through archaeological methods. By considering data from the most diverse possible sample of human cultures he attempts to arrive at more valid generalizations about human nature than would be possible otherwise. For example, some have thought it inevitable for a boy to feel hostility toward his father due to the father's sexual access to the mother and its denial to the son. The late Bronislaw Malinowski, an anthropologist of international reputation, found that boys among the Trobriand Islanders of the South Pacific were not hostile toward their fathers but toward their maternal uncles, who were responsible for disciplining their nephews. On this basis he suggested that the hostility might be associated with the resentment of authority rather than sexual jealousy (1937: 41 ff.). The anthropologist always feels compelled to make cross-cultural tests of assumptions about human nature, and to do this he must take into account the variety and total known range of ways in which humans have responded to the problems of existence. One of the main purposes of this book is to introduce the reader to some of the variety of designs for living which man has developed.

In the United States, as well as in other places, the commitment of anthropologists to the biocultural and comparative emphases is revealed in their insistence that professionally trained anthropologists become familiar with all branches of the discipline. The physical anthropologist must be familiar with the methods and findings of ethnology, archaeology, and other subdivisions of cultural anthropology, so that he will recognize when he comes against a problem on which he needs help from a cultural anthropologist and so that he will avoid unwarranted and distorting reliance on biological explanations of human behavior. The ethnologist, linguist, archaeologist, or other cultural anthropologist, in turn, must be able to recognize the possible significance of genetically inherited characteristics in the cultural problems he investigates.

Within cultural anthropology the archaeologist must be familiar with the methods and findings of ethnology, for only by a knowledge of living cultures can he interpret the cultures of the past. The ethnologist, in trying to understand the cultures of the present, can add time depth to his conclusions by incorporating archaeological findings. To generalize about the processes by which languages operate the linguist must remain aware of the larger cultural context of which language is a part. Moreover, he must be acquainted with how languages work in all parts of the world. Any aspect of human nature can be understood adequately only as man is viewed as a biocultural being and in the full range and variety of human life in different times and places.

In line with the cross-cultural method, and adding to the diversity of the field, is the fact that many anthropologists have taken to the study of literate communities in Euroamerican and other advanced societies. Both rural and urban groups in the United States and other modern nations have been investigated, partly because of the desire to apply concepts and methods distinctive of anthropology and partly because ethnologists are interested in understanding the impact of complex communities on peasant and non-literate cultures.

Admittedly, no one anthropologist can be expert in all aspects of his field. Each must specialize in one or a few areas. This necessity for specialization tends to tear anthropology apart, but the ideal of viewing man as a whole is maintained strongly enough to provide a compensating force for unity, and in spite of repeated expressions of concern that it might disintegrate, anthropology remains a single discipline.

2

CUSTOMS
AND
CULTURES

Cultural anthropologists are labeled that because they are concerned primarily with the investigation of what they call cultures. In popular terms a culture may be thought of as the way of life of a community or other group. An anthropologist learns about a culture by living in the community and observing what goes on. The late Robert Lowie, prominent ethnologist at the University of California, lived among the Crow Indians and published several volumes describing their culture. Franz Boas of Columbia University, sometimes known as the father of American anthropology, described the culture of the Kwakiutl Indians of British Columbia. His student, Margaret Mead, investigated the culture of the mountain Arapesh of New Guinea and wrote an ethnography of several volumes about it. In view of the fact that anthropologists study and talk about them so extensively, it behooves us to understand as clearly as possible what cultures are.

INDIVIDUAL CUSTOMS

If a culture is defined as the sum total of the cultural traits of any group, the problem may be approached by discovering what a cultural trait is. And perhaps the most useful way of understanding the nature of a cultural trait is to ask just what it is that ethnographers experience which makes it possible for them to suppose that cultural traits exist. Imagine that an ethnographer, coming upon the first Crow he has ever seen, finds him in disguise and stalking a deer. At this point he has witnessed a single event only, and he has no way of knowing certainly whether or not that Crow has ever stalked a deer before or whether or not he will ever do so again. For all he knows it may be a unique event. However, some days later he again may observe the same Crow stalking deer in the same fashion. Strictly speaking, and this is important, the second activity is not the first, but a unique occurrence. Nevertheless, the ethnographer rightly views it as a repetition of the first because it is closely similar to it. Further observation of the same Crow reveals that he repeats this action over and over again, in fact, whenever he hunts deer by himself. Though each action or event remains distinct from all the others, the close similarity among them and the fact that they are used in similar circumstances justifies the ethnographer's conclusion that stalking deer in this way is customary for this person. It is one of his personal customs or, alternatively, personality traits. It is important to keep in mind that it is the ethnographer's perception of the similarities among the repeated actions of this individual which has enabled him to come to this conclusion.

MULTI-INDIVIDUAL CUSTOMS

Similarities among the actions of an individual remain in the sphere of personality. We move to the cultural sphere only by observing that the personal customs of a plurality of the members of a society are similar. Continuing with the previous example, the ethnographer beginning his work among the Crow may observe that it is customary for other Crow hunters to pursue deer by stalking them while in disguise (Lowie, 1935: 72). In other words, he perceives a similarity among the customs of a plural number of Crow hunters in respect to the manner of hunting deer. This observation makes it possible for him to conclude that he has found not just an individual custom but a multi-individual or social custom. Such a socially standardized custom is usually referred to by anthropologists as a cultural trait.

It is important to remember that without the observation of similarities among the distinct actions of given individuals and among the customary actions of a plural number of individuals the ethnographer would not be able to conceive of the existence of the cultural trait.

EMPIRICAL INDICATORS OF CUSTOMS

The actions observed by ethnographers may be thought of as one kind of empirical indicator of personal and social customs. There are, however, at least two other major kinds of empirical indicators of customs, namely, utterances and artifacts.

Actions are movements of the human body which can be observed. Though movement is involved in utterances, it seems useful to treat them as a different category, since the bodily movement which can be seen is limited and the utterances are experienced primarily as auditory stimuli. As an example of an utterance the ethnographer may hear one Crow taunting another for violating the taboo against marrying a woman of his own clan (Lowie, 1935: 45f.). The taunting may be repeated, and it may be done by other Crow as well. It becomes apparent to the ethnographer that it is the personal custom of many or, perhaps, most of the Crow to utter this taunt as a sanction against those who violate this important marriage taboo, and, since a plurality of the Crow practice this utterance in such circumstances, he has evidence of the existence of a cultural trait.

Utterances are of great importance in anthropological field work, for there are many traits which can be communicated to the ethnographer only through language. Only through utterances can the anthropologist learn what ideas and motives lie behind many of the people's behaviors, and only in this way can he learn about ideas and feelings not manifested directly in observable bodily movements or which, for various reasons, he does not have the opportunity to learn about by other means during his term in the field. The Crow informant can explain to the anthropologist why the man whose wife was kidnapped did not show resentment or try to take her back. He can explain that mourners preparing for the Sun Dance abstain from food and drink for several days, a fact which the ethnographer may not have an opportunity to observe. He can explain that all war plunder belongs to the captain of the war party, in spite of the observable fact that it is always divided among the members of the party (Lowie, 1935). The fact is that many of the customs reported in ethnographies have not been observed by the anthropologist; they have been learned from the explanatory utterances of informants.

Actions and utterances are alike in that the observer must be able to see or hear the person who performs them in order to detect a trait's existence. *Artifacts*, which are the material objects resulting from some human actions, can be observed in the absence of the persons who make and use them. In archaeological field work, for example, all persons who made and used the artifacts are deceased, so that it is not possible to observe the actions by which they were made and used or hear the utterances which would reveal the meanings associated with them. The ethnographer, by contrast, is frequently able to see people manufacturing and using bows and arrows, pots, baskets, and other artifacts; and he even may be given a demonstration which includes utterances in explanation of the manufacture, use, and meanings of an artifact. In such case the ethnographer enjoys the advantage of having all three major kinds of empirical indicators—actions, utterances, and artifacts. In other cases, the anthropologist must infer the existence of customs by observing similar artifacts in various places in the community, as when, for example, wooden bowls are seen time after time in Crow tipis.

It is significant that one kind of artifact is notably more informative than all others, and this is the artifact to which writing has been applied. When people have recorded their ideas and told of their actions on clay tablets or paper, it is possible for researchers to learn much more about the culture in the absence of the artifact's maker than is usually the case. A book is one of the most informative of all artifacts. In anthropology, however, both ethnologists and archaeologists have worked most often with cultures with little or no writing. The ethnologist traditionally has worked with *existing* nonliterate peoples, and the archaeologist works with *extinct* nonliterate cultures, that is, prehistoric cultures.

An investigator, whether ethnographer, sociologist, or casual observer, experiences customs as similar utterances, actions, or artifacts. These three kinds of phenomena are the empirical manifestations or indicators of cultural traits, which are classes of personal customs which are so closely similar to one another that they are thought of as the same custom. It is these of which cultures are composed.

THE ESSENTIAL NATURE OF CULTURAL TRAITS

So far customs have been defined without dealing explicitly with the question of their essential nature, and on this anthropologists have been unable to agree. Some have included artifacts as elements of cultures, but others have insisted that artifacts are simply material results of cultures. Whatever the answer, it is well to keep in mind that artifacts cannot come into existence without human actions and that actions often occur without producing artifacts. Since, in these ways, actions seem more basic than artifacts, some have insisted that culture consists of behavior, that is, actions and utterances. Still others, a minority among anthropologists, have thought of customs as being ideas.

At this point it is important to note and remember that neither utterances, actions, or artifacts can occur or come into existence except as the result of counterpart forces or conditions internal to specific persons. A mother will not utter a reprimand of her child for not kissing his godfather's hand unless she has the idea that her child should do this and that it is the thing to do to reprimand a child for not performing in such a way. A man will not put on a wide-brimmed hat (as opposed to a narrow-brimmed one) unless he has the notion, an internal factor, of doing such a thing.

There has been some disagreement about whether cultural traits consist of ideas, behaviors, and artifacts or only one or two of these. This is a misleading formulation of the problem, because behavior (actions and utterances) and artifacts are empirical phenomena, that is, they can be observed directly by the senses. Ideas, by contrast, cannot be observed but must be inferred from behavior and artifacts. We do not observe the ideas of others. Yet we are compelled to suppose that behaviors and artifacts are consequences of ideas or something like them within individuals. For this reason it seems useful to think of the observable phenomena as empirical indicators of customs and to distinguish among three major kinds — utterances, actions, and artifacts. *Ideas or some kind of internal forces are always present in customs, and they may be expressed either as utterances or as actions; and sometimes the actions are of the kind that result in artifacts.*

An additional reason for regarding the internal forces as more basic than the empirical events they produce is that the latter are repeated at intervals rather than being continuous. Yet most anthropologists seem to assume that cultural traits have some kind of continuity. One might ask, however, where the custom of stalking a deer in a certain fashion is between the times the actions are performed. If the custom is regarded as internal to the individual, this question can be answered by saying that, essentially, the custom is a continuously existent force within individuals. The continuity is provided internally; otherwise the action would not be repeated each time the hunter found himself securing deer. When a Zapotec Indian of Mexico utters an invitation to an unexpected mealtime visitor to join him in eating, he does so because of an internal notion or idea that is a continuous part of his personality. It seems that there is a good case for regarding the internal factors, whatever they are, as the essential elements in cultural traits. They explain the standardization of personal customs, and many are multi-individual.

On such grounds there are those who define cultural traits as multi-individual ideas. There is difficulty with this, however, since ideas are ordinarily thought of as psychological notions of which one is conscious, which is not always so. Many motor habits, for example, seem to operate below the level of consciousness or at a very low level. Many Ecuadorian Indians walk with short, choppy steps, little arm movement, and with the trunk bent slightly forward. In this respect they are culturally different from most Americans, who walk with a longer stride and a pronounced arm swing. Many of the Indians probably have never thought about how they walk; no one has set out to teach them to walk that way, and they have not intentionally learned it. They become conscious of their mode of walking only as they have opportunities to compare it with the walk of culturally different persons. This certainly is a trait of Ecuadorian Indian cultures, but if such motor actions are not consciously learned and maintained, it may not be appropriate to refer to the essential internal forces underlying them as ideas. Nevertheless, the action seems to be a manifestation of some continuous internal condition. It is a trait of those who practice the walk in question, and it is internal. The term *esotrait* seems a useful designation for all learned, continuous, internal forces which produce standardized utterances and actions.

At this point the definition of a cultural trait may be revised. It may be defined as any set of similar, individual, customary esotraits, which are manifested empirically as repeated utterances, actions, and the artifacts which result from some actions.

Though few social scientists have adopted the notion that cultural traits are basically esotraits, it is still possible for them to discuss cultural phenomena with those who have by simply using the neutral terms *custom* or *cultural trait*. When it is said that boiling grasshoppers in lemon juice is a part of the culture of a Zapotec community, one anthropologist may mean the actual behavior and another may mean the esotrait which produces the behavior. In this book the reader may assume that terms such as cultural trait, social custom, or cultural element refer to multi-individual esotraits.

THE CONCEPT OF THE SUPERORGANIC

Some social scientists have insisted that culture is superorganic, by which they mean that it belongs to a level of reality distinct in its nature from the biological and psychological level from which it is derived. By this view it is just as surely different from the organic as the organic is from the inorganic, or as steam is from water (Kroeber, 1917: 210). This means that a culture operates according to superorganic principles and must be explained in terms of such principles rather than by reference to the biology or psychology of individuals. Those who adhere to the concept of the superorganic reject the kind of definition of cultural traits just set forth.

Those who hold to the superorganic view make a number of points in support of their position. They suggest that every culture normally outlasts the particular generation of individuals who participate in it, indicating thereby that the culture has a kind of life of its own. It is pointed out that any culture is more than any given human can understand or participate in. It is affirmed that the individual is born into a kind of cultural stream, lives out his life being carried along by it and dies having influenced his way of life little or none.

Expressing such notions in these ways too often communicates a feeling that a culture is some kind of mystical entity which operates independently of individuals. The mystery disappears, however, if other modes of expression are used. The culture which outlasts a generation of people is merely a culture that is similar to that of the previous generation because its bearers have learned their customs from members of that generation. Though a given individual cannot know or participate in all of his society's culture, other individuals in his society *do* know and participate in the other customs. The person who does little to change his culture is somewhat like the single voter. His lone contribution may count for little, but combined with the contributions of the remainder of the members of that society, a major change may result.

All this is not to say that the culture concept is not valid or that it is not useful for many purposes to deal with human behavior in purely supra-individual terms; but it is necessary to include the contributions of individuals in groups to understand adequately how cultures work. This is because of the previously emphasized fact that cultures are composed of sets of similar individual traits.

3

THE CONTENT
AND STRUCTURE
OF CULTURE

When considering the content of culture the neophyte in anthropology sometimes forgets the limitations imposed by anthropological definitions. In the first chapter it was stated that cultural phenomena are not biologically inherited. The anthropologist defines culture as being *learned*; that is, acquired by man as a member of society; and it is important to exclude genetically inherited characteristics when dealing with the content of cultures.

Secondly, anthropologists define cultural phenomena as being *shared*. In the previous chapter the word *shared* was not employed, for it was considered more accurate to picture cultural traits as sets of similar individual customs rather than as uniform entities, thus allowing for the fact that the personal traits of which cultural traits are composed vary slightly from one another. The point emphasized now, however, is that cultural traits are not unique to individuals. If they were they would be nothing more than personality traits. When, however, a plural number of the members of a society manifest closely similar personality traits it is useful to group these into a single category called a cultural trait.

With few exceptions, then, anthropological definitions limit cultural phenomena to those which are learned and those which are social, thus excluding those which are genetically inherited and those which are solely individual.

A MODEL OF A CULTURE

No ethnographer has found a way to detect all of the learned, multi-individual customs of any culture, and it is believed that there is no culture so simple that it can be described in its entirety. Consequently, any ethnography is only a partial description of the culture in question.

Figure 1 is a simple chart designed to communicate some of what has been said about the nature and composition of cultures, using only a few Crow traits to represent the culture's entire content (Lowie, 1935). The traits are listed at the left side, and the individual members of the society are indicated by the letters at the top.

	A	B	C	D	E	F	G	H	I	J	K	L	M	N	O	P	Q	R	S
Ceremonial objects inherited by eldest son		x	x		x	x			x										
Changing one's name after an outstanding feat	x	x	x	x		x	x	x											
High valuation of a perfectly straight nose	x	x	x	x	x	x	x	x	x	x	x	x	x	x	x	x	x	x	x
Believing water to have medicinal value	x	x		x	x	x	x	x			x		x	x	x	x	x	x	
Making arrowheads	x	x	x	x	x	x	x	x	x										
Stripping bark from tipi poles									x	x	x	x	x	x	x	x			
Throwing dung at clowns																		x	x
Belonging to a club		x			x	x	x	x		x									
Believing that four is a mystic number	x	x	x			x	x	x	x	x	x	x	x		x	x	x	x	x

Figure 1 — Model of Crow Culture

The model illustrates the definition of a cultural trait which has been employed. Some of the traits are participated in by all or nearly all of the Crow, and others by a smaller proportion. Many customs cannot be participated in universally because they are confined to one sex only. Among the Crow, for example, the arrowheads are made by men; only women strip the bark from tipi poles; and only boys throw dung at clowns. A truly complete description of any community's culture in this form would have a minimum of tens of thousands of customs listed, and for every member of the community who participates in a custom an X would have to be entered in the appropriate space below his name. Of course, no such description has been accomplished. In fact, and this is important, one of the main reasons that the culture concept is so useful is that it enables one to deal with large numbers of people without making a complete study of the socially acquired personality traits of each individual.

IDENTIFYING AND DISTINGUISHING CULTURAL TRAITS

The cultural trait commonly is thought of as the smallest, most basic element in a culture. In a sense this is true, but it is necessary to realize that many of the cultural elements which anthropologists refer to as traits can be subdivided into culturally significant parts which, in turn, might be called cultural traits. The smoking of the ceremonial pipe as a symbol in the declaration of peace among some Indian tribes would seem to be a fairly basic unit of culture, but it can be analyzed into a number of parts meaningful to the people. There is the formation of the circle of men to whom the pipe is to be passed; there is the fact that the pipe is to be passed in a clockwise direction; there is the singing and dancing which accompanies the smoking; and a number of other elements, all of which may be viewed as traits (Lowie, 1954: 29 f.).

A conceivable way to deal with this would be to reserve the use of the term *cultural trait* for those elements which cannot be broken down into parts meaningful to the people. This has not proven to be particularly useful for the simple reason that a given cultural element may be treated as an indivisible unit under some circumstances and under other conditions will be divided into parts and one or more of the parts thought of as indivisible units. When an Arunta of Australia is explaining how a kangaroo is dispatched, he will refer to and think of the spear as an indivisible unit. But a spear also may be analyzed into the point, shaft, binding, and so on, and when an Arunta is describing how a spear is made he will analyze it into such parts. The upshot of this is that what a cultural trait is depends on how the observer is viewing things at a given moment for given purposes. It seems most useful to define the scope of a cultural trait as that which at some time, in some context, is customarily viewed by the people as an indivisible unit. Clearly, the scope of a trait is determined by its context at given times rather than by any objective quality of the trait itself.

CULTURAL COMPLEXES

It is apparent that many cultural traits actually are configurations or complexes which can be analyzed into traits more limited in scope, but they are called traits because they are ordinarily thought of by the people who practice them as indivisible units. Since so many traits are complexes in some sense, it is impossible to make a precise distinction between a trait and a complex. In fact, some anthropologists have used the term *trait-complex* (Wissler, 1923: 52). In spite of the difficulty, anthropologists have found the term *cultural complex* useful to refer to cultural units which obviously consist of a relatively large number of interrelated traits. The term is used particularly when it is desired to call attention to the fact that there is a configuration of interdependent traits. An example of such a complex would be the buffalo hunting complex of the Crow and other Plains Indians. There are the time of year when the hunting is done, the ways of locating the herd, the kinds of weapons that are used and how they are handled, the ways in which the horses are handled, and a large number of other elements. On American campuses a dating complex can be identified, which includes many specific traits which nearly any university student could describe. Cultures, then, may be viewed as consisting not only of cultural traits but of complexes of traits as well.

CULTURAL LINKAGE

In considering structure it is important to remember that the traits and complexes which make up a culture are linked to one another. Some anthropologists, in fact, have viewed an entire culture as though it were a single unit of linked elements. They have emphasized that cultures are not just collections of unrelated customs, but that each custom has a functional relationship with other customs in the culture. This emphasis is one aspect of an anthropological doctrine known as *functionalism*. In anthropology this point of view is closely associated with the names of Bronislaw Malinowski and A. R. Radcliffe-Brown. Beginning in the 1920's, Malinowski vigorously attacked the tendency of some anthropologists to view cultures as little more than aggregations of unrelated traits. He insisted on viewing cultures as *systemic* in nature and emphasized the importance of explaining any cultural element in terms of its functions in relation to other elements in the system and its contribution to the operation of the system (1944: 150ff.).

The other aspect of functionalism is its emphasis on the relationships between cultural phenomena and noncultural features, notably, man's biological makeup, the natural habitat, and population characteristics. Malinowski, particularly, viewed the ultimate function of culture as the satisfaction of biological needs. The functionalist point of view in both its aspects is now firmly established in anthropology, and, though earlier views have been somewhat modified, anthropologists regularly try to understand traits in reference to the cultural and noncultural contexts within which they function.

Studies of cultural change have demonstrated the systemic nature of cultures by showing how a change in one custom produces changes in related elements, the degree of change depending on the number and the strength of the linkages. A new custom or the removal or modification of an old one often undermines the old system of linkages or permits, promotes, or necessitates a new system. The substitution of single family homes in the place of the multi-family dwellings once used by the Yakima Indians of Washington undermined the intimate modes of interaction and feelings of unity which formerly characterized the culture (Barnett, 1953: 92). As the Tanala of Madagascar switched from dry rice cultivation to the production of wet rice a series of changes was precipitated because of the many connections between rice production and other cultural elements. Wet rice growing, for example, led to permanent villages, which, in turn, required more effective patterns of defensive warfare (Linton, 1939: 283). Many of the American Indian tribes which took up the custom of riding horses experienced far-reaching cultural changes of a variety of kinds. Some cultures were modified slightly, and others were extensively reformulated, the differences depending partly on what the cultures were like previously. Among the Shoshone tribes horse riding made possible larger, more permanent villages, warfare, and more clearly defined political leadership — all of which were weak or lacking in pre-contact times. The horse was used to transport food farther and more rapidly, making the villages possible. The warfare which resulted from the use of the horse also promoted the gathering of people into larger social units; and both the warfare and the larger concentrations of people required more effective leadership, resulting in the emergence of chiefs (Steward, 1937: 630, 632). Certainly, linkage is one of the most significant aspects of cultural phenomena.

THE NATURE OF LINKAGES

The links among customs may be themselves multi-individual esotraits. Cultural elements are functionally linked in the sense that a plurality of members of the society entertain in their minds such a connection, whether they are aware of it or not. There could be no connection between male dominance and the use of stone axes without those concerned sharing that notion, either explicitly or implicitly. This esotrait itself, because it is a socially acquired set of similar individual customs, is a cultural trait and may be referred to as a *linking trait*.

Linkages are always basically psychological, and some seem to be solely that, since there is no current, non-psychological reason for them. The idea in our own culture that women wear colorful clothing, necklaces, and earrings is not made necessary by any external conditions. In fact, in some cultures the men wear the more colorful clothing and ornaments (Mead, 1935: 245).

Many linking traits, while essentially internal, are encouraged or necessitated by external interdependence. Some of these are functional only, without direct physical contact. In the United States, for example, there is a linkage between the air transportation complex and major league baseball scheduling. Because of space-time factors it is possible to have baseball teams located three thousand miles apart and still maintain the desired game schedules. Even more obvious, perhaps, is the functional linkage between a canoe and its paddle. Other linkages, such as that between an arrowhead and its shaft, are based on direct physical connections.

THEMES

One kind of linking trait is the *theme*, which may be defined as a multi-individual value or orientation, sometimes with emotional content and sometimes with little or none, which is linked to a significant plurality of other traits in the culture in question. Morris E. Opler, who proposed this concept, regarded a theme as a ". . . postulate or position . . .", either implicit or explicit, which usually controls behavior or stimulates activity (1945: 161). Accordingly, it seems appropriate to think of themes as linking the various traits they control and stimulate.

One of the significant themes of Chiricahua Apache culture is long life (Opler, 1945: 203ff.). The Chiricahua place the umbilical cord and the afterbirth in a young tree to bring long life to the child. They are particularly pleased when an old person blesses a child, for that brings long life. Nearly every song and prayer in the puberty rites mentions long life, and every time the word for long life is mentioned in a ceremony the old women applaud. People have dreams about long life, and one of their main reasons for fear of witches, ghosts, and other evil supernatural beings is that they will deprive them of long life. The old are consistently deferred to among the Chiricahua. These and other traits are linked to the long life orientation, so that it is appropriate to say that the theme permeates or flavors much of the Chiricahua way of life. Other themes of Chiricahua culture are activism, the superiority of males, the value of women, and the importance of shared family responsibility.

In her widely read book, *Patterns of Culture*, Ruth Benedict suggested that the Plains Indian cultures manifest a Dionysian quality (1934: 79). This is an emphasis upon emotional and physical exuberance, excess aggressiveness, and reckless activism. This emotional theme was traced through a number of aspects of the cultures. Fasting and torture are used to bring on supernaturalistic visions; men gain prestige by daring and reckless risking of their lives in war; and death results in uninhibited and prolonged expression of grief. By contrast, Benedict suggested, the Pueblo Indian tribes of the Southwest manifest an Apollonian orientation, which emphasizes emotional control and moderation in all aspects of life.

Many anthropologists are of the opinion that Benedict went too far toward leaving the impression that a whole culture might be dominated by a single quality or *ethos*, a concept which is sometimes referred to by anthropologists as *configurationalism*. It is now felt that there are few if any cultures in which a single theme prevails greatly over all others and that most manifest a number of themes of varying importance. In Lipan Apache culture, for example, Opler was able to discover twenty major themes (1946: 161).

CONTEXTS AND PURPOSES

Many cultural traits are linked into complexes because they occur in the same context or contribute to the realization of the same purpose. The customs that are brought into play at a machinist's lathe may be linked in the minds of machinists and others because they occur in the same context, that is, at and around the lathe while the machinist is doing his work. A courtship complex consists of many specific traits which may be considered interrelated because all of them have to do with the purpose of winning a spouse. All cultural complexes seem to exist because their constituent traits occur together or contribute to a central goal. The *institutions* dealt with by sociologists, such as education, the family, economics, and the like, appear to be vast complexes of customs linked with one another around basic purposes in the life of the society.

ASPECTS OF CULTURE AND LINKAGE

The phenomena of any culture are so diverse that anthropologists and others have felt compelled to classify the content of culture into more manageable categories. This subdivision of cultural content into aspects is done on the popular level as well. Science, industry, education, government, religion, recreation, and such categories are familiar to everyone.

The danger in this is that we will forget that customs in one aspect are linked to and interdependent with those in other aspects. In conformity with the functionalist view of cultures as systems it behooves us to remember, when we are studying economic life, for example, that many economic customs are interdependent with political, religious, educational and other such elements. It is impossible to understand how cultures work without keeping the principle of linkage in mind.

4

CONCEPTS FOR CULTURAL ANALYSIS

A culture has been defined as the sum total of the sets of similar individual esotraits manifested by the members of a society. These sets of individual customs are called cultural traits, and within any culture they are linked with one another into complexes, which, in turn, are interrelated with one another to form the whole culture. This chapter will introduce some concepts about traits employed by anthropologists in thinking about cultures and analyzing them. They should be understood as notions which can be used to understand better how cultures work and how they affect the lives of the persons who create and participate in them.

OVERT AND COVERT CUSTOMS

These contrasting kinds of traits must be defined from the observer's point of view (Honigmann, 1959: 121). Obviously, artifacts are easily observable, making it possible to infer readily from the object to an underlying esotrait; and the same is true of actions. Thus, customs which have easily observable empirical indicators can be said to be *overt customs*. Also, idea esotraits which are expressed in utterances which correspond closely to the thoughts in the person's mind and which are frequently expressed are highly overt.

   Covert customs are those which are not expressed directly in actions, artifacts, or utterances of the kinds just mentioned. Their empirical manifestations do not correspond to some of the esotraits behind them in such a way as to allow the observer to infer directly from the empirical indicator to the esotrait. Or, if they are ideas almost never expressed directly by utterances, they are relatively covert. Among the Teotitlán

Zapotecs of Mexico actions and utterances may be outwardly friendly, but it may be impossible to tell whether this is a direct expression of true friendliness or whether it reflects a desire to avoid unpleasant interpersonal exchanges, which are much devalued by these people. The esotrait behind the action is covert or hidden.

It should be noted that there is no precise division between overt and covert customs but that a cultural element is either more overt or less overt than other customs.

EXPLICIT AND IMPLICIT TRAITS

By contrast with overt and covert traits, *implicit* and *explicit customs* must be defined from the participant's standpoint. Explicit customs are those which the participant is sufficiently aware of to be able to express verbally (Kluckhohn, 1949: 31ff.). A Crow woman, for example, can explain how to erect a tipi; it is very explicit in her mind. Implicit customs, however, are those which the participant is not aware of. The previously mentioned mode of walking of the Ecuadorian Indians is an excellent example of an implicit trait. The rules of grammar which govern utterances are implicit to the speakers of every language, except in those cases where language has been analyzed and made explicit by grammarians or linguists. Any culture has many implicit customs, and it often is easier for a culturally alien observer to discover them than it is for the native. As with covert and overt customs there are varying degrees of explicitness and implicitness among a culture's traits.

IDEAL TRAITS

Ideal culture consists of traits manifested in utterances and written statements by a society's members as to what they do, what they believe, or what they ought to do or believe. They are ideal in the sense that they often are found to contradict what the people actually think and do. The latter is what many anthropologists have called *real culture*, but this sometimes has led to the false conclusion that ideal traits are somehow less than genuine cultural phenomena.

The Teotitlán Zapotecs repeatedly declare that interpersonal physical violence does not occur among them. This is the ideal, but such violence does take place; there is a contradiction between their utterances about their actions and the actions themselves. All cultures exhibit such discrepancies between their ideas and correlative thought and behavior, some more than others. In anthropological field work informants often give ethnographers the ideal picture of their culture, a fact which must be taken into account carefully. Both what people announce that they believe and do and the commitments and behaviors which contradict such ideal statements must be recorded in ethnographic work if the goal is the completest possible picture of the culture, for both are part of the culture.

EFFECTIVE AND NON-EFFECTIVE CUSTOMS

The distinction between effective and non-effective customs is seldom if ever made by anthropologists, but the concepts are useful for indicating something quite significant about the nature of cultures. Much of the content of any culture consists of knowledge of all kinds of things and ideas which have potential but unrealized consequences in the lives of the participants. There are many peoples in the world, for example, who know about and even can explain the germ theory of disease; but they do not accept it. It is *non-effective* in terms of the unrealized potential of being believed.

Many customs remain in the non-effective category simply because the resources—physical, monetary, mental, or in respect to supporting knowledge and skill—are not available (Barnett, 1953: 360). Many of the peoples of the world know of and mentally accept automobiles, television viewing, fertilizing, gasoline lanterns, and a host of other alien elements, but they have not been able to act upon this acceptance because of the lack of money or other resources. The esotraits are part of the culture, but they are not effective. Many of the newly developing nations and peoples of the world today hold in their cultures vast funds of ideas and desires which are awaiting only the necessary conditions and resources for them to become effective in the culture.

PROMOTIVE AND RESTRICTIVE TRAITS

Some writers have made a useful distinction between customs which support and extend human potentialities and inclinations and those which limit or reduce them (Bidney, 1953: 10f.). Customs involving artifacts facilitate man's control over nature. Even a simple hand knife is promotive in that it enables man to transcend the limitations of his biological makeup. Among the more impressive promotive artifacts of modern times are space craft and computers.

In all societies there are customs which have the effect of restraining aggressive and sexual inclinations. The ancient custom of foot binding among the Chinese prevented the women from making use of the natural potential of the foot, even as the American custom of wearing shoes results in failure to develop possible uses for the toes.

UNIVERSALS, SPECIALTIES, AND ALTERNATIVES

Social scientists have made extensive use of Ralph Linton's threefold distinction among cultural traits in terms of degree of participation

(1936: 272ff.). *Universals* are those customs practiced by all normal adult members of a society. *Alternatives* are traits among which people are allowed to choose, as, for example, different modes of transportation or different kinds of footwear. *Specialties* are customs associated with some particular subgroup. For example, there are customs associated with being a woman, man, or child; and others are associated with being a policeman, carpenter, canoe maker, craft guild member, medicine man, secret society member, or member of some other special group.

5

OBTAINING CULTURAL DATA

Any given culture consists of all of the learned, multi-individual esotraits of a society, including those by which they are linked together to form a whole cultural system. Anthropologists doing *ethnography* try to discover what these cultural traits are and how the culture operates. They do so by careful observation and recording of utterances, actions, and artifacts. Among the vast number of empirical indicators observed the ethnographer must be sure, first, that they are repeated, that is, customary or standardized rather than unique, and that they are multi-individual rather than idiosyncratic. While in the field he will do all he can to detect and learn the nature of the linking customs. He will do what he can to learn whether or not the traits are universals and, if not, he will try to determine whether or not they are optional or whether they are associated with a subgroup. He will take into account the fact that many of the customs are covert to him or implicit to the participants and, consequently, make a special effort to detect and understand them. He will try to distinguish the ideal customs as well as those which contradict them. Some of these and other decisions about the nature of the culture can be made after the anthropologist leaves the field, but this can be done only if an excellent set of field notes is kept. It can be achieved only by high quality field methods.

PARTICIPANT OBSERVATION

A cardinal practice of ethnography is to learn about the culture by participating in the customs to some degree and, while participating, to observe. This ordinarily means that the anthropologist lives among the people themselves and makes himself as much like them culturally as they will permit and as is compatible with the maintenance of mental and physical health and scientific objectivity. Participation often has the advantage of helping the investigator establish good relationships with the people so that the channels of communication will be opened. By actually taking part in and trying to experience the culture as the native participants do he gets an inside view that is not possible otherwise. And by constantly being among the people he has the opportunity to learn many things that he would miss ordinarily. He makes close friends, and he overhears and participates in a multitude of casual conversations which supply him with a wealth of clues, many of them subtle, by which he can infer the existence of customs which are highly covert.

Such a procedure is an ideal never fully realized. For one thing, some groups will not permit participation, or they limit it. In other cases too much participation is not well accepted and may inhibit communication or arouse suspicion. In some instances the ethnographer may experience *cultural shock*, the mental stress which results from the ambiguity and insecurity of one's position in an unfamiliar cultural environment. Some ethnographers can stand more of this kind of stress than others. And not only must the anthropologist consider his mental health, he must also maintain physical health—often a difficult matter. The ethnographer has no choice but to take some risks, a fact which has prompted one writer to characterize anthropologists as people who refuse to believe in the germ theory of disease (Service, 1958: v.).

A major difficulty with participant observation is that one may begin to identify himself with the local values and lose the detachment necessary to achieve an accurate and objective description of the culture. This is handled by remaining aware of the danger and limiting participation or periodically withdrawing from the community in order to recover objectivity.

The use of language may be considered a special aspect of participation, since the language is part of the culture. Sometimes, because of time limitations or the limited nature of the research, the ethnographer uses interpreters or some language other than that of the community under study which is known to some or all of the people. The best field work, however, is done by use of the indigenous language if it is still the everyday language. Only by employing the idiom which is the natural vehicle for the culture can the anthropologist get the most accurate view of it, and only in this way can he understand and participate in the casual everyday conversations which are so revealing.

THE USE OF INFORMANTS

Participant observation is time consuming, and it does not reveal some things which, for one reason or another, the ethnographer does not have the opportunity to observe. There are many things which occur only at certain times of the year or for some other reason only infrequently. There are things that occur only at certain places, and it is not possible for the ethnographer to be everywhere at once. Since the ethnographer may not have the opportunity to witness some things, he must depend on informants to tell him about them. Also, many of the covert customs can be learned and understood adequately only by questioning and conversing with persons with whom the ethnographer has relationships of mutual trust.

A number of principles are observed in the use of informants. Whenever possible it is important to use *multiple informants,* so that their statements can be compared for possible discrepancies. If possible, informants from *various age levels,* from *both sexes,* and from other subcategories which may exist should be secured. It is also important to regularly check the *internal consistency* of a particular informant's testimony. If an informant understands and accepts it, the anthropologist may take complete notes in his presence, but often the anthropologist must keep his notebook out of sight or take sketchy notes in a casual fashion so as not to destroy rapport. In such cases the ethnographer must construct full notes from his memory as soon as possible after leaving the informant. There are some cases, however, in which informants have worked over an anthropologist's notes with him to be sure everything was correct. In interviewing informants anthropologists often find it impossible to go through a list of questions or use anything in the nature of a sociological schedule. In many societies this approach dries up the source of information, or the informant intentionally gives false information. The only alternative is to engage in casual conversation, trying to follow up crucial points when one can and, for the rest, taking what comes.

OTHER TECHNIQUES

A complete account of all the problems and techniques of field work cannot be given here. In addition to the above recital of a few of the main principles and problems of the two chief ethnographic techniques, a few more matters of interest may be noted.

Anthropologists usually aim at spending at least a year in the field in order to have the opportunity to learn about many customs which are seasonal in occurrence. They may leave the community for a time, either to restore mental or physical health or to recover their objectivity. They often engage in the collection of nonsensitive data through village mapping, the study of artifacts, the collection of genealogies or study of the language. Not only is such information of value in itself, it often opens doors to information about which the people are more sensitive. Ethnographers may collect biographies and autobiographies. If written documents are available, they will use them. Some have used psychological tests of various kinds, and tape recorders and cameras have been employed. Anthropologists are experimenting with a variety of additional field techniques, some of them highly sophisticated, but participant observation and the interviewing of informants continue to be the basic approaches.

THE NEW ETHNOGRAPHY

Sometimes field work has been regarded as nothing more than the collection of cultural facts. In recent years there has been increasing emphasis on the formulation of hypotheses and theories to govern the data collection process. A hypothesis to account for the cultural behavior of the group under study is set up and data by which to test the hypothesis is gathered. Another aspect of the new emphasis is seeing things from the point of view of the people being studied rather than imposing externally obtained categories. The so-called *new ethnography* is actually rather old, but the consistency and explicitness with which the new approach is set forth among anthropologists is new.

CULTURAL VARIABILITY

It has been noted previously that the cross-cultural approach is one of the most distinctive emphases of anthropology. It is the fact that mankind manifests so much variability from one group to another that prompts anthropologists to insist on a representative sample of this variability as the only adequate basis on which to generalize about man's nature. Whether it be how to get enough to eat, how to explain the existence of the universe, how to behave toward one's relatives, how to dispose of the dead, or any other of the vast number of such problems of living, the anthropologist wants to know the range and variety of ways in which people have solved them. He feels that this approach yields a superior view of the potentialities and limitations with which humans are born. And the applied anthropologist feels that such understanding will be of special value in this day of contact among culturally different peoples. This chapter explores some of the concepts and problems of cultural variability.

CULTURAL BOUNDARIES

As one moves from place to place on the earth and within any nation or region he finds that groups vary from one another in their customs. Cultural variability is an obvious fact, but there remains the sometimes vexing question of whether or not boundaries between one culture and another are detectable and, if so, how they can be defined.

As one views humanity in any area of the globe he finds that it is possible to put people into categories according to their behavioral similarities and differences. More specifically, it is observed that there are clusters of individuals who, in some of their customs, are more like one another than they are others. These similar individuals constitute a group, and the sum total of their customs is their culture.

Some of these groups are distinguishable from other groups by a large number of their customs and in all major areas of life—technological, economic, social, religious, and aesthetic. This may be true of what is often called a *community*, and it is often true of a *tribe*, which consists of a number of local communities. Groupings of this kind probably are fairly easy to differentiate from one another culturally, but even their cultures will in many respects be similar to those of other communities or tribes. Thus there is overlapping, and no absolute boundary can be drawn.

Other culturally distinguishable groups may differ from one another in a relatively small proportion of their customs, and these may not involve all major areas of life. This is often true of families, cliques and friendship groups, various kinds of formal organizations, and, perhaps, even nations and groupings of culturally similar nations. Among these we have rather clearly functional units whose members are aware of one another and are similar to one another as a consequence of their regular and intimate interaction. Families are this kind of grouping, and it seems appropriate to speak of family cultures. Sedentary settlements, the populations of which are small enough to provide for close interaction within the community, also are of this kind. Nations and categories of culturally similar nations (Western as opposed to Oriental, for example) consist of subdivisions which interact relatively little with one another and can be put in the same category only by virtue of their cultural similarity or an identifying feature such as common government.

The families of which communities are composed and the groupings of communities which make up tribes and nations are commonly closely similar to one another in a high proportion of their customs. In this sense there is extensive overlap among family cultures and among community cultures. Also, any individual family member's personality in some ways may be more like members of other groups to which he belongs, such as friendship groups or clubs. Another way in which there is overlapping, then, is that an individual actually belongs to more than one group and participates in more than one culture.

It is clear that cultures are not mutually exclusive bodies of custom among which precise boundaries can be drawn. Cultures overlap; there are cultures within cultures; and some differ from others only in a small proportion of their customs. For the sake of study the anthropologist selects groups or categories of people which are distinguishable from others in respect to *some proportion* of their customs and refers to all of their customs as their culture. Sometimes the customs by which a subgroup is distinguishable from a larger group of which it is a part are referred to as a *subculture*.

NONLITERATE CULTURES

One important way in which cultures vary from one another is in respect to whether or not the people have reduced their language to writing. Those cultures which lack writing are sometimes called *nonliterate*, a term which some anthropologists prefer to primitive. The latter word implies inferiority to many who use it, and it sometimes implies that the people are representative of the earliest human cultures. This second implication obscures the important fact that they actually are different in many specific ways from whatever they have been in the past. Lay descriptions of so-called primitives often imply that their customs are identical to what they were tens of thousands of years ago, a position which anthropologists reject. For these reasons many anthropologists refuse to use the word *primitive* or use it reluctantly. Others regard it as a legitimate designation of cultures which, in general ways, are representative of earlier stages of human culture. This book uses the term *nonliterate* in preference to primitive. The word *illiterate* is best reserved for persons whose language is written but who are unable to read or write it.

FOLK AND URBAN CULTURES

Robert Redfield's concept that communities and cultures can be ranged along a continuum from strongly folk cultures to strongly urban ones provides a useful device for exploring the differences between nonliterate cultures and civilized cultures. Nonliterate cultures, of course, fall near the folk end of the continuum.

The folk community is small, and its members have few contacts with outsiders. Its culture is homogeneous, that is to say, the customs of its participants are closely similar. The people are bound together largely by kinship ties, which are sometimes rather extensive. Technology is relatively simple and economic exchange is limited, since production is largely for use. Tradition rules; the people do not reflect upon or question their well integrated culture. Highly urban cultures manifest substantially the opposite of such traits (Redfield, 1947: 297ff.).

It is important to realize that this is an ideal concept. The cultures of nonliterate communities, as a matter of fact, do exhibit a degree of heterogeneity; trade is rather extensive in some of them; and kinship is rather less important in some than is sometimes realized. Actual cultures fall at different points along the ideal continuum from the folk extreme to the urban extreme but never at either end point. Moreover, the continuum involves a number of dimensions, as just indicated, and Redfield himself noted that a given culture may be placed at different points along the continuum depending on which dimensions are given greatest weight.

The significant point is that many of the world's groups exhibit cultures which, in general, are relatively more homogeneous, kinship oriented, economically unspecialized, and traditional than many others. Such cultures, in fact, are those which have been most frequently investigated by anthropologists, and a term for them is desirable. The cultures of the nonliterate communities and of many literate rural communities of the world fall relatively closer to the folk end of this ideal continuum than most towns and cities and can be referred to appropriately as folk cultures.

PEASANT CULTURES

There has been a recent surge of interest among anthropologists in the study of what is known as the peasant society. Peasant societies are rural, but they lie within the sphere of power of literate civilizations and are dependent upon them (Foster, 1967: 6). The culture of the peasant community, though influenced by and dependent upon the larger, more complex society of which it is a part, remains relatively more homogeneous and simple. Some of these are nonliterate communities which have been incorporated within the sphere of influence of a literate civilization, and others have been peasant communities from the beginnings of civilization in the area in question. Among the peasant communities which have been studied by anthropologists are rural Indian villages in Mexico, some present day African communities, fishing villages of Southeast Asia, and village communities in China and India. Such peasant cultures are of great interest to anthropologists, not only because, as Foster estimates, half or more of all people who have existed since man's origin have lived a peasant life, but also because peasant cultures, like nonliterate cultures, are passing from the world scene.

CIVILIZATION

Civilization sometimes has been used as a synonym for culture, but when anthropologists refer to civilization as a type of culture, they ordinarily mean cultures which manifest city life. A difficulty with this usage is that there have been some rather large cities which failed to exhibit the style of life commonly thought of as characteristic of city dwellers. The Yoruba of West Africa had population concentrations of over 100,000 consisting mostly of farmers (Bascom, 1955: 256, 258). They fell far short of the degree of diversity and general complexity of industrial cities, but the Yoruba city's residents were economically interdependent as manifested both in craft specialization and trade. Most agree that industrial cities characterized by great occupational and social heterogeneity are manifestations of civilization; and some refer to cultures such as those of West Africa as civilizations, while others choose not to.

Aside from this problem, it is important to remember that anthropologists avoid defining civilized peoples as those exhibiting refined, rational, and nonviolent behavior. Were this criterion applied, a number of so-called savage groups would be rated more civilized than many Euroamerican societies.

CULTURAL VARIABILITY AND THE CULTURAL FIELD

All cultures are similar in the general categories of phenomena of which they are composed. All have customs which can be classified as technological, economic, social, political, legal, religious, aesthetic, recreational, educational. Anthropologists sometimes say that there is in this sense a *universal pattern* for cultures, and the aspects they employ to classify customs reflect this concept.

The obvious reason for such universal categories of cultural phenomena is that men everywhere are born with similar biological and physiological characteristics and into similar natural habitats. Habitat and biology, however, often differ from one place and from one group to another, which helps account for cultural variability. Other factors, such as demographic, distributional, and cultural-historical influences, also play a part.

Earlier it was noted that one aspect of the functionalist approach was the recognition that the elements of a culture are linked to one another so as to form a kind of system. Thus any custom is a function of other customs. In dealing with the cultural field we are involved in the second aspect of functionalism, the fact that cultural traits are linked with noncultural features, that is, to elements of the cultural field. Any culture is linked into and part of a larger configuration of interdependent elements consisting of habitat characteristics, biologically inherited traits and conditions, and population size and distribution. Some examples of links between cultural factors and the systemic field within which cultures arise and operate are found in the subsequent discussion.

The following paradigm of relationships between culture and its field may be useful.

1. *The field factor provides limitations.* Certain things are culturally impossible or difficult because of biological, habitat, or other noncultural conditions. Due to the size of the human body and the size of walnut shells it is culturally impossible for people to dwell in a walnut shell. Bamboo houses are impossible for Eskimo culture, as is going without clothing. In some cases, however, culture has a way of overcoming apparent limitations. It once seemed that there was no possibility of moving through the atmosphere, but this is now a cultural reality.

2. *The field factor allows for a variety of possibilities.* No biological or habitat factor determines precisely how food will be transported to the mouth. The fingers alone, leaves, tortillas, chopsticks, and metal implements are among the variety of objects which have been employed. Some habitats provide the possibility of using bark cloth, woven fabrics, or skin for clothing, though only one or none may be used. Psychologically it is possible to believe in one god, a hundred, or none.

3. *The field factor may provide tendencies.* Though many things may be possible culturally, some things are more likely than others. A few societies are said to be ignorant of the male role in conception, but the tendency seems to be otherwise. Human respiration is such that most people stay under water, if at all, only for short periods; but in a few cultures biological means for staying under water for long periods of time have been exploited. Biologically, the tendency is for people to use flat-soled footwear, if they wear any at all, but some peoples wear shoes with extremely long supports beneath the heel, which hold the foot in a basically uncomfortable position and make walking difficult.

4. *In building their cultures people have selected among the possibilities and tendencies.* Since the field factor allows for a variety of possibilities, there is more than one way of solving many problems of living. Moreover, the variety of possibilities is so great that no single culture can utilize all of them. Every society, in effect, has selected a relatively small proportion of the customs which human beings are born with the equipment to learn and practice in their earthly environment. Some have selected the habit of eating two meals a day from among the several possibilities. Some groups have chosen to associate each person with his mother's line of descent, some with his father's, and still others with both lines.

5. *Field factors are altered by cultural means.* Men have destroyed and modified many habitat features. Non-literate peoples have deforested large areas by slash-and-burn agriculture. The face of the earth has been altered radically in many modern nations, the once desert areas which now produce vegetable and other specialty crops being an example. Some peoples bind the heads of their infants to give them unnaturally elongated heads, and modern medical research has produced artificial organs. Most significant of all, perhaps, is the future possibility of scientific manipulation of the genetic code to produce individuals with the desired characteristics, whatever those may be.

BIOLOGICAL DIFFERENCES

AND CULTURAL VARIABILITY

Biological differences among groups undoubtedly are associated with some minor cultural differences. The lack of tatooing among Negro groups, for example, is partially related to the fact that the foreign matter introduced beneath the skin would not contrast well with the dark pigmentation. The linear build of some groups may be reflected culturally in a tendency to stand on one leg.

There seem to be few significant differences of this kind, however, and the races of the world are closely similar anatomically, physiologically, and psychologically. Supposed differences such as the greater visual acuity of some nonliterates and their ability to track game and other humans turn out, in most cases, to be due to acquired powers of observation not appreciated by a culturally alien observer. Psychologically, anthropologists believe that all major races inherit about the same mental potential. This belief is based largely on their experiences as participant observers, by which they sense that people of all races manifest the same kind and degree of ingenuity and intelligence in solving their problems. On these grounds they feel that racially inherited psychological differences cannot be invoked to account for the differences between complex and simple cultures. African Negro cultures, in fact, are about as complex as cultures can be without writing. Why Negroid peoples apparently failed to develop writing in pre-modern times is not known, but it is possible that only one or two societies in human history invented writing without opportunity to learn of the basic concept from others, and most Caucasoid groups did not initiate systems of writing on their own (Kroeber, 1948: 514). It also may be significant that Negro Africa was very sparsely settled in pre-modern times, for complex cultural developments are most apt to occur in areas of high population density and intense cultural contact. In the Old World such cultural developments took place around the eastern end of the Mediterranean Sea, and in the New World they occurred in and between the southern and northern margins of North America and South America respectively.

Of key importance in respect to inherited psychological potential is the extreme *plasticity* of human nature. With relatively weak inherited predispositions and highly developed ability to learn and to symbolize, man's cultural potentialities are manifold. Anthropologists proceed with the study of the range and variety of cultural phenomena on the assumption that all major racial categories have about the same range of inherited intelligence potential.

NATURAL HABITAT AND CULTURAL VARIABILITY

Anthropologists long have rejected the notion that the content of a culture is determined mostly by the natural environment. This is because they have found culturally different groups in closely similar habitats and very different cultures at different times in the same location. Apache hunters and Pueblo agriculturalists both are found in the Southwest. The cultures of present day American communities are greatly different from those of the Indian communities of three hundred years ago in the same places. Obviously, factors other than the habitat must be considered.

Anthropologists now devote proportionately less of their energies to the refutation of the notion that natural habitat determines cultural content and relatively more to understanding the many ways in which culture is interdependent with or independent of the habitat. Among other things, they note that some customs or kinds of customs are more directly dependent on habitat than others. The types of canoes may reflect the sizes of trees and the kind of bark available, but religious belief seems much less dependent on habitat characteristics.

DEMOGRAPHIC FACTORS AND
CULTURAL VARIABILITY

Large population size has been found to be associated positively with cultural heterogeneity and a high rate of innovation. The relationship seems to be circular. Population cannot increase beyond the ability of the technology to support it, but once the population has grown sufficiently it is possible to develop a more complex technology and social organization. This again provides a basis for further population growth.

CULTURAL HISTORY AND VARIABILITY

This category embraces all kinds of phenomena. Neither biology, habitat, or population, nor even all three of these field factors together, can account for most of the specific differences among contemporary cultures. Most are to be explained by specific events and conditions relative to the culture's history which, for most cultures, are unrecoverable. Many such specifics fall in the category of what are called accidents, a word used to indicate unpredicted factors. A man just happens to shake with emotion during a religious ceremony, and shaking becomes a culturally standardized expression of spiritual possession. A starving man is forced to eat a tomato, and tomatoes become a regular food. A canoe builder experiments with different keel shapes to see which provides the greatest stability, and others adopt his solution. Such specific factors have been observed to be the stuff of cultural change during historical times, and it must be assumed that such have given rise to cultural differences in all times and places.

ISOLATION AND CONTACT

Spatial isolation of a society from others permits accidental cultural-historical factors to operate in such a way that the culture follows its own course of change without interruption from other groups. Thus, it becomes ever more distinct from other cultures. When a culture is in contact with another culture it becomes similar to it by borrowing and, at the same time, increasingly different from cultures with which it is not in contact.

UNDERSTANDING AND EVALUATING
CULTURAL DIFFERENCES

One of the most cherished themes in the anthropological subculture is *cultural relativism*, which is the practice of perceiving and understanding any element or aspect of a culture by relating it to the cultural context of which it is a part. Such an approach to understanding customs avoids the natural, more common procedure of viewing alien customs by applying the concepts and values of one's own culture, a practice which may be termed *ethnocentrism*.

Anthropologists have reported many instances of ethnocentrism. The Hopi Indians of northern Arizona make three dimensional images of supernaturals known as kachinas and give these to their children at the time of the ceremonies honoring those supernaturals. Americans, viewing this custom in terms of their own culture, which includes giving three dimensional images to children at Christmas time, have come to regard the Hopi figures as dolls. They commonly are referred to as kachina dolls, and readers of popular magazines are sometimes told how the Hopi give these dolls to their children, just as we give dolls to our children at Christmas. Cultural relativism as a mode of interpreting customs avoids the distortion and misunderstanding produced by such an ethnocentric approach. Instead the anthropologist tries to understand this custom by noting all relevant elements in the context of Hopi culture. Such inquiry reveals that the kachina images are not made for children to play with and, in this sense at least, they are not properly viewed as dolls. They are not even decorative dolls. Instead, they are provided for the children to become familiar with the appearances of the different kinds of kachina costumes worn by Hopi men as they impersonate the kachina beings in their ceremonial dances. Rather than being given to the children to play with, the images are hung from the rafters in the child's home (Oswalt, 1966: 359).

One of the main emphases of anthropological training is the avoidance of the distortions of ethnocentrism and the utilization of cultural relativism as the best way of minimizing such distortion. If it is of practical importance for us to understand the peoples of other parts of the world, it is imperative to get more of us, especially the world's decision-makers, to utilize the anthropological mode of understanding other cultures. Obviously, it is of basic importance to the validity of the conclusions of anthropological science to avoid ethnocentric interpretations.

While cultural relativism is most usefully defined as a mode of observation and understanding rather than evaluation, the fact remains that people compare and evaluate cultures and customs. The ethnocentric viewing of alien traits commonly leads to the notion that one's own culture is superior to others. Not only does the observer interpret an alien custom erroneously as a consequence of ethnocentrism, he often concludes that it is inferior. Negro African groups often have been misunderstood as buying wives, directly followed by the feeling that this is a reprehensible way of treating women. The relativistic approach reveals that the African is not purchasing a wife but compensating her relatives for her loss and the loss of her children. The compensation, in fact, may be regarded as evidence of respect for the bride and the valuable contributions women make to family life. Unfavorable judgements based on ethnocentrism help account for the refusals of tourists and other aliens to understand and adjust to the culture of the people they are visiting, and it also lies behind the *cultural imperialism* of Americans, Russians, and some others who want to urge their way of life on culturally different groups.

Anthropologists and others who, as the result of familiarity with cultural differences, have gained an appreciation of cultural relativism are apt to question ethical and religious beliefs and find it difficult to remain committed to any culture or religious faith. Many anthropologists see all supernaturalism as a cultural phenomenon only, and those who still hold to religious beliefs are prompted to re-evaluate them carefully in the list of cultural relativism. Generally, it can be said that anthropologists tend to be highly tolerant of cultural differences, though some are rather intolerant of those who are not tolerant. It seems, also, that many have made a kind of dogmatic or religious commitment to cultural equality, which actually is no more justifiable scientifically than any other faith. Some have concluded erroneously that cultural relativism demonstrates the fallacy of supernaturalistic concepts, whereas the truth is that it demonstrates neither their validity or their falsity. Nevertheless, for any who agree that cross-cultural intolerance and misunderstanding are dangerous and destructive, cultural relativism serves as a concept to combat the unwarranted ethnocentrism which tends to produce them.

LANGUAGE
IN CULTURE

Any natural language is a functioning aspect of some culture. Languages are learned rather than biologically inherited, and the utterances of a group are expressions of multi-individual esotraits. A language occupies a special place in its culture, however, since it is the vehicle by which most of the elements of the culture are transmitted from one person to another and from one generation to another. Many of the implicit elements of a culture are transmitted mainly by various kinds of actions, but most multi-individual esotraits probably are or can be expressed by utterances.

The human mind and vocal apparatus are such that a great diversity of languages is possible and, in fact, exists. Moreover, all races are born with the biological equipment for learning any language in existence. Linguistic phenomena can be understood most adequately, then, by considering the range and variety of languages in all kinds of cultures.

DESCRIPTIVE LINGUISTICS

Most of the peoples studied by anthropologists lack writing, that is, they are nonliterate. This means that it is not possible to learn about their cultures by examining anything written in their language. The most effective way to study such cultures is, in harmony with the idea of participant observation, to learn the native language and use it to interact with the people being studied. As the result of using native languages in field work, anthropologists have been led into the study of the sounds and combinations of sounds of a given language and how they are employed to communicate ideas. This study forms an important aspect of linguistic anthropology known most commonly as *descriptive linguistics*.

It is part of linguistic anthropology not only because field study has forced linguistic analysis but also because variability in linguistic structures is an integral part of the general anthropological concern with cultural variability. Accordingly, we will be concerned primarily with giving some notion of the diversity of structures which anthropologists and other descriptive linguists have found among the world's languages. To understand this structural variety it is desirable to become familiar with the concepts *phone, phoneme, morph,* and *morpheme.* When these are understood it will be possible to gain a deeper appreciation of the range and variety of ways in which human beings can formulate the meaningful utterances we commonly think of in terms of sounds, syllables, words, phrases, and sentences.

PHONETIC VARIATION

The minimal element of speech is the *phone,* and this must be understood as what is heard by a person expertly familiar with how the human organism produces sounds and who is practiced in distinguishing them from one another. This is important because the native speaker of a language lacks the ability to detect and distinguish from one another all of the sounds he uses. This is another way of saying that many phonetic customs are part of the implicit culture.

A phone may be defined as a minimal element of sound consistently employed by the speakers of a given language and distinguishable by the linguist from other such sounds in the language. In English, for example, a qualified phonetician will hear repeatedly a sound which is made by closing both lips to stop the stream of air being emitted through the mouth, then opening the lips to permit the stream to resume with a puff. The vocal cords do not vibrate. This, of course, is the sound which we usually write as p. The linguist describes it as a voiceless, bilabial stop with aspiration, and he records it as p', since this is the symbol in a widely used phonetic alphabet employed to indicate voiceless consonants produced by closing both lips to stop the air flow and then releasing the flow with a puff.

The phonetician would also hear another voiceless bilabial stop being used repeatedly by speakers of English. The only way this consistently uttered sound differs from p', is that it is not followed by a puff of air; it is unaspirated. He would record this sound by using p without the mark indicating aspiration. The layman may wonder why the linguist bothers distinguishing between the two, and the full answer must be postponed for a bit. It is enough at this point to note that the linguist distinguishes between these two closely similar sounds because they are produced differently and because he hears these differences repeatedly. We can say that the difference is patterned or habitual. Later it will become apparent that awareness of such consistent differences may be necessary to understand how the language works.

The *unaspirated,* voiceless, bilabial stop p and the *aspirated,* voiceless, bilabial stop p ' are, obviously, only two of many sounds employed consistently by speakers of English. The linguist also will recognize the voiced bilabial stop, which we write with the letter b. He will distinguish the lingua-alveolar stops produced by placing the tip of tongue against the ridge just behind the upper teeth, which we indicate with the letter t if the voiceless sound is used and by the letter d if it is voiced. Another pair of stops is made by raising the back portion of the tongue against the palate to produce the sounds we indicate with the letters k and g. Several other English sounds are *fricative* consonants. That is, the stream of air through the throat and mouth is not stopped completely but merely constricted so as to produce friction. Examples would be the sounds indicated in English writing by f, v, s, z, th, and sh. The nasal sounds of English are m, n, and ŋ (as the last sound in words ending with *ing*).

The vowel sounds involve a variety of positions of tongue and lips and are differentiated from one another largely in how high or low the tongue is held, whether this involves the front, central, or back portions of the tongue, and whether the lips are rounded or unrounded. One of our English vowels, for example, is the long e used in words such as *beet* and *sea*. It is produced with unrounded lips and with the front portion of the tongue in a high, tense position. In the International Phonetic Alphabet it is indicated by the symbol i, and it is described as a voiced, front, high, tense, unrounded vowel.

Keeping in mind the fact that anthropologists are interested in cultural differences and their significance, we find that the study of phones used in the various languages of the world provides additional evidence of cultural variation and a greater appreciation of the variety of sounds which the human is born with the ability to learn to produce. Languages vary from one another in the basic sounds they include, and no language uses more than a fraction of those which it is possible for the human organism to produce. Any normal infant utters at random a number of sounds which the adult members of his society do not produce. As he grows older, by imitation and by inculcation, he loses the ability to use some of these and acquires the ability to produce other sounds which he did not utter as an infant. The specific sounds a normal individual can use in speech depend not on his race or peculiar genetic background but upon the phonetic customs he has learned as a member of the group into which he was born. Phonetic abilities are acquired, multi-individual esotraits just as surely as other elements of culture.

Among the sounds which speakers of English would be able to produce perfectly well had they been born into a group with a language using those sounds is the voiceless, bilabial fricative. This is produced like the bilabial stop p except that the lips do not close completely, thus permitting a thin flow of air to continue. When English speakers come across this phone in a foreign language they tend to confuse it with that English phone which sounds most like it, namely, f. But f is produced by using the upper teeth and the lower lip, not both lips. The f is labio-dental, but the non-English sound, which may be written ⏀ is bilabial. This bilabial fricative, then, is one of many sounds which people of all genetic backgrounds are born equipped to pronounce but which is not used in English and some other languages.

One vowel sound not found in English is the voiced, front, high, tense, rounded vowel. A comparison of this description with that of the long e described earlier will indicate that the only difference is that the former is unrounded and the latter (written phonetically as ü) rounded. Though it is a non-English sound, users of English can learn to pronounce it simply by producing our so-called long e but rounding the lips instead of leaving them unrounded. This example illustrates how phonetic study of alien sounds can help one learn to speak a foreign language with a minimum of accent.

The voiceless bilabial fricative ⏀, and the front, high, rounded vowel ü, are only two of a great number of sounds absent from English but found in other languages. Since the position of the tongue can be varied continuously from its lowest to its highest possible position, there are at least as many vowels as there are aurally distinguishable heights. Moreover, each of these positions may be modified by the movement of the tongue forward or backward, by the shape of the lips, or by eliminating voice so as to produce voiceless vowels. Any given language uses only a fraction of the vowels all normal humans are born with the ability to learn to pronounce.

PHONEMIC VARIATION

In the structural analysis of a language the first thing the linguist does is to discover as many as possible of its phones. Having done this, he could assign some letter or symbol to each phone and use those symbols to write the language. This would be a *phonetic alphabet*. A phonetic alphabet is not necessary, however, as we shall see presently.

Any language uses a rather large number of phones. In fact, as we noted earlier, a native speaker of a language is not able to distinguish from one another all of the phones that he uses. There are scores of phones in the speech of a given group, but not all of the differences among these phones make a difference in meaning; that is, not all of the phonetic differences among them are meaningfully significant. At the beginning the linguist does not know which differences make a difference in meaning, so he keeps them separate in his analysis until certain procedures reveal which are meaningfully significant and which are not. In English the difference between the unaspirated, voiceless, bilabial stop p and the aspirated, voiceless, bilabial stop p' is not meaningfully significant. That is, whether one uses the aspirated sound or the unaspirated sound in a given utterance makes no difference in the utterance's meaning. The unaspirated sound in this pair of closely similar phones is found, for example, in the word *spill*. On rare occasions, though, the aspirated form may occur in this word, as when a mother exclaims in

exasperation, "Oh-h-h, Johnny, you sp(*puff of air*)*illed* your milk."
While this is an unusual way of pronouncing *spill*, it does not change
its meaning. Actually what we have in English is that the unaspirated,
bilabial stop is used following s, whereas the aspirated stop is used
at the beginning of a word, as in the word *pill*. If you suspend a thin
piece of paper just before your lips and pronounce the two words, *spill*
and *pill* alternately, you will be able to detect the puff of air with the
latter word and its absence with the former. This difference is an example of what is called *conditioned variation*, which means that one
sound is found only in one kind of sound environment, whereas the
other similar sound is used only in a different kind of sound context
(Pittman, 1948: 60ff.).

Another example of how a difference between similar phones may
not be meaningfully significant may be taken from the language of
the Ottawa Indians (Pittman, 1948: 58). The Ottawa word for *hello*
may be written phonetically either as boǯo or as ƀoǯo. (Pronounce the o
like that in *so*, and the ǯ like the g in *beige*). The initial sound in
the first utterance is the English b, and the initial sound of the second
utterance is the voiced, bilabial fricative, similar except for its voicing
to the voiceless bilabial fricative described previously. The only phonetic
difference between the two initial sounds is that one is a stop and the
other is a fricative, but this difference does not make a difference in
meaning. An Ottawa can use either sound in this word and it still means
hello. This is an example of what is called *free variation*. The Ottawa
speaker makes no differentiation between the bilabial fricative and the
bilabial stop and, in fact, may even regard them as one sound.

Whenever, as in these two examples, the linguist finds similar
phones the differences between which are not meaningfully significant
he puts them together into a single category of sounds which he calls
a *phoneme*. In English, for example, the aspirated p' and the unaspirated
p are included in the same phoneme, which may be indicated in an
alphabet by a single symbol. A phoneme, then, may be defined as a
category of *alternative* phones, variation within which makes no difference in meaning. As noted, the difference between the two phones p
and p' makes no difference in meaning in English utterances; and the
difference between the two phones b and ƀ makes no difference in the
meaning of Ottawa utterances. In each example we have a phoneme
which includes at least two alternative sounds, and no matter which
sound is used in a given utterance, the meaning is unchanged. Such
alternative phones are known as *allophones*.

Use of a similar phone which *does* change the meaning, however,
indicates that the phone must be regarded as in a different phoneme.
In English b differs from p only slightly, mainly in that the b is a bilabial
stop *with* voicing and the p is a bilabial stop *without* voice. If one says
bill rather than *pill* the meaning of the utterance is changed; therefore,
it is impossible to include b in the same phoneme with the kinds of p
we have in English. Variation from the sounds of a phoneme, therefore,
makes a difference in meaning.

The essential point to be derived from this discussion is that languages differ from one another in which sounds belong to the same phoneme and which belong to different phonemes. Here is another way in which cultures differ. In some cultures the difference between *b* and *p* makes a difference in the meanings of the utterances in which the sounds are used; but in some it does not, with the result that *b* and *p* may be placed in the same phoneme. In some languages the difference between *b* and *ƀ* is meaningfully significant, whereas in others, as in Ottawa, it is not. In the Turkish language, the vowels in our English words *bet* and *bat* are not distinguished. A linguist will hear both of these vowel phones used repeatedly in Turkish, but analysis will show that the difference between them makes no difference in meaning; they may be included as alternative phones within a phoneme (Swift and Ağrali, 1966: 6f.).

A native speaker of a language uses any of the phones in a phoneme, varying from one to another according to the conditioning effect of neighboring sounds or other influences, and, in all probability, he does this quite unconsciously. With this in mind it is possible to understand why it is unnecessary to use a phonetic alphabet. A separate alphabetic symbol for each distinguishable phone is unnecessarily cumbersome. All that is required is a symbol for each phoneme and, after learning the value of the symbols, the native reader will use whichever allophone suits him or whichever one fits the sound environment in which he is using it. In English we do not need separate letters for the two kinds of *p*; one will suffice. It is this kind of analysis which makes it possible for descriptive linguists to provide an alphabet for previously unwritten languages. A *phonemic alphabet* is easily learned by a native for both reading and writing his language.

MORPHOLOGICAL VARIATION

So far, it has been emphasized that languages vary from one another *phonetically*, that is, in regard to what sounds they employ, and *phonemically*, that is, in respect to how the sounds they use are classified into categories of alternative phones. Just as the meaning of the concept of phone must be understood to learn what a phoneme is, so the meaning of the phoneme concept must be kept in mind to understand *morphs* and *morphemes*.

It is important at this point to remember that a phoneme does not have a specific meaning; it merely makes a difference in meaning. The smallest unit of language which has a specific meaning is the *morph*. A morph may consist of only one phoneme, but commonly it is made up of more than one. To avoid confusion it is essential to remember that a morph may be composed of a combination of parts, that is, a combination of phonemes. The phoneme, however, is *not a combination* of parts but a category of alternative sounds. The morph may be defined as a linguistic unit composed of either one phoneme or a combination of phonemes plus a specific meaning. It cannot be divided without destroying or greatly modifying its meaning.

An English morph which consists of only one phoneme is the plural s sound, which is used in connection with other linguistic units to indicate more than one of whatever is being named. For example, it is employed with words such as *bat*, *book*, and *turnip*, which are understood to mean one of each, to produce *bats*, *books*, and *turnips*, which are understood to mean more than one of each. Most English morphs, however, consist of a combination of more than one phoneme. *Bat* is a morph consisting of three phonemes and the meaning, "wooden implement for hitting the ball in certain games." Another morph, one which always must be used in connection with other morphs, is *in*, as in the words *inflexible* and *inactive*. *In* is a combination of two phonemes and the meaning, "not."

Linguistic studies have shown, however, that morphs may differ somewhat from one another without a change in meaning. For example, the English plural of *bat*, as already noted, uses the s sound; but the plural of *bag*, *song*, *telephone*, and many other English words is the z sound. We do not write it as z in such words, but that is the way we pronounce it. It will take only a little experimenting on the reader's part to ascertain that we use the s sound for some plurals and z for others. The meaning, however, is still plural; and it is apparent that we have two morphs, similar soundwise, but still somewhat different, and the sound difference makes no difference in the meaning. These examples show that different morphs can often be put into a single category because they have the same meaning, and this category is what linguists refer to as a *morpheme*. The plural morpheme in English consists of the two morphs mentioned above as well as at least one other morph we haven't mentioned. The previously mentioned morph *in* also is an *allomorph* (alternative morph) of a morpheme. Another form of this morpheme is the *im* in *immoral*. A morpheme, then, may be defined as consisting of a morph or a set of alternative morphs and a meaning which remains the same regardless of which morph is used.

Morphemes are combined in various ways to form words. Languages vary from one another in regard to the combinations of phonemes they use to form morphs and morphemes, the specific meanings associated with these combinations, and the means by which the morphemes are combined to form words. In English the morpheme indicating plurality and the morpheme meaning *not* (*in*, *im*, etc.) are examples of bound morphemes, since they cannot be used except by attachment to other morphemes. *Boy*, however, is a free morpheme, since it can be used alone as a word. The word *boys* is made up of two morphemes, *boy*, and the plural morpheme, the former being a free morpheme and the latter a bound morpheme. *Boy*, of course, is a combination of phonemes rather than only one. Other words may be composed of two or more free morphemes, such as the word *hatrack*. Still other words are composed of two or more bound morphemes, such as *retain*—*re* meaning back and *tain* indicating keeping or holding.

Languages vary from one another in respect to the kinds of words most often used. Some languages make much use of words composed of bound morphemes or combinations of bound with free morphemes, English being an example. Others make much more use of words which consist of one morpheme only. Instead of using bound morphemes, they tend to use additional words, each consisting of only one morpheme. Chinese is an example. Languages also may differ from one another in respect to the frequency with which they construct words of two or more free morphemes. Some, in fact, commonly put free morphemes together in long strings which are regarded as making up a single unit, that is, a word.

Some of the morphemes of a language may be called *root morphemes*; that is, they are basic morphemes with important meanings, and are altered or added to in various ways to form words which utilize these basic meanings. The various ways in which root morphemes are altered to form words are called *morphological processes*. Prefixation is the process of adding a morpheme to the beginning of another morpheme to form a word. *Trans* is a prefix widely used in English, and *transport* is an example of a word in which it is used. *Suffixation* is the addition of a unit to the end of the root, the *ly* in *quickly* being an example. *Infixation* is the insertion of a morpheme within another one to modify its meaning. The Sioux word *cheti* means "to build a fire." *Chewati* means "I build a fire" (Sapir, 1921: 73). Analysis reveals that *wa* is a morpheme indicating first person. Some languages are tonal, which means that the meaning of words is regularly modified by shifting the pitch of one or more syllables. Other morphological processes are *vowel change, consonantal change, reduplication* of a morpheme, and *accent shift*. Some morphological processes are not found in some languages. Tone shift and infixation, for example, are not used in the formulation of English words. Cultures vary extensively in the kinds of morphological processes used and the degree to which they use them.

SYNTACTICAL VARIATION

Languages also vary from one another in the ways they combine words with one another to form phrases and sentences, that is, in syntax. It is not possible to substitute word equivalents in the same position from one language to another. In the Nbaka language of the Northern Congo to say, "I will never make a home with you," one must say, "Not I make will house with you." (Nida, 1957: 165). Otherwise it won't make any more sense to a speaker of Nbaka than his way would be to a speaker of English. Word order often makes a difference in meaning within the same language. "The man bites the dog" does not convey the same message as, "The dog bites the man." Word order is much more important in some languages for the conveyance of meaning than it is in others.

ASPECTS OF DESCRIPTIVE ANALYSIS

When a linguist has analyzed the language in terms of the various elements discussed above he has a full picture of the structure of the language and the functional relationships among its parts. Descriptive analysis of a language consists of four phases corresponding with the four aspects of variation: 1) *phonetic analysis* to determine the minimal sounds used, 2) *phonemic analysis* to determine how the phones can be classified into meaningful units known as phonemes, 3) *morphological analysis* to identify the morphs and morphemes of the language and the ways they are used to form words, and 4) *syntactical analysis* to determine how words are combined with one another to form phrases and sentences.

Applied linguists carry out such analysis of a language and assign symbols to each phoneme to construct an alphabet. Then the people can be taught to read and write, and, knowing the structures and processes of their language, the linguist can compose or translate works in the indigenous language, whether they be history, sacred writings, agricultural instructions, fiction, or a wide variety of practical treatises of value to the people.

TRANSFORMATIONAL-GENERATIVE GRAMMAR

Students of cultural anthropology should be aware of a relatively new and controversial linguistic approach which emphasizes the study of the phrase structure of sentences as the basis for ascertaining the grammar of a language. Noam Chomsky, linguist at the Massachusetts Institute of Technology, has challenged a number of the assumptions associated with the methods of descriptive linguistics, though these assumptions have not been specified in this brief treatment. Chomsky and those of like mind feel that the descriptive linguists have failed to give adequate attention to syntax as the basis for understanding any language's grammar and, in fact, insist that the phonemic and morphological arrangements of a language can be understood adequately only within the context of its syntax (Chomsky, 1957: 13ff.). The transformation theorists allege that the arrangement of the components of sentences is governed by basic rules intuitively known to the speakers of a language by the time they are five or six years of age. They see a language as composed of a number of kernel sentences (op. cit. 46). Kernel sentences are simple, which means that they consist of only a noun phrase (composed of a noun and, sometimes, an article) and a verb phrase (composed of main verb and whatever auxiliary form is necessary to complete the thought).

Secondly, kernel sentences are active (rather than passive) and thirdly, declarative (rather than interrogative, etc.) (Thomas, 1962: 198). The speakers of a language, the transformationists emphasize, can distinguish kernel sentences which are grammatical from arrangements of words which are not grammatical. In doing so they are governed by rules which make it possible to determine or evaluate grammatically an utterance. *David runs. The boys have caught the horse,* and *The coyote chases the mouse* are examples of grammatical kernel sentences in English. *The mouse coyote the chases* and *Have caught the boys the horse,* however, violate the phrase structure rules and are, consequently, not grammatical.

Transformational-generative grammar takes its name from the fact that the kernel sentences of a language can be modified or transformed in various ways to generate the infinite variety of utterances possible in all languages. These transformations involve the rearrangement of the parts and/or addition of elements such as adverbs, adjectives, and pre-positional phrases; all this according to invariable abstract rules intuitively understood by the speakers of the language. Conformity to these rules results in grammatically acceptable sentences; violation of them results in ungrammatical or nonsense utterances. Transformationists insist that languages can be analyzed in terms of these rules and that the relations among the smaller elements of which the language is composed can be understood fully only in terms of the principles of sentence structure.

It is impossible here to evaluate transformational linguistics as applied cross-culturally. It has proven useful for teaching language, particularly languages foreign to the student; and it has applications in teaching machines to work with linguistic materials. It remains to be seen what degree of success transformationism will have in discovering rules governing the transformation processes of the world's languages; and only if this is done successfully will it be possible to describe the range and variety of transformation rules employed in the world's cultures. The assessment of the theoretical disagreement between the descriptive linguist and the transformation theorists is beyond the scope of this introduction.

COMPARATIVE AND HISTORICAL LINGUISTICS

Careful comparisons of languages with one another in terms of their phonetic, phonemic, morphological, and syntactical characteristics enable linguists to classify languages into families according to their varying degrees of similarity. It is then assumed that those languages which are similar enough to one another to be put in the same family have a common origin. Presumably, different families of languages may have common origins but this is not demonstrable from a comparison of them.

About nine language families are spoken by close to ninety per cent of the world's population (Nida, 1954: 203). One of these is Dravidian and includes Tamil, Malayalam, Telugu, and Brahui, all languages of the subcontinent of India. Another is Indo-European, which includes Hindi, Sanskrit, Greek, Russian, French, German, English, and a number of others. Some areas of the world are far more variable linguistically than others. A recent classification indicates nineteen different families for North America (Driver, 1961: 576); and it has been alleged that there are more than eighty families in South America (Beals and Hoijer, 1965: 613). Many of these are represented by only a few hundred speakers.

Some historical linguists have tried to determine whether or not vocabulary and grammatical changes occur at constant rates, hoping that they will be able to determine how long ago similar languages split off from one another. *Lexicostatistics*, also known as *glottochronology*, is such a method. It is based on research into the history of written languages, which shows that the "basic vocabulary" of a language may be expected to change at the rate of nineteen per cent every thousand years. This basic vocabulary consists of words for a sample of a hundred concepts regarded as universal in human culture. Glottochronology, for example, indicates that the Navaho language of the southwestern part of the United States became separate from the Kutchin language of Alaska about 850 years ago (Beals, 1965: 629). Not all linguists accept glottochronology as a valid technique, but it continues to be used, and it remains to see how it will stand the test of time.

METALINGUISTICS

In addition to *descriptive linguists* and *comparative linguistics*, a third branch of linguistic anthropology is *metalinguistics*, which explores the relationship between a language and the way its speakers view their total environment. How people think about and perceive the world in which they live is thought by some to be largely a consequence of the way they refer to their environment linguistically. The brand of metalinguistics of greatest concern to anthropologists is *ethnolinguistics*, which has to do with the linkages between linguistic customs and non-linguistic elements of cultures. Problems in this area frequently are discussed under the rubric *language and culture*, though it always must be kept in mind that linguistic traits are learned and multi-individual just as surely as any other cultural trait. Language is an aspect of culture.

The notion that language influences people's thought and experience is commonly known as the *Sapir-Whorf hypothesis*, for it was promoted extensively by the anthropologist-linguist, Edward Sapir, and by an engineer turned linguist by the name of Benjamin L. Whorf. Whorf became interested in the problem as a consequence of his observations that behavior is influenced by the words people use. He noted that a workman handling barrels of gasoline was very careful about his matches and cigarettes, but after the barrels were emptied, that is, when they could be defined linguistically as *empty*, he was no longer careful (1941: 75). As the result of this kind of thing, accidents occurred.

Such observations prompted Whorf to study other languages to see to what extent there were cross-cultural differences of this kind. From his study of Hopi, for example, he reported that temporary events such as lightning, wave, flame, meteor, pulsation, etc. are all referred to by using verbs, thus clearly indicating short duration. In English, on the other hand, we express these by nouns, disposing us thereby to think of them as having a degree of stability and permanence apparently not attributed to them by the Hopi (1956: 215). Dorothy Lee, using linguistic data secured by Bronislaw Malinowski, has pointed out that the language of the Trobriand Islanders of the South Pacific does not provide ready ways of expressing change or causation (1949: 401ff.). There is no word for becoming or for being, for the Trobrianders are concerned with being only and do not feel any need for words to distinguish between being and becoming. Neither does their language provide ready ways to distiguish among the past, present, and future, for being is timeless. An examination of Trobriand syntax shows that the sentences are formed by arranging the words discretely without additional elements to show the relationships among them. They lack the subject-verb-predicate sequence which disposes English speakers to interpret the world in cause and effect terms. The Trobrianders are capable of expressing a sequence in terms of cause and effect, but their language does not encourage them to do so. Thus, they view their world of experience much differently than speakers of English, who cannot satisfactorily comprehend Trobriand experience because the structures of the English language do not provide them with satisfactory tools by which to think about it or discuss it. This consideration of the relationship between language and experience as expressed in the culture suggests the importance of knowing the language if one wishes to understand a culture and, also, knowing the culture as an aid to the analysis of a language.

Anthropologists always have realized the importance of the relationship between a language and its cultural context, but there remains some disagreement as to the degree of validity of the Sapir-Whorf hypothesis and the specifics of the linkages between linguistic and non-linguistic customs. Nevertheless, anthropologists are experiencing increasing appreciation of the language in culture approach, and there are calls for more explicit, more refined methods of study and theoretical analysis. Dell Hymes has called for an ". . . *ethnography of speaking* . . .", which approaches languages not just as systems of utterance units but in terms of the culturally defined meanings, behavioral contexts, and social functions of utterances (1962: 13ff.). One anthropological method which moves along these lines, now enjoying some popularity, is known as *componential analysis*. Native terms are identified and their entire range of meanings in the culture explored. The approach is essentially an investigation of how people divide and classify experience through their language. That different cultures do this differently is well-known to anthropologists, and componential analysis is a method of exploring these differences.

VARIATION IN COMPLEXITY AND VOCABULARY SIZE

Languages vary in complexity of grammar and in the number of words in the vocabulary. Some nonliterate languages are more complex than those of some civilized cultures. In fact, all languages are complex. Navaho was used by the United States during World War II as an unbreakable code and is one of the most difficult of languages to learn. Since civilized cultures have larger numbers of customs, they may be expected to have a larger number of words than simpler cultures. This does not mean, however, that given individuals in nonliterate societies may not have larger vocabularies than many individuals in civilized societies. There is no language which consists of only a few hundred words; all have vocabularies of many thousands.

 **TECHNOLOGY**

Technology, in its basic cultural meaning, refers to all of the social customs by which people manipulate material entities and substances of all kinds. It includes techniques of manipulating raw materials to produce artifacts, ways of handling or modifying artifacts, and means of manipulating animal and human bodies, including one's own body (Honigmann, 1959: 290). This concept means that technology extends into all areas of culture. The manner in which water is applied in baptism, the kissing of the hand in greeting a respected elder, a way of mixing art pigments, or the means of holding a saxophone are all techniques. Conventionally, however, anthropologists confine technology as an aspect of culture mainly to the production and utilization of foodstuffs, shelter, clothing, and the containers and implements desired to satisfy physical wants. These will be the concern of this chapter.

EVALUATION OF TECHNOLOGIES

Euroamerican cultures have developed exceedingly complex technologies. One anthropologist has said that the focus of American culture, that is, the aspect in which Americans are most interested, is technology (Herskovits, 1948: 544). This focus seems to be accompanied by the thought that cultures of simple technology are inferior.

There is no question but that many of the artifacts produced by today's advanced civilizations are superior in the sense that they make possible greater control over the physical world. This is not a scientific criterion for evaluating cultures, however, since some could argue that greater control of the material world has not brought greater happiness, which may be preferred as the greater goal. This is an issue which has not been settled by scientific method, since there is no agreed upon scientific means of establishing what goals are most important.

Yet a dispassionate and careful look at the techniques of nonliterate cultures provides occasion for admiration even by the standards of Western civilization. Melville Herskovits has pointed out that non-literate peoples utilize a very large proportion of the fundamental principles of engineering (1952: 241). Moreover, many techniques which appear at first glance to be crude are far from it when one takes into account the skills and intelligence demanded. In fact, so-called primitives manifest an ingenuity and proficiency in dealing directly with sometimes rather harsh environments which most civilized persons are unable to match. In Euroamerican societies most of the technology has been turned over to specialists, many individuals actually being much less accomplished technologically than many members of nonliterate groups. And a given Euroamerican technologist may be quite ignorant and unskilled in technological areas other than that in which he specializes.

PRODUCTION OF ARTIFACTS

No human group is so simple as to live without planned production of tools, weapons, implements, containers, and other artifacts. A rather wide variety of objects is produced from stone—knives, scrapers, axe heads, lance and projectile points, drills, adze heads, and many more. Some of these are produced by chipping hunks of stone which can be fractured easily without disintegrating, such as flint or obsidian. Other tools may be made by grinding or rubbing the surface of a fine-grained stone, a process which takes more time than chipping but which produces a more durable tool.

Large numbers of objects, especially where trees are abundant, are made of wood, the variety of items being so great that there is little point in enumerating them. A number of the wooden items produced by nonliterate peoples manifest considerable skill, particularly when it is remembered that the basic tools are the axe, the adze (which has the blade running at right angles to the length of the handle), and the knife. Maori craftsmen are famous for the intricate carving with which they covered the panels and posts of their council houses. Woodworking is highly developed, not only in the South Pacific, but in parts of Africa and along the Coast of British Columbia. Among the many well-crafted items produced by the Mangbettu of the Congo was a man's bench produced by stitching the parts together with reeds (Schweinfurth, 1874: 114f.). They also followed the practice of burying wood in moist earth to darken it. The Indians of British Columbia make planks of red cedar, smoothing the sides with adzes, and polishing them with stones and dogfish skin. A number of objects, including a box made from a single piece of wood, are made by heating and steaming the wood until it can be bent to the desired shape. The edges of planks are sometimes stitched together and worked in such a way that the joint is hardly noticeable (Drucker, 1965: 30).

Objects of bone and horn also are employed extensively by non-literate peoples. Needles, awls, hide scrapers, hoe blades, and harpoon heads are among the great diversity of objects which have been produced.

Animal skins are employed to make bags, bottles, shields, pouches, cases in which to store food, clothing, and numerous other items. Some items are made of rawhide, but hides are often tanned to produce leather. The fatty tissue and, if desired, the hair, is removed with a scraper to expose the portion of the skin which is to be treated chemically. Urine, brain substances, flour and sour milk mush, and tannin from bark are among the several substances which have been used to treat skins. Some peoples employ only mechanical means to make the skins flexible, such as kneading and chewing.

The production and use of felt is of importance among Tibetans, Turks, and other pastoral nomads who have an adequate supply of wool or hair. The material is rolled, beaten, and pressed into compact, even sheets. Tents, blankets, rugs, mattresses, mittens, boots, hats, and rain coats of felt have been common among various peoples.

Though felting originally was found only in Asia and Europe, the somewhat similar process of making bark cloth is practiced in Africa, Central and South America, Indonesia, and Oceania. The inner bark of suitable trees is beaten with mallets, usually grooved, so that the bark will be worked into a thin mat of criss-crossing fibers. The anvil usually is of wood, often a log. The commonest use of bark cloth is in clothing, though it is used for a number of other purposes, too. Since not all species of trees provide suitable bark, the cloth is produced only in those regions where these trees are found. Decorative designs often are applied to the cloth. In some places, rather than being beaten into fabric, bark is used for clothing in some other state, commonly in shredded form.

Containers and mats often are produced by the interlacing of relatively stiff and wide splints of materials, commonly grass, but also many other things such as roots, twigs, or leaf strips. Such containers are known as *baskets* and the techniques by which the elements are interwoven whether the items produced are containers or otherwise, as *basketry*.

Plaiting as a basketry technique is the weaving by hand of strands which are about equally pliant so that they cross one another at right angles. This sometimes is done by hanging the warp strands from a frame and pulling the woof strands through by hand. If the criss-crossing strands are alternated one at a time, *checkerwork* is produced. If more than one of the strands is regularly crossed, the result is *twilled work* and the technique is *twilling*.

In these two forms of plaiting warp and woof strands cannot be distinguished. In *twining*, however, strands are worked onto a frame of rigid warp strands, and this can be done so tightly and finely that the basket will hold water. The pliant woof strands also can be wrapped around each warp element, producing *wrapped basketry*, or twining and wrapping can be combined in the same basket. When heavy strands are coiled and the coils bound tightly to one another by looping pliant elements around two or more of them, the technique is known as *coiling*. Plaiting, twining and wrapping, and coiling are three basic techniques, but they are combined and varied to produce a number of different kinds of weaves. Moreover, elements of different color and form are employed to vary the basket's appearance.

In a number of communities or regions one technique or another is dominant or used exclusively. Coiling, for example, was not found in northern California, though twining was common. A central California group, the Pomo, utilized a variety of weaves and produced what are said to be the finest baskets in the world (Kroeber, 1962: 263). This is in spite of the fact that the culture was relatively simple in most other aspects.

True weaving must be distinguished from plaiting, even when a frame is used. Weaving differs in that the warp threads, that is, the base threads which are stretched parallel to one another on the loom frame, are divided into alternating sets which can be raised and lowered in relation to one another so as to insert woof threads between them in one movement rather than passing it alternately over and under each thread. A rod called a *heddle* is attached by means of short threads to every other warp thread. This makes it possible to raise this set of threads away from the rest of them so that a *shuttle*, a small implement containing the bobbin on which the woof thread is wound, can be passed between the two sets of warp threads. A second heddle is attached to the other half of the warp threads in the same way, making it possible to raise that set. This reversal of the relative positions of the two sets of warp threads secures the previously inserted woof thread in place and makes possible the passage of the shuttle with its thread in the opposite direction. After a woof thread has been inserted it may be packed tightly against the previous one by means of a *batten*, a bar which extends the width of the loom. If the design being woven is complex there may be several shuttles, one for each color of yarn.

The threads used in weaving are spun, though spun threads also can be used in plaiting. Many peoples produce yarn and string by rolling the fibers between the hand and the thigh, though this method is slow and may produce lumpy thread. The *spindle whorl* is used in many places to produce better yarns faster than is possible with the hand and thigh. The spinner twists a little fiber into a short length of yarn and fastens it to a slender rod to which is attached a disk of clay or wood in the manner of a wheel to an axle. The disk is closer to the bottom end of the rod than the top and acts as a flywheel to keep the rod turning when the spinner has given it a twist. As the rod spins, twisting the yarn, the spinner adds additional fiber, manipulating it so that it twists into the previously spun yarn to produce a continuous, tightly twisted thread. When a length of yarn has been spun it is wound around the spindle near the whorl, and the spinning is continued by giving the implement another twist and adding more fiber. Peoples of the Old World allow the spindle to fall toward the ground while turning, whereas those of the New World commonly permit it to spin on the ground or in a bowl.

The *belt loom* is a widely used type in which the warp is tensioned between two bars, one of which is attached to a stationary object and the other of which is fastened to a belt around the weaver's waist. Tension is maintained by the weaver's body. This type of loom was common in the New World. In some parts of the Old World various improvements on the basic loom were made, including foot pedals to operate heddles, revolving beams instead of stationary bars, and complete frames to which the various loom parts can be attached.

Among the fibers which have been woven on looms are cotton, flax, wool, hair, and bark.

A wide variety of objects of fired clay are made by sedentary non-literate groups. Nomadic peoples find it more practicable to use less breakable materials such as stone, wood, hide, basketry, or sheets of bark, and the few who utilize pottery ordinarily produce only a few objects. The most common use of fired clay is for pots, but a variety of other items such as figurines, smoking pipes, spindle whorls, and various kinds of ornaments may be produced.

Pottery-making is a highly developed skill. The clays must include the proper proportions of substances so that the pot will not crack during drying and firing. Tempers of various materials—sand, pulverized pieces of broken pots, and the like—commonly are added for this purpose. The pot also must be properly shaped to avoid breaking during firing or during use. Sometimes this is done by *molding*, that is, applying the clay to a mold such as a basket or old pot. Pots are also shaped with the fingers alone from a lump of clay, a process known as *modeling*. The *coiling* method of shaping pots consists of building up a spiral of rolled pieces of clay. These are pinched together and the shaping completed by smoothing the inner and outer surfaces by rubbing or scraping. Wheel-made pottery is limited to literate cultures of Europe and Asia.

After shaping, the pottery is dried, but it is useless until fired so as to transform it into a water- and heat-resistant item. This process, too, requires much skill. Some people fire ceramic items in open fireplaces, but many place them in a furnace or kiln, which makes possible greater control and higher temperatures.

Untreated pottery is porous and allows liquids to seep through slowly. Some groups waterproof the pots by applying a glaze, which also adds to the appearance. Glazing involves adding a thin coating of clay containing a mineral and firing a second time. Porcelain, invented by the Chinese, is a highly developed type of glazing in which the added substance penetrates the entire utensil, making it glasslike. Some peoples who do not glaze pots augment a pot's ability to retain liquid by applying a surface coat of finer clay (a slip), rubbing melted resin on the surface, or smoking the pot and smearing it with fat. Glazing or the addition of other substances is often done for the purpose of making it easier to paint the pot.

Pots may be elaborated by the addition of bases, legs, handles, or other elements. Various designs may be incised in the clay or painted on before firing. Cultures vary from one another widely in the shapes of pottery and the designs applied.

In modern times machine-produced containers of metal have widely replaced pots of fired clay. True metallurgy, however, was known in both the Old and the New Worlds. This involves the smelting of metals from ore rather than their use in the natural state. Iron working was not developed in the New World, but it is outstanding in most of the Negro cultures of Africa and among the nonliterate peoples of southern and eastern Asia. The industry is so highly developed in Africa that some have felt that it was an independent development there, but it is now generally thought that the basic concept of iron working diffused to Africa from Asia Minor.

FIRES

Ordinarily fires have not been considered as artifacts, but though they are not of well-defined shape and last only a short time unless fed, usable fires ordinarily require technological production. All nonliterate peoples use fires and only a rare few are unable to produce them. Some groups use percussion methods to strike a spark and thereby ignite tinder. Others use various kinds of friction methods. The fire drill, which involves spinning a rod of wood in a depression in another piece of wood to create enough heat to ignite tinder, is widespread. The rod may be rotated between the hands or it may be operated by wrapping a bow string around it and moving the bow back and forth. The latter device is called the bow drill. Some peoples utilize what is called a pump drill. Two cords are attached to the top of the rod and twisted around it, the other end of each cord being secured to a horizontal cross bar. The bar is then worked up and down to wind and unwind the cords so as to turn the drill. The fire saw is another friction device and involves drawing a stick back and forth across the grain of another piece of wood. The fire plow consists of rubbing the end of a stick back and forth along a groove in the direction of the wood grain.

SUBSISTENCE TECHNOLOGY

Every human group must include as a part of the culture some system of customs whereby they wrest a food supply from their habitat. The kinds of foods secured obviously must depend on what is available. No society, however, lives a life of leisure, simply plucking luscious food from trees or bushes at will whenever they hunger. Some work harder than others, but all groups work for a living.

Several major kinds of technologies for the securing of foodstuffs are distinguished. *Collecting* involves the gathering of primarily wild plant items, though the capture of insects and, sometimes, the smallest forms of animal life might be included. Hunting, fishing, agriculture, and stock-raising are the other major subsistence modes. It is important to remember that a given subsistence system includes more than one of these. Hunting, collecting, and fishing are frequently found in combination among those peoples who gather animals and plants from the natural environment rather than producing them as is done in agriculture and stock-raising. Even producers of foodstuffs often employ one or more of the food gathering techniques as well.

A wide variety of specific techniques and utensils is used in collecting wild products, depending partly on what is being obtained. The collection of berries or mushrooms, for example, might require no more than a basket or other receptacle to put them in during picking. Pointed *digging sticks* are used by many peoples to unearth roots, bulbs, grubs, and the like. *Beaters*, often of plaited basketry, are used in the collection of seeds. Long, hooked *poles* may be used to secure nuts, cones and such from trees. *Knives*, of course, are useful for cutting various products from the bushes or trees on which they grow. Nets may be used for catching insects or birds.

Simple collection of wild foods seems crude to most peoples with technologically complex cultures, but competence is, in fact, required in collecting. Knowledge of where and when to find wild plant foods, including the ability to distinguish edible from poisonous species, and the means of obtaining them is transmitted from generation to generation as part of the culture. Such knowledge, gathered by ethnographers, has been incorporated into survival manuals for military or other personnel who might become lost in an alien habitat (Kluckhohn, 1949: 173).

The hunting of wild game generally involves the use of equipment of greater bulk and complexity than the collecting of wild plants and insects. Large, strong animals such as the bison, deer, bear, guanaco, kangaroo, caribou, or whale ordinarily are brought down with substantial weapons which are thrown or by weapons propelled by mechanical contrivances. A *club*, a *knife*, or a *lance* can be used to dispatch game, but these require the hunter to approach the animal more closely than is usually possible or safe. Some groups use knives or clubs specially designed for throwing, making close approach unnecessary. The *boomerang* is a flattish, angular throwing stick, rare models being designed for return. The *bola* consists of several weights connected with one another by cords, which wrap around the legs of an animal when thrown at it. The *harpoon*, which has a point to which a cord is attached and which separates from the shaft when it penetrates the animal, can either be thrust like a lance or thrown like the *spear*. Spears commonly are thrown by means of the *spear thrower*, also known as the *atlatl*, which is one solution to the problem of how to propel a projectile a greater distance or with greater force. This device is simply a stick with a hook or other arrangement at one end to receive the basal extremity of the spear shaft. In throwing, the spearman retains the front end of the spear thrower in his hand, using the atlatl as an extension of his arm.

The most widespread mechanical device for propelling a missile is the *bow*. It occasionally is used to project pellets, but its usual use is with the *arrow*. Anthropologists commonly distinguish two basic types, the *self bow*, which is of one piece, and the *compound bow*, which is built up of layers of wood, bone, or sinews. A skillfully made compound bow has considerable power. The bowstrings are made of a variety of vegetal and animal fibers. A good deal of skill goes into the making of good bows and arrows. There is a variety of techniques for handling the weapon. Different groups hold the string and arrow in different ways when shooting, and a number use special devices to pull back the string and arrow against the tension of very powerful bows.

The *sling* is a fairly widely used device for augmenting the projection of pellets or stones. The *blowgun* employs concentrated air power to propel darts. In modern times the gun, which utilizes explosive chemicals for high speed propulsion of specially designed missiles, has been acquired by many of the world's nonliterate groups and has replaced their aboriginal weapons. Poisons are not infrequently used on the points of spears, arrows, or blowgun darts.

Traps differ from weapons in that they can operate in the absence of the individual using them. There is a large variety of traps, many quite ingenious, but the common types are the *pitfall*, the *snare*, and the *deadfall*. Animals which fall into the camouflaged pits may find themselves impaled on sharp stakes. A snare consists of a loop arranged in such a way that when the animal enters it it will tighten and hold him. The common procedure is to attach one end of a cord to a bent sapling, though there are other means. The deadfall consists of a weight which, when tripped by the animal, falls on it and holds it down. The weight may have a spear mounted in it so as to transfix the animal. One North American group trapped wolves by building two concentric circles of stakes with a door opening inward in the outer wall. When the wolf entered and secured the bait he would go forward between the walls until he pushed the door shut, thus trapping himself.

There is a variety of other arrangements by which animals are taken. Eskimos place a bloody knife in the ground with the blade up. A wolf may lick the knife, cutting his tongue, and excitedly gorge himself to death on his own blood. Very common is the use of various kinds of lures and disguises. Hunters often reproduce the animal's call or masquerade in its skin in order to approach it closely. Nets are used in hunting as well. It is common in the hunting of grazing animals to drive them into a pen or corner them in the V of converging fences or the end of a blind canyon. Herds also may be driven over cliffs or into rivers and lakes, where they can be dispatched while swimming, perhaps from canoes. Animals may also be driven into the open or into an ambush by setting fire to the vegetation. Anthropologists are impressed with the keen observation and ingenuity which lies behind the hunting techniques of nonliterate peoples.

Fishing commonly is secondary to hunting and collecting or to agriculture, but there are some groups which depend mainly on fishing. A number of the techniques already mentioned in connection with hunting are used for taking fish. Some groups shoot them with the bow and arrow, or they may be impaled on spears, usually with multiple prongs. Fish traps often consist of a cage with a small opening at the end of a cone or a V through which the fish easily enter but find it difficult to locate the way out. The traps frequently are set in openings in weirs or dams. Poisons often are placed in water so that the stupefied fish can be gathered at will. Fishing by means of nets is widespread, the nets being either thrown or fixed in streams or other places where fish may be entangled in them. The hook and line is fairly widely used also. Hooks may be carved from bone or wood or made of metal. Both barbed and unbarbed hooks are found.

One of the most highly developed fishing areas of the world is coastal British Columbia, where the Indians secured such an abundant supply of salmon, herring, and other fish that they had the leisure to develop their social and ceremonial system and their arts to a degree unusual for nonagricultural peoples.

The main tasks in *hand agriculture* are preparation of the fields, planting, caring for the growing crops, and harvesting. Nonliterate peoples in all parts of the world use what is usually called *slash-and-burn* techniques, though it is sometimes known as *shifting* or *swidden* cultivation. This involves the cutting and burning of the trees and other vegetation in the area to be utilized. When the plot's fertility has been exhausted, the process is repeated in another place. Deforestation and erosion have been the consequences of this in many regions. In some places the land may be renewed by floods or by artificial means. The *digging stick* and the *hoe* are the most widely found soil preparation and planting implements among nonliterate farmers. The digging stick is used to loosen the soil or to poke a hole into which the seed is deposited. A few groups have added a foot bar to the stick to gain added leverage. Hoe blades are made of bone, stone, wood, or metal. African farmers use a short-handled hoe with an iron blade, and many American Indian groups used the shoulder blade of the bison as a hoe blade. In modern times, of course, many nonliterate peoples have adopted the plow and other animal-drawn equipment, but plow agriculture was indigenous only to Europe, North Africa, and parts of Asia, including Indonesia.

Particularly important during crop growth are weeding and protection of the plants from pests. In some groups people live in the fields during this time. A few nonliterate peoples, such as some of the Indians of the American Southwest and some Philippine tribes, irrigate their crops, but large scale irrigation systems are not frequent among simpler groups. The harvesting of those crops which survive the growth period may involve no more than the use of the hands, though a knife or a sickle is necessary for some crops.

Hand agriculture is found widely among nonliterates, and a wide variety of crops is grown. The Americas are distinctive for the large number of domesticated plants, maize being the most important. Other well known New World plants are beans, squash, pumpkins, white potatoes, sweet potatoes, manioc, peanuts, pineapples, tomatoes, and tobacco (Driver, 1961: 43f.). These and other Western Hemisphere crops are now grown extensively by nonliterate groups in Africa and Asia as well as by Euroamericans. The white potato, in fact, was grown so extensively in Europe before being brought across the Atlantic by English-speaking whites that many do not realize that it was originated in South America. From the Old World, mainly Asia, have come wheat, barley, oats, rye, peas, several fruits, soy beans, millet, rice, and sugar cane. The coconut, taro, yams, and breadfruit are grown extensively in the islands of the Pacific, though just where they were domesticated is uncertain (Linton, 1955: 91ff.).

It is significant that all of these crops were domesticated by so-called primitives. Civilized cultures are the beneficiaries of the keen observation and experimental activities of nonliterate peoples.

The most widespread domesticated animal is the dog. Dogs are eaten in a number of societies and sometimes are raised for that reason. In no group, apparently, were they raised as a major source of food. Among the Indians of North America some groups ate dog flesh only for ceremonies or when starving. Among the main domesticated animals are sheep, goats, cattle, horses, donkeys, camels, and reindeer, all of which can be herded. These animals are raised by pastoral nomads, who secure crop foods and manufactured items by trading the products of their herds. Sedentary farmers also utilize some of these animals in combination with crop production. The pig and the water buffalo are not well adapted to pastoral nomadism. The main pastoral area of the Old World is the belt of desert and grassland including part of North Africa, Arabia, the central Asiatic steppes, and portions of southern Siberia and Mongolia. The Kazak people of Central Asia raise mainly sheep and cattle but also have horses, camels, and goats (Murdock, 1934: 139). These same animals are herded in Southwest Asia and in North Africa, but the camel is relatively more important among many of the groups of the latter areas. Reindeer are important in northern Siberia, and cattle are of major importance in much of Negro Africa. In the New World only llamas and alpacas were of any importance; and they were found only in the Andes, where they supplemented a basically non-pastoral subsistence system. Guinea pigs, musk ducks, and turkeys also were raised in parts of the Americas. Bees were kept for their honey in both the Old and New Worlds.

When one considers the means man utilizes to obtain foodstuffs, the great variety of items available for human ingestion, either by direct exploitation of the natural habitat or by the humanly contrived and controlled methods of producing crops and animals for meat or milk, becomes apparent. Only some of these foods are eaten without modification, however, for the variety of specific foods prepared by man is great; the possibilities are virtually infinite. Societies have been selective in regard to what foodstuffs they secure from the habitat and how they prepare them for consumption. Some of the North American Indians ate acorns, and some didn't; and those who did had to leach the acorn flour to remove the bitter tannic acid. Boiled grasshoppers, lizards, and angleworm soup are consumed in some societies, but ordinarily not by North American whites. In the United States eggs are defined culturally as of basic dietary importance, but some of the people of Asia regard them as excrement and, accordingly, unfit for human consumption. These differences, of course, are not a matter of biologically inherited tendencies or limitations. What any man considers as food or can successfully ingest and digest is not a reflection of universal human nature but a consequence of his cultural conditioning.

All cultures incorporate customs for modifying foods before eating. A number, such as acorns and manioc, are not fit for human consumption until certain elements are removed. People who produce grains or collect seeds pulverize them by means of a mortar and pestle or grind them between stones. The flour then may be made into a gruel, formed into cakes, or incorporated into some mixture. Meat and fish commonly are cut up into small strips or pieces and dried by air or over the fire. Both may be smoked. A number of vegetable items must be scraped, peeled, or cut open before using. Cooking is done with or without vessels. Many broil meat or other items by placing the piece on a stick or otherwise arranging it near a fire. Many things are baked in hot ashes or heated sand. A number of groups, notably in Oceania, steam or bake food in pit ovens. People without pottery may boil food in wooden, hide, or basketry containers by placing red hot stones in the water. In Indonesia cooking is done in bamboo tubes.

Techniques of serving and consuming food vary culturally as well. Some people eat with their fingers; others eat with implements. Many have only two meals a day or, perhaps, one big meal with snacking at other times. Inherited human nature does not dictate precisely what we eat, how we eat, or when we eat. It is apparent that a great variety of possibilities exist and, in fact, are utilized in various cultures.

CLOTHING AND ORNAMENTATION

One of the functions of clothing is concealment of some portion of the body, but there is great cultural variability as to what portions are concealed. Some groups go without clothing, though all adorn the body in one way or another. In most societies it is no shame for a woman's face to be uncovered, but in some it is; and in the same society it may be quite acceptable for the woman to expose her breasts. Those who live in societies in which they are accustomed to seeing people with little or nothing on are not ordinarily aroused sexually by the sight of the bodies of persons of the opposite sex. Other stimuli, such as certain postures or expressions are necessary for such arousal. Modesty, then, is culturally defined and not the basic reason for the existence of clothing.

Neither is protection from the weather a universal reason for wearing clothing. In the very coldest environments clothing is necessary to survival, but many groups get along with far less than is considered adequate by many others and without notable discomfort. There is plasticity in respect to how much cold one can stand or is willing to put up with. Moreover, some people in hot climates wear far more than is necessary. This is not to say that protection is not an important function of clothing, for rain capes, leggings, and other such items obviously have this purpose. The point is that how much protection is needed is culturally defined, and, within limits, human physiology is adjustable to these definitions.

Most anthropologists feel that two other factors, social identification and adornment, are far more basic functions of clothing than either concealment or protection. People of all cultures ornament the body by attaching aesthetically pleasing objects or by mutilating the body, and clothing often serves this function. Clothing and other ornamentation, being highly visible, serve ideally to emphasize social differences. All societies distinguish between the sexes thereby, though there is no specific way of doing this that is universal. In some societies men wear skirts, and in others women wear trousers. Dress and adornment also may indicate age, marital status, social class, occupation, religious or political office, and other social positions. The same person, of course, may wear different clothing at different times, depending on his role at the moment. Special ceremonial clothing and adornment, for example, are common.

Animal skins, basketry, woven fabrics, felt, grass or other vegetal materials, and bark cloth have been used for clothing.

A wide variety of objects may be attached to the body for ornamental or identification reasons. Necklaces, anklets, plugs, rings, pins, feathers and the like in the nose, lips or ears, arm bands, and wrist bands of all kinds may be found. The appearance of the body may be modified by staining the skin or the teeth, plucking the body hair, tatooing or scarifying the skin, stretching the ear lobes, binding the feet, deforming the head, or severing fingers. The hair is worn in a great variety of ways also. Again the rule is cultural diversity, thereby illustrating the large number of cultural alternatives allowed for by inherited human nature.

HOUSING

In regard to shelter, nonliterate cultures manifest everything from utilization of natural places to large architecturally elaborate structures. Some have used caves as their homes, even in recent times. Many nomadic societies use simple wind breaks, commonly with a fire built on one side so that one can sleep between the wind screen and the fire. A variety of shapes and materials have been used. Many, of course, are rectangular with vertical walls. Some are cylindrical, some cone-shaped, and a few octagonal. Some have flat roofs, and others have cone-shaped or gabled roofs. Some consist of gables with no walls, the eaves sitting on the ground. Brush, wood, bamboo, stone, brick, reeds, felt, and hide are among the many materials used. Neither the shape nor the materials are precisely determined by the natural habitat, for different sorts of houses sometimes are found within the same habitat.

Housing has the obvious function of providing protection, but a number of additional functions, such as privacy, aesthetic satisfaction, social identification, and modes of interaction are linked to house types. The multi-storied apartment houses of the Pueblo tribes of the American Southwest are thought to be linked to their cooperative interaction patterns, their unilineal kinship organization, and, perhaps, their need for protection from the raiding Athabaskan tribes (Steward, 1955: 167f.). The individualistic Navahos, on the other hand, live in widely scattered hogans.

House furnishings vary so much from culture to culture that a good deal of space would be required to give an adequate picture of their diversity. The houses of nonliterate groups generally use the earth as the floor, though various kinds of mats, blankets, and the like are employed. In larger dwellings it is common to have raised banks or benches against the walls for sleeping. A fireplace usually is found near the center of such dwellings. Raised bedsteads and tables and chairs are uncommon; instead, people sit and sleep on the floor or on the raised areas previously mentioned. Goods are usually kept in baskets hung from the supporting structures of the roof or from wall fixtures or placed on the benches.

TRANSPORTATION ARTIFACTS

Bodies and artifacts are moved from place to place without benefit of the wheel in most nonliterate cultures. Some people, of course, wear footgear regularly, but those who go barefoot ordinarily have some kind of footwear for traveling, even if they only be moccasins or sandals. Perhaps the most specialized footgear in nonliterate cultures is the snowshoe, found among the Indians of northern North America.

A number of devices for carrying loads on the person have been developed. Head rings for transporting heavy objects are found in some places. Some groups simply use a rolled up blanket, shawl, or other cloth to support the head load. Objects commonly are carried on the back by means of bags, packs, baskets, and other containers held in place by means of shoulder, chest, or forehead straps. A number of societies use a pole balanced on the shoulder with loads hanging from each end.

Domesticated animals also may be used, various kinds of packing gear being employed on animals such as camels, horses, donkeys, reindeer, or llamas. The *travois*, which consists of two poles tied to the sides of the animal and dragging behind on the ground, was used on dogs by the American Indians of the Great Plains before the introduction of the horse. Later, of course, it was transferred to the horse. Both dogs and reindeer have been used extensively with sleds.

For water transportation, rafts of various sorts have been used, the *balsa* of several parts of the Americas being among the most interesting. This consists of several bundles of reeds tied together to form a cigar-shaped craft. Rafts, obviously, are not water tight, but air buoyant craft are used extensively by nonliterates. The two main kinds are dugouts and those with a frame with skins or bark stretched over it. The birch-bark canoe, as found among the Indians of Canada, is so light as to be transported easily when a portage is necessary. The dugout, which consists of a log hollowed with fire and an adze, is the most widespread water craft. The skin *kayak* is one of the most complex boats made by nonliterate peoples. The Polynesians may be the most expert navigators, having settled the Pacific Islands by covering long distances across the seas. They observed the stars and the ocean currents and made navigation charts.

Even this brief summary should make it clear that man has developed a notably great range and variety of techniques and artifacts in order to survive and to satisfy the many material wants he has developed; and in the course of doing so he has utilized a great deal of practical intelligence. The technology of nonliterate peoples may be simple and crude as compared with that of modern civilization, but it is much more complex and ingenious than most Euroamericans realize. In fact, the average so-called primitive may be a more expert technician than most Euroamericans. Given the mobility of the human hand, the flexibility of the human mind, and the variety of natural materials, it is not difficult to understand the variety and ingenuity of human technology. A study of the technologies of nonliterate groups can provide one with a better understanding and appreciation of the human mind.

ECONOMIC
ORGANIZATION

Economics sometimes is used to include technology, but it is better employed to refer to the ways in which people, time, and materials are organized for the purposes of producing, distributing, and consuming goods and services. It is apparent that the linkages between technological and economic customs are both numerous and strong; and it is quite impossible to discuss one of these without slipping frequently into the other.

With economic organization we move more certainly into the area of social organization. In technology the main concern is with how people relate themselves to substances and objects, both natural and artificial; but in this chapter there will be relatively greater emphasis on how people relate themselves to one another for the production, distribution, and utilization of technological items.

WORK AND LABOR

One of the most extensively held notions about so-called primitives is that they work as little as possible. They are thought of by some as existing at a kind of "pre-economic" level, each person working just enough to satisfy his immediate needs for food and shelter. The fact is that in every culture people have developed desires which prompt them to go beyond what would be necessary for mere survival, and the volume of work is adjusted to meet these desires. The potter works to produce a container and also to produce one pleasing to the eyes of himself and others, as well as for the sheer satisfaction of manipulating materials. The grower of yams works to secure a food supply and also, as is true in Ponape and much of the rest of the South Pacific, to produce enough yams to put on big displays which will enhance his prestige (Bascom, 1948: 212). Moreover, many nonliterate groups, including those living in the supposedly easy tropics, live in environments so harsh that satisfaction of their desires requires considerable planning and sustained effort. In other words, they not only work, but they work hard.

A significant feature of work in nonliterate cultures is the lack of time orientation. There will be variation from day to day in the times that work is begun as well as the times it is abandoned. On some days the work may total only a couple of hours, and on other occasions it may last most of the day. The total daily work period also may be interrupted by a number of breaks of varying duration, either for rest or for engaging in nonproductive activity such as conversation. The number and length of the interruptions may well depend on factors such as how demanding the work is at that season or the physical condition of the worker. This is in contrast to the concept in industrialized cultures of working regularly for so many hours a day, so many days a week, with scheduled breaks for rest, refreshment, and vacations. This may be difficult for the Euroamerican to understand, but it is well to realize that the notion that time is of monetary or economic value is pretty much a peculiarity of industrialized groups. Nonliterate cultures lack machine technology, which must be employed efficiently if producers are to realize a return from their investment in expensive equipment (Dalton, 1961: 8).

The practice of paying wages to other persons in return for their work is unimportant or absent in nonliterate groups. Assistance with a major task may be rewarded in some way, but the laborer does not regard himself as selling his services to provide himself a living. Wage labor is characteristic of those cultures, such as our own, which have market economies.

Cooperative work is employed rather extensively in nonliterate cultures. One of the most common forms is the informal working side by side of relatives, members of a family, or neighbors as they clear their gardens, pursue a game animal, or accomplish whatever task is at hand. There also may be cooperative labor for special occasions such as raising a roof or harvesting a big crop. Typically a host invites large numbers of people to help with such jobs and rewards them with a feast. Some cultures even have permanently organized cooperative work groups, such as the dokpwe of the Dahomeans of West Africa. This is a society of mostly young men who work in groups of forty or a hundred in the fields and in building houses (Herskovits, 1938: 63ff.). The obvious reason for cooperative labor is that it enables the accomplishment of jobs almost impossible for one or a few. Beyond that it may be more efficient, even for those tasks which can be done fairly easily by one or a few persons. One of the reasons for the greater efficiency may be the enjoyment of working with others; an ordinarily onerous task may be undertaken with a greater will in the group situation. Working in rhythm to music or to a chant is sometimes involved, and people may work harder in anticipation of feasting and recreation to follow. It is also true, however, that group labor sometimes is less efficient, particularly if the social function comes to override the technological goal, and some cooperative labor is arranged more for recreational than economic reasons.

SPECIALIZATION

Economic specialization of some kind and degree is found in every culture, but sexual division is the salient feature in nonliterate groups. This is largely a function of kinship organization, particularly the family. The husband ordinarily is concerned with those tasks requiring greater strength and mobility or those which are more dangerous. This is probably connected with the fact that women are generally less muscular than men and are less mobile due to the physiology of reproduction. Accordingly, women are most often involved in the tasks which make it possible for them to stay fairly close to home and children. It is the men who do the hunting of wild animals in the hunting and gathering cultures, and the women collect the wild plant foods and, perhaps, a few small animals, and prepare the meals. Among agricultural peoples the men usually do only the heaviest work, and the women commonly take care of the rest. In herding cultures men usually care for the animals. This is not to leave the impression that women in nonliterate societies don't work as hard as men, for they frequently engage in tasks which require a good deal of endurance.

Too much can be made of the biological distinction in accounting for sexual division of labor. Biology necessitates that there be a differentiation and that heavier and more dangerous tasks requiring mobility more often go to the men. Beyond this there are other reasons for the association of specific pursuits with one sex or another which seem more dependent on various unique cultural-historical factors. It has been suggested that women usually take the main responsibility for crop production because at the hunting and collecting stage they were the plant gatherers. At the same time, in some groups, the Pueblo tribes of the southwestern United States, for example, the men are the farmers. In other words, for many tasks there is variation from one culture to another in regard to which sex they are assigned. In some cases we have historical evidence explaining the division; in other cases we can infer the possible reason; and in still others we have no way of knowing or inferring the reason. The biological explanation seems least applicable to the crafts, where work is ordinarily restricted to one sex or the other in spite of the fact that one is as physiologically adequate to the task as the other. Functionally, the important thing about sexual division of labor is that it maintains reciprocal dependency between men and women, thus providing a strong bond between husband and wife (Levi-Strauss, 1956: 277).

Another universal physiological factor underlying division of labor is age difference. Obviously, there are some tasks for which the youngest and the oldest members of a society lack the strength, endurance, or other performance qualifications. The old men of Tiwi society in Australia leave the kangaroo hunting to the younger males, since they lack the keen eyesight and coordination necessary. Instead, they remain in camp and manufacture spears, canoes, throwing sticks, and other Tiwi artifacts (Hart and Pilling, 1960: 33f., 46). Children assist with or take full responsibility for a diversity of technological activities. Samoan children, for example, are given the task of gathering the small land crabs (Mead, 1930: 67).

Many cultures manifest little in the way of specialization other than the sexual dichotomy and age differentiation, but other forms are by no means absent. Hunting and collecting peoples undoubtedly exhibit the least in the way of occupational specialization. Though voluntary or part-time specialists may be found, it usually is necessary for each person to put most or all of his effort into the satisfaction of the group's wants. Those who produce something more of a surplus than most hunters and collectors show more evidence of occupational specialization. The farming societies of Africa, for example, have full time specialization in iron working, pottery, basketry, wood carving, and other activities. The Nupe of Nigeria have craft guilds which enjoy official status and have definite political privileges (Nadel, 1942: 257). In most nonliterate societies, however, there are few if any persons who are expected to gain their entire livelihood from a specific craft.

PROPERTY

Just as in our own culture, the property of nonliterate groups consists of land, the products of exploitive activities, and intangibles. The idea that so-called primitives are generally communal is false. Land usually is owned by the community or the tribe as a whole, particularly among hunters and gatherers of wild animals and plants. Farming groups also tend to hold land communally, though they grant families, lineages, or other groups the right to use the land as long as they cultivate it. They do not have the right to sell it or otherwise dispose of it, for it belongs to the community. Herding peoples frequently lack a concept of land ownership at any level.

Products from hunting and gathering, agricultural produce, livestock, and artifacts such as clothing, ornaments, containers, implements, and weapons are not owned communally. The basic criterion of ownership here seems to be usage, and food and artifacts are generally owned by the person, family, kinship group, or association which employs them. Many nonliterate groups are generous with food and other items, sharing with relatives and, perhaps, other members of the community, but this should not be confused with communal ownership. Private property is a universal among human cultures.

Knowledge of curing processes, technical skills, religious knowledge, myths, songs, dances, and many other intangibles are found as property among nonliterates. Nonmaterial property is often owned by individuals but also may be owned by kinship and other groups.

CAPITAL, CREDIT, AND INTEREST

Nonliterate societies do apply certain types of goods to production, and in this sense it may be appropriate to say that they have capital. It is necessary to recognize, however, that many are very poor in capital goods as compared with modern civilizations. Hunting peoples have their weapons; farmers have their implements and storage facilities; but perhaps some fishing communities, such as those of coastal British Columbia, maintain more capital goods than most agriculturalists, pastoralists, or hunters. Ocean-going peoples, especially, have various kinds of water craft, elaborate netting and trapping devices, hooks and lines, and other items, all of which represent a great investment of labor and give long-lasting service.

The investment of goods with the notion of getting a return is not absent in nonliterature cultures. The Kwakiutl of Vancouver Island might lend five blankets with the expectation that six will be returned after a few months. The borrower, in turn, might make loans in order to realize a return (Boas, 1895: 341). There are a number of other examples of the concept of interest among nonliterates, but more widespread by far is the idea of lending without interest.

DISTRIBUTION AND EXCHANGE

A variety of modes of allocating goods and services are found in the world's cultures, though different cultures emphasize different modes. Euroamerican and other advanced cultures emphasize what has been called the *market system* of exchange. Such cultures are characterized by an economy-wide operation of the market principle involving general purpose money and prices governed by supply and demand. Other means of allocation, such as gift exchange and direct exchange of one item for another, occur, but are not dominant and tend to function within the context of the market principle.

The market system should not be confused with market places. Sites where people assemble for trade are found among a number of nonliterate groups which lack a market economy, and exchanges in those societies having an economy-wide market system commonly occur without the exchanging parties meeting or directly communicating with one another.

The market system is associated with what has been called *general purpose money*. One purpose of money is to provide a medium of exchange for buying and selling. This, of course, is its main use in Euroamerican cultures. Second, it may be used to discharge obligations, such as taxes, fines, or debts. Third, money may provide a standard of value, that is, a way of comparing the value of different kinds of goods and services. There are other functions, but these may be considered the three main ones. Money is general purpose money if it serves all of these functions; if it serves only one or two, it may be called *limited purpose money* (Dalton, 1965: 48). General purpose money is found among nonliterate groups, though it is uncommon. Peasant peoples utilize the general purpose money of the civilization which dominates them economically and politically.

The money objects employed by societies operating by the market system and having general purpose money serve the functions of money most effectively if they manifest physical characteristics and relationships of certain kinds. These have been defined as homogeneity, divisibility, portability, and durability (Gregory, 1933: 602). Euroamerican coinage exhibits these features, and a few nonliterate groups have been found with money forms of this kind. Cowry shells were used by the Yurok of Northern California, and dogs' teeth were used in the Admiralty Islands. Such were definite monetary systems which, in some cases, have been translated in terms of other systems (Herskovits, 1948: 277f.). A larger number of groups have utilized objects as media of exchange which do not meet all the above requirements. Pigs, for example, are neither very durable nor very portable. Rice was used as a medium of exchange among the Ifugao of the Philippines, but it, too, is lacking as compared with more durable money objects. Herskovits has referred to the use of such media of exchange as *money barter* (1952: 211ff.). Limited purpose money which fails to manifest all four physical characteristics and relationships mentioned is found in a fair proportion of nonliterate cultures and in widely scattered places.

Another significant fact about money in nonliterate cultures is that it seldom functions for more than a limited number of exchangeable items, whereas money in modern civilized cultures is used for a great variety of things. Even the money of Euroamerican societies, however, is not used for the buying and selling of all items exchanged (Burling, 1962: 820).

Many cultures have what is called a *multicentric* type of economy, which means that there are two or more distinct sectors having different kinds of items and modes of exchange. Monetary exchange may be used in one sphere and non-monetary means of allocation in other areas: or one sphere may be characterized by one kind of money object and another by a different kind. Bohannan found three such economic areas in the economy of the West African Tiv (1963: 248ff.). One consisted of food items, household utensils, some kinds of tools, and raw materials for producing any of these; and exchange for these was by gift or market barter. Another economic sector concerned slaves, cattle, medicines, and several other things; and brass rods served as general purpose money for the items within that sphere. The third area involved rights in human beings other than slaves, mainly women, and the exchange had to do largely with various marriage obligations and arrangements.

While the cultures of the nonliterate world almost always lack economies dominated by the market principle along with general purpose money used for a wide variety of exchangeable items, such cultures are not entirely absent among them. The Kapauku Papuans of the western portion of New Guinea are a notable example. The Kapauku are strongly capitalistic in their economic orientation and organization; and among the features reported for them are general purpose money exhibiting the four physical characteristics of Euroamerican money— cowrie shells in this case—savings, market places, operation of the law of supply and demand, exchange of commodities through sale, paid labor, and lease contracts (Pospisil, 1963: 29).

The market system of exchange is one of the fundamental principles of allocation which may dominate in a given economy. In the economies of many cultures, *reciprocity* is the fundamental means of allocation (Polanyi, 1944: 54ff.). This involves exchange of items between units of about the same kind, for example, among individuals, households, kinship groups, or communities. In a great number of nonliterate cultures most economic items are transferred by a form of reciprocity known as *gift exchange*. Distribution of goods is not the main purpose of gift exchange; rather the items are distributed as a consequence of the reciprocal social and ceremonial obligations that the members of a community have toward one another. Though the economic consequences are extensive, the main reason for the exchanges is the establishment or maintenance of social bonds which are important to those involved. This well illustrates the functional interdependence of economics with other aspects of a culture. Food sharing with one's relatives and other persons is a case in point. One person maintains good social relationships with another and gains prestige by sharing whatever surplus he might have with his fellows. If the occasion arises, the recipients of such gifts are expected to respond in kind. Forde has suggested that this may be viewed as an elementary form of credit (Forde, 1956: 337).

Marriage arrangements also may be accompanied by gift transfer. Often a groom and his relatives must make substantial gifts to the family of the bride, and sometimes there is a two-way exchange of items, both before the wedding and at designated times during the earlier period of married life.

In modern civilized societies many economic transfers take place in which the social relationships between the parties are quite incidental, but gift exchange as a function of social reciprocity is found here as well.

In addition to gift exchange, there are a number of occasions for exchange of items without money or gift giving being involved. Face-to-face barter is the most common form, but some societies have developed what is known as *silent trade* or, sometimes, *dumb barter*. One party leaves the items he has to trade at a designated spot and withdraws, sometimes to watch unobserved. The other party then comes, examines the goods, and, if satisfied, leaves what he has to trade in their place. The fact that this system has been known in various parts of the world for hundreds of years attests to its workability.

Face-to-face barter may or may not be attended by bargaining and haggling, and it may or may not occur at special places where those who have goods to exchange assemble for that purpose. Hunters and collectors, especially, do not have market places, what trade there is being occasional and individual. Agricultural peoples, of course, are more apt to have the food surpluses necessary to the development of occupational specialization and, consequently, markets. Among such peoples market places are mainly for the facilitation of exchange between members of different communities, for within the community trade usually can be handled satisfactorily without a special place for traders to assemble. Markets have been important among nonliterate peoples in several parts of the world, but, as already noted, their presence does not mean that the market principle of exchange is dominant. It has been pointed out, for example, that the markets which are so striking a feature of West African cultures are *peripheral* in the sense that non-economic functions are more important than economic transactions. Markets are places where the West Africans meet in large numbers and exchange news and gossip with friends and relatives, make political decisions, or engage in recreational and religious activities (Bohannan, 1963: 242). Barter was prohibited in the markets of the Dahomeans of West Africa, but even there the use of money was not an aspect of an economy wide system of exchange based on the market principle (Polanyi, 1966: 81).

Another fundamental mode of allocation distinguished by Polanyi is *redistribution* (1944: 54ff.). In those cultures using this principle there is a central point to which economic items flow and from which they are redistributed among the society. Some African chiefs and kings, for example, are expected to give generously to their subjects on ceremonial and other occasions, thereby maintaining their loyalty. In turn a chief's subjects pay tribute to him, with the result that he is provided with the goods necessary to bestow on his people. Thus, economic redistribution is carried on and inequalities of production within the chiefdom are evened out. The people know that if they have met their obligations to contribute their surpluses to the chief's granary they will be provided what they need in case of scarcity. It is apparent that this institution performs both economic and political functions.

Cultures vary from one another in the relative importance of reciprocity, redistribution, market exchange, or other modes of allocation. Only one fundamental mechanism is used in some, and more than one in others. In some cultures one principle dominates, whereas, in others two or more may be of roughly equal importance.

CONSUMPTION

Reflection on the nature of distribution and exchange in nonliterate societies reveals that the unit of consumption is not always identical with the unit of production. For example, a given family as a unit may not consume all that its members cooperate to produce and may also consume items which it did not produce. This is true even of the relatively simple hunting and collecting groups, for, as noted previously, they may share food rather extensively.

The quantity of food consumption at various times in relation to the amount of food available is a matter that is sometimes misunderstood. Nonliterate peoples are often pictured as improvident, consuming all that is available as it becomes available rather than saving for leaner times. Any implication that this is due to natural lack of discipline must be rejected. It must be remembered that nonliterate technology embodies few effective techniques for the preservation and storage of food surpluses, and nonliterate peoples often find themselves in the position of having to consume great quantities within a short period if they are going to consume it at all. This is compounded by the fact that many groups depend mainly on one or two major resources, particularly hunters and collectors or herders, and they consequently are in rather difficult circumstances during that portion of the year when these resources are not in season or when they fail. However this may be, the assumption of natural improvidence of "primitives" is invalidated further by the fact that many groups do what they can with the preservation techniques available. Some storage of fish, grain, meat, and other foodstuffs is, as a matter of fact, practiced by many nonliterate groups.

It is incorrect to assume that nonliterates consume only for biological maintenance. As is the case with civilized peoples, there are a number of functions of consumption. For some the preparation and consumption of food becomes something of an art, and the enjoyment of taste may be highly emphasized. In addition to this aesthetic function, utilization of food and other things also may be a matter of sociability. Most important of all the reasons, other than satisfactions of biological needs, is *prestige consumption*. This function, of course, can be most highly developed in cultures with the necessary surpluses, but in such cultures it is common. Upper class members of American society, for example, commonly exhibit their social position by the cars they drive, the houses they live in, the clothing they wear, the art they own, and the money they spend on parties, vacations, and philanthropy. This sort of thing also is found among nonliterate peoples. Some Melanesians, for example, put on great public displays of yams which, though they are not eaten but left eventually to rot, serve their purpose of bringing prestige to the owner. On the Polynesian island of Samoa the netting of pigeons became a prestige sport engaged in only by chiefs (Murdock, 1934: 50f.). Perhaps the most famous example of prestige consumption in anthropology is the *potlatch* of the Northwest Coast Culture Area of North

America. A person who inherited chiefly status had to validate that position by giving away and contemptuously destroying great quantities of valuables at potlatches. Not only was the prestige of the giver confirmed and enhanced on such ceremonial occasions, the receivers of the gifts might feel shamed by receiving so much at the hands of a rival in the prestige system (Codere, 1950: 62ff.).

10

SOCIAL
ORGANIZATION

The chapter on technology focused on the range and variety of socially standardized ways by which men have related themselves to objects in the solution of the problems of life. It was seen that economic organization involves greater concern with the customary ways by which people relate themselves to one another. It might be possible to classify customs by whether they pertain specifically to man-to-man relationships or man-to-non-man relations. If this were done most technological customs would fall in the latter category. Most kinship, political, associational, religious, and many economic customs would fall in the former class. It is apparent that customs in any of the conventional aspects of culture used by anthropologists would cut across this dichotomy, and this certainly is true of the aspect known as social organization. This term is a poorly defined one used by anthropologists to designate several categories of custom which most extensively involve interpersonal relations and the groups that form thereby. Inevitably included under this heading are marriage and family relations; kinship groups such as the lineage, clan, phratry, and kindred; age groups; and the variety of non-kinship groupings such as clubs and secret societies. Not infrequently, economic organization, political organization, legal customs and social stratification are included, but they are sometimes held out for separate treatment. It is well to remember that, since any culture is a system of interdependent elements, it is impossible to carve it into mutually exclusive categories without doing some violence to the facts.

STATUSES AND ROLES

Anthropologists and other social scientists have come to make extensive use of the practice of viewing social relations in terms of statuses and roles. A status probably is most usefully understood as a label by which some kind of member of a group is identified, either by a participant in the group or an outside observer. The status is some aspect of some kind of person's relationship with another kind of person, which is useful for identifying the person's total set of relationships with the other. The identification term, husband, in our culture immediately calls forth the notion of an adult male legally having a permanent and specially intimate relationship with an adult female. This basic identification aspect (that is, the status) of the male's relationship to the female either reveals to us or provides a basis for us to explore the ideal and actual behaviors associated with it (that is, the roles). Briefly, being a husband is the status one occupies, and the associated behaviors are the roles. Using the identification, husband, enables us to predict some of the behaviors associated with being a husband—this on the basis that husbands live out similar roles in nearly all of the world's cultures. For a given culture, however, it is necessary for the outside observer to study the family relationships to determine some of the husband roles which more often differ from culture to culture.

A significant aspect of the status-role concept is the difference from one kind of member of a group to another. The husband does not behave toward his wife in just the same ways that she behaves toward him. In other words, they occupy different statuses (identification roles), and they live out different but *complementary* roles in relation to one another. This status-role differentiation and consequent interdependence binds members of groups together.

In economic organization we already have seen that roles differ from person to person. Men perform different tasks from those of women; adults perform tasks different from those of children, and some persons specialize in one or another craft. Such status-role differentiation is implicit also in family and kinship organization, associations, political and legal systems, religion, and other aspects of culture to the degree that they directly involve complementary intragroup and intergroup interaction.

THE FAMILY

Anthropologists have not been able to agree fully on a definition of the family. Commonly it is thought of as the social unit established by a man and woman entering into a permanent relationship with one another which consists of living together, cooperating economically, and producing and rearing children. In harmony with this the family often has been viewed as a residential unit. Usually it is, but there are some social units which seem to perform the functions of a family without all members of that unit residing together. Among the Ashanti of Africa spouses were found to live in different households. Man and wife lived with their brothers and sisters rather than with one another, and the children divided their time between the two households (Fortes, Steel and Ady, 1947: 168). There are other groups, to be mentioned later, which lack an adult male as a functioning member of the unit, therefore consisting of only a woman and her children. While such groups are in the minority they occur frequently enough in widely scattered places to justify including them as families. It seems useful to regard the family as a group consisting of at least one parent with offspring and providing for the physical care, affectional support, and socialization of its members.

Most families consist at least of a man and wife with children, and this unit has been treated by most anthropologists as the basic family group. Many have come to refer to this unit as the *nuclear family*; nuclear in the sense that it is a basic unit which may be expanded in various ways to form larger units sometimes known as *composite families*. One way in which the nuclear family may be expanded is to include the children's children in the same social unit to form what anthropologists usually call the *extended family*. This means that when a young person marries he brings his spouse into the family group into which he was born rather than breaking his ties with his parents; and his children, in turn, become members of this group, making it a three-generation unit.

Extended families are formed and their composition determined by the operation of a *residence rule*. If the cultural rule is for the groom to bring his bride into the family into which he was born, *patrilocal* residence prevails and a patrilocal extended family is formed. If the bride continues to live with her parents, bringing her husband into the family, we have what is known as a *matrilocal* residence rule, with matrilocal extended families resulting. The *bilocal* residence rule provides that the couple may take up membership with either parental family. The result may be a bilocal extended family including married daughters who have brought their husbands into the group and married sons who have brought their wives into the group. Figure 2 shows the composition of these three kinds of extended family. There also are societies in which a boy takes up residence with his mother's brother at an early age, and, when he marries, brings his wife to live with that family. This forms what is known as the *avunculocal* extended family. The patrilocal extended family seems to be by far the most common form and is also much more frequent than the independent nuclear family, which prevails in the United States and other modern nations. Independent nuclear families result from what is called *neolocal* residence, and if husband and wife reside in different domestic units, we have what is known as *duolocal* residence.

Many anthropologists have come to feel that the term *virilocal* is more satisfactory than *patrilocal* and that *uxorilocal* is to be preferred to the word *matrilocal* (Adam, 1947: 678). In view of the large number of anthropologists who prefer the newer set of terms and use them in their writing, it is well to become familiar with them. Distinctions between patrilocal and virilocal residence on the one hand and matrilocal and uxorilocal residence on the other have been suggested, but these cannot

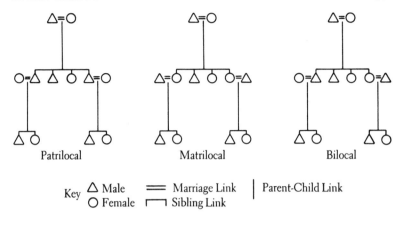

Patrilocal   Matrilocal   Bilocal

Key △ Male   === Marriage Link | Parent-Child Link
    ○ Female ⌐¬ Sibling Link

Figure 2 — Extended Families

be explored here. The result in terms of the composition of the resulting extended families is the same in either case.

Another way of forming a composite family is for brothers or cousins to bring their wives and children together in a single functional unit. Two terms, *joint family* and *agnatic family*, have been applied to this kind of group. Joint families sometimes result from the elimination by death of the elderly parents, thereby leaving brothers with their spouses and children as the functioning unit. Such units become extended families again when the children marry and have offspring.

A third way of expanding the family beyond the nuclear unit is to add one or more spouses. If a man takes an additional wife we have what is known as *polygyny*, and a *polygynous* family results. *Polyandry* is the marriage of a woman to two or more men and results in a *polyandrous* family. Another logical possibility is for a plurality of men to be married to a plurality of women, in which case the term used is *group marriage*. Rare cases have been reported but not as the prevailing, permanent arrangement. The three forms of plural marriage are different kinds of *polygamy*, and any family involving multiple spouses is referred to as a *polygamous* family.

Consideration of the extended family, the joint family, and the polygamous family shows that all of them can be interpreted as complexes of nuclear subunits and that each contains individuals who belong to more than one nuclear family (see Figure 3). It also should be apparent that extended families and joint families also may be polygamous.

As noted previously, the prevailing situation among the world's peoples is some composite family arrangement rather than the independent nuclear unit. The economic and technological activities are carried out collectively to some degree and are commonly directed by the older members. The group functions to provide its members secure status and affectional support and it operates as a unit in the care and training of children. The composite family, especially the extended unit, is able to

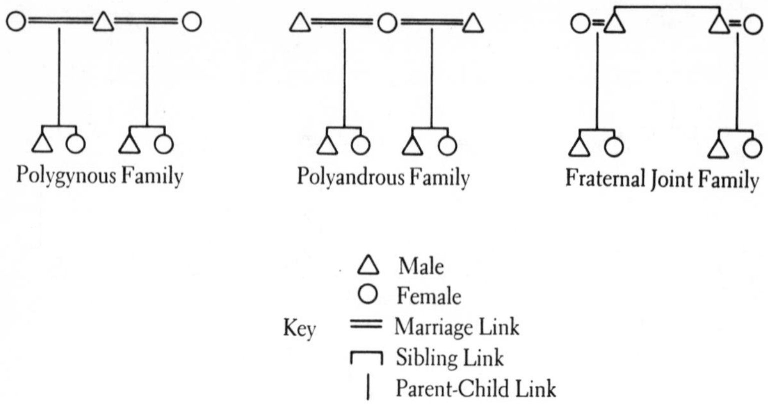

Polygynous Family   Polyandrous Family   Fraternal Joint Family

Key

△ Male
○ Female
═ Marriage Link
⌐¬ Sibling Link
| Parent-Child Link

Figure 3 — Polygamous and Joint Families

do these things more effectively than the independent nuclear type because it contains a greater number of persons to fall back on in the event of sickness or other failure on the part of one person. If a mother becomes ill there are other women, perhaps her mother and her sisters, to care for her and for her children. If the elderly father no longer is able to carry his share of the work load, others will compensate. The circle of intimacy is larger, and the strains of sustained and intense inter-action with a small number of individuals which are so common in the independent nuclear family are avoided. In fact, it is possible to view the independent nuclear family as a rather unstable arrangement not well suited to the functions it is called upon to perform and, for that reason, of low incidence in human society. The prominent French student of social structure, Claude Levi-Strauss, prefers not to view the larger family types as built of nuclear families but alleges that it is more realistic to think of the nuclear unit as a *restricted family* which appears in those societies in which the family is given little functional value (Levi-Strauss, 1956: 272f.).

Further restriction, by eliminating the male parent as a functioning member of the group, would do away with the nuclear family, and this has happened to some extent in a number of cultures. The most cele-brated case is that of some of the Nayar caste groups of the Malabar coast in India. As warriors it was difficult for the men to establish families in which they would function regularly as husband and father. A lifelong ritual relationship between husband and wife was established by a marriage ceremony, but the two did not live together. The wife continued to reside in the social unit composed of her brothers and sisters, her mother, and her maternal uncles and aunts. She was per-mitted to establish ritually initiated relationships with other men, some-times maintaining a relationship with more than one at a time. The original husband might or might not become one of these *visiting hus-bands*. Her children and those of her sisters were reared within the previously mentioned group (Gough, 1961: 357 ff.). Negro groups of

British Guiana manifest a similar tendency for different reasons. In a minority of cases a woman sets up a household consisting only of herself and her unmarried children (Smith, 1956: 257ff.). The man who fathered the children may function as a part of another unit within which he has responsibility to his mother. There are other cases of units without functioning father or husband, which leads Levi-Strauss and some others to question the assertion of many anthropologists that the nuclear family is universal in human culture.

It remains significant that some type of family group incorporating coresident husband and wife is nearly universal. Apparently there are certain functions or combinations of functions which are performed more satisfactorily in the long run by a unit which includes both parents and children than by any other arrangement. Sexual satisfaction, economic cooperation, the rearing of children, and emotional gratification may be regarded as the main functions of the family. Investigation shows that any one of these functions may be provided for by arrangements other than the family, but the formation of family groups, most commonly composite families, seems to be the most effective way of serving all of these functions together.

MARRIAGE

Marriage designates the socially recognized relationship between a man and woman which is expected to result in the establishment of a family, usually consisting of both parents and their children at least but sometimes only of mother and children.

No culture allows complete freedom in the selection of a spouse. The universally found *incest taboo*, for example, always prohibits sexual relations between siblings (brothers and sisters) or parent and child, though the proscription is often extended to other relatives. This, of course, means that one must marry outside his nuclear family. Beyond this there is the fact that marriage in many cultures is much more than a relationship between two persons. It is a union between social groups, namely the relatives of the bride and the relatives of the groom. Those relatives affected by the union—parents, brothers and sisters, uncles and aunts, and cousins—may have a right to involve themselves in the decision on who will marry whom. In some cultures specified relatives, commonly the young person's parents, negotiate with another young person's family without consulting the future spouses, though it is usual to take into account their wishes to some degree. In a few cultures the parents decide who their children will marry while they are still infants, or even before they are born. Frequently, the young people are permitted to make their own decisions within the bounds of certain culturally defined rules and as long as they do not seek marriage with someone their families disapprove. Once the decision is made, the two families make whatever arrangements are defined or permitted in the culture in question.

The rule against marrying within the nuclear family is an example of exogamy, which is the anthropological term for marrying outside of a specified group to which one belongs. Many societies have kinship groups larger than the family which are exogamous, the so-called clan being a common example. The effect of exogamy is to link to one another the married couples' respective groups, whether they be families, clans, or communities. The opposite of exogamy is endogamy, which refers to marriage within one's own group. Obviously the family cannot be endogamous, though some larger kinship groups are. It is not rare for communities to be endogamous. Both exogamy and endogamy may be either required or preferred.

Often it is preferred that one marry a certain kind of relative. Many groups, for example, require any person (commonly referred to by anthropologists as Ego) to marry his cross cousin, that is, one related to him through siblings of opposite sex. Many groups distinguish terminologically between cross cousins and parallel cousins, the latter being offspring of siblings of the same sex (see Figure 4). In most cultures parallel cousins may not marry, though among some Arab groups a man has the right to marry his father's brother's daughter.

Two kinds of secondary marriage illustrate the previously mentioned fact that marriage establishes a relationship between groups. In some cultures a man who loses his wife by death may replace her by marrying one of her sisters, a custom known as the sororate. The levirate is the practice by which a woman who loses her husband by death marries his brother. Both of these continue the union between the same two sets of relatives which were joined when the original partners married, thereby reflecting the importance attributed to the linkage between the two groups.

In most societies some kind of wedding ceremony marks the initiation of a marriage relationship. These take such a diversity of specific forms that no attempt is made here to delineate their range and variety. In some communities the ceremony does not take place at the time the couple take up residence with one another but, perhaps, after the first child has arrived. In a few places all that is required is that the couple live together, and people recognize that a marriage has begun.

Aside from the matter of wedding ceremonies, there is a variety of arrangements by which a marriage relationship is ratified. Some kind of property transfer is found in all parts of the world, and this most frequently takes the form of what anthropologists call either bride price or bride wealth. This is paid by the relatives or the kinship group of the groom to the bride's group, not only in compensation for the loss of the woman but also for the loss of the children she will bear. This transaction between groups reinforces the previously mentioned fact that marriage may be more a group than an individual affair, especially since the wealth is received and used by the parents or other relatives of the bride rather than by the bride herself. Almost never is this correctly viewed as wife buying, since the woman is not thought of as property by those involved.

Another marriage arrangement is *gift exchange* between the pair's relatives. Such exchanges seem to symbolize the unity between the two groups which are establishing an alliance through the marriage of their respective members. It has been suggested that it is similar to the exchange of gifts at Christmas between those who maintain a valued social relationship.

There are a number of groups which require that the groom work for the bride's family, either before or after coresidence begins or both. This is known as *bride service* or, sometimes, *suitor service*. As with the bride price, this involves the idea of compensation to the bride's relatives.

Another fairly common arrangement, functionally more similar to bride price and suitor service than it may seem, is *sister exchange*. A family of a groom may give one of his sisters to his bride's relatives to be the wife of one of their men, perhaps the bride's brother.

Marriage by *capture* is not important among nonliterate peoples. In fact, it is not the usual or approved way for securing a wife in any community. It occurs to some degree among warlike groups. Mock capture is sometimes a feature of weddings and may be a ritual means of expressing the reluctance of the bride and her relatives to initiate the new relationship.

There are few cultures in which *elopement* is the standard way of getting a spouse, but elopements do take place in virtually all societies. It appears to be a way out sometimes utilized when one is unhappy with the partner chosen for him, when a strongly desired marriage is not approved by one of the families involved, or the standard marriage rules are otherwise viewed as too burdensome. In some Australian cultures the marriage possibilities are so limited that it is hard for a young man to locate a desirable girl he would be allowed to marry. As a result elopement has become the usual way to get married.

Among other sanctioned ways of acquiring a wife is *inheritance*, both the levirate and the sororate being examples. A very few groups permit a son to inherit the wife of his father, provided that she is not his biological mother. In still other cultures a man may acquire a wife by being adopted into her family, whereby he becomes not only the woman's husband but the legal heir of his in-laws.

Cultures vary widely in the degree of marital stability. In many nonliterate groups the marriage relationship is exceedingly brittle, and one may have several spouses during his lifetime. Often divorce is simple, termination of coresidence being all that is required. Divorce is often somewhat difficult in societies in which groups of relatives have an investment in the continuation of the marriage. If divorce necessitates a return of the bride price a woman's relatives are apt to exert pressure on a woman to stay with her husband. Many nonliterate groups appear to have a higher divorce rate than modern American society.

UNILINEAL DESCENT GROUPS

Unilineal descent groups are produced by the operation of unilineal descent rules. These prescribe that an individual belongs either to his mother's group or to his father's group, and which group he belongs to depends on the prevailing rule in his society. For such a rule to have operational significance the descent group must be consistently exogamous, which means that father and mother belong to different unilineal groups, and all of the children belong either to the father's group or to the mother's, not both. When the unilineal rule is followed without exception or complication it produces a group of consanguineal (genetic) relatives who have descended from a common ancestor and who are related to one another through only male links or only female links. Since the relationships are biological, each individual ideally remains a member of the group into which he was born for his entire life. One does not marry into or out of purely unilineal descent groups because they consist of consanguineal relatives.

If the rule of descent is patrilineal all members of the society in question are born into and remain in one of the two or more patrilineal descent groups existing in the society. Each individual, whether male or female, will belong to his father's patrilineal group, while his mother belongs to a different group, specifically, her father's patrilineal group. Examination of Figure 4 will reveal that any individual (Ego) belongs to a patrilineal descent group which includes:

1. his brothers and sisters (siblings)
2. his father (but not his mother)
3. his father's brothers and sisters
4. the children of his father's brothers (but not the children of his father's sisters, since the latter would be female links)
5. the children of the sons of his father's brothers
6. Ego's father's father
7. the brothers and sisters of his father's father
8. the children of his father's father's brothers
9. the children of the sons of his father's father's brothers
10. the children of Ego's brothers (but not those of his sisters)
11. Ego's own children
12. Ego's son's children (but not his daughter's children).

This list does not include quite all of the members of this patrilineal descent group which are on the chart, but if the list is followed carefully the notion of how the members of the group are linked through males only should become clear. Note the basic fact that the sons and daughters of any male member of Ego's patrilineal descent group belong to that male member's group. On the other hand, the sons and daughters of any female member of Ego's patrilineal descent group are excluded; they belong to their father's group.

Due to lack of space the full variety and number of persons who can be members of a given patrilineal group are not shown, but such

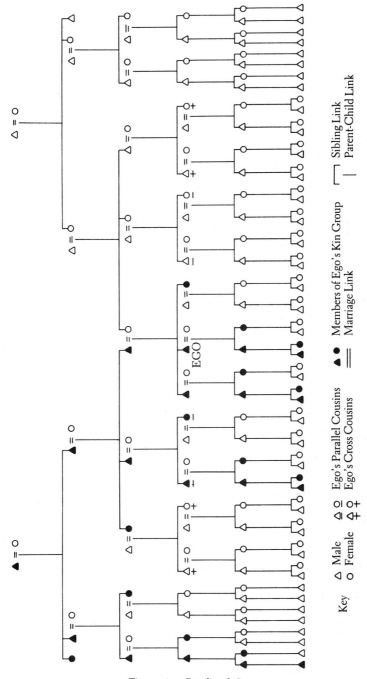

Key

△ Male
○ Female

⊴ ○ Ego's Parallel Cousins
⊲+ ♀+ Ego's Cross Cousins

▲ ● Members of Ego's Kin Group
═══ Marriage Link

⌐ Sibling Link
| Parent-Child Link

Figure 4 — Patrilineal Group

groups range in size from a small handful to many hundreds. By cultural definition each member of the group is linked consanguineally to each other member of the group through males only. The most remotely related members must trace their relationship through males back through the generations to a common ancestor, who would be a common ancester not only to the two members in question but to the rest of the members. Thus, the patrilineal descent group is composed of those who have descended from a common ancestor through male links. It should be noted for later reference that some such groups are so large that the links several generations back have been forgotten. The result is a unilineal group with a tradition of having descended from a common ancestor but whose members cannot trace the relationships. Some cultures have both groups whose members can trace the relationships and groups whose members cannot trace the relationships. The larger group may be composed of two or more of the smaller kind.

A matrilineal descent group is identical in structure to a patrilineal descent group, except that all links are female. Every member of the group is born into and remains a member of his mother's group. Again, since the group is exogamous, one's father belongs to a different matrilineal group, specifically, his mother's. The basic formula is that the sons and daughters of any female member of Ego's matrilineal descent group belong to the group in question. The sons and daughters of any male member of Ego's matrilineal group, however, are excluded (see Figure 5).

Before going further, three things should be noted and kept in mind as a basis for understanding these and kinship groups to be discussed later. An examination of Figure 4 will reveal that the unilineal descent group incorporates *only a portion* of Ego's *patrilateral* relatives. The neophyte often falls into the error of supposing that unilineal groups include all of the relatives on one side of a person's family. The second point is that the membership of one unilineal descent group does not overlap that of other unilineal descent groups of the same type and magnitude in the society. Thus, if a tribe or other society is divided into ten patrilineal groups, each individual belongs to only one of the ten groups. Note that this means that no matter which member of a given group one starts tracing relationships from he will come out with exactly the same persons as members. The third point to remember is that the unilineal group is not a residence group in the sense that a unit of space is occupied by all members of the group in question and no members of other groups of the same kind. If husband and wife live together, this obviously necessitates the presence in the same residential unit of members of more than one of the exogamous unilineal groups, for husband and wife belong to different groups. It frequently is true that a large number of the members of a given group reside in a common territory, but there are nearly always members of other unilineal groups residing there also.

It has been necessary to spend so much time on the composition of the consanguineal, unilineal descent group because there is nothing like

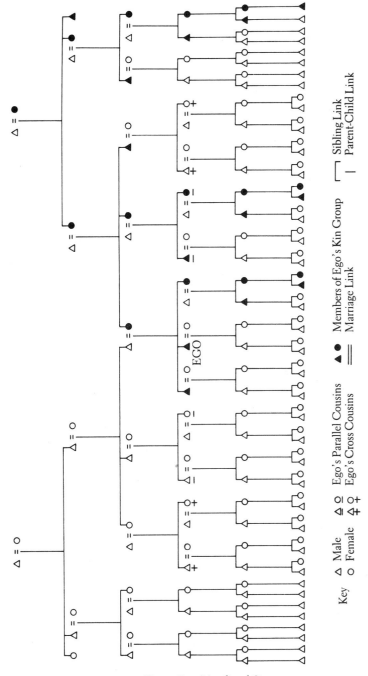

Figure 5 — Matrilineal Group

it in American society, but the ultimately important concern is how such groups function. Certainly one of the major functions is the *regulation of marriage* through the rule of exogamy. This is why siblings belong to the same group and husband and wife do not, and these facts affect the behavior of the members of the nuclear family toward one another. The regulation of marriage is structurally important because, were exogamy not maintained with reasonable faithfulness, the composition of the group would change until it ceased to exist as such. This function is also important in that it promotes the solidarity of a tribe or community by linking the kin groups of which it is composed with one another.

Another major function of unilineal descent groups is *mutual aid.* The group is a kind of second line of defense for its members in time of need, and it supports them on important occasions in the life cycle. If one gets in trouble or has a legitimate need which cannot be handled otherwise, he may well turn to the other members of his unilineal descent group; or they may come to his aid voluntarily out of recognition of their kinship to him. If one of the members of the group is murdered or injured it ordinarily is the duty of his descent group to see that restitution is made, if necessary by killing or injuring a member of the group to which the perpetrator of the act belongs.

Beyond the two functions just explored a number of others may be assumed. Unilineal groups often have ceremonial and religious functions. Such a group may have its own gods, its own priests, and its own rituals and ceremonial paraphernalia for dealing with the supernatural. The ceremonial functions may have to do with *totemism,* for it is common for a unilineal group, especially the larger type, to have a *totem.* The totem is an animal, plant, or other object with which the group believes they have a special mystical relationship. It may be a mythological common ancestor, and it may be taboo to kill or eat the totem. Ceremonial and religious functions may involve the ownership of songs, rituals, myths, or totemic symbols.

In some societies the unilineal descent group may own land and other economically valuable property and control its use and inheritance. Finally, one or more of the unilineal groups may exercise governmental responsibilities, perhaps the provision of the chief or other governmental functionary.

There is another type of kinship grouping formed by the combining of two or more of the larger size unilineal descent groups into still larger units. Such a unit is known as a *phratry.* Some phratries seem to involve little more than the regulation of marriage through exogamy, though they may have other specific functions.

If there are only two unilineal descent groups in a society, or only two phratries, each division or half may be referred to as a *moiety.* It should be realized, however, that the word *moiety* may be applied to any group identified as one of two divisions of a larger unit, whether it is a descent group or not.

DOUBLE DESCENT AND MIXED DESCENT GROUPS

A rather unusual kind of kinship arrangement, resulting from what is called *double descent*, is found in Australia and a few other places. It is the consequence of the overlapping of matrilineal with patrilineal groups, and the categories of persons sometimes formed by this overlapping are variously referred to as *marriage classes*, *sections*, or *bilinear kin groups* (Murdock, 1949: 51). In those societies which have both patrilineal groups and matrilineal groups Ego belongs to his father's consanguineal group for one purpose and his mother's for another purpose. He, along with all the people who belong to his patrilineal group and all who belong to his matrilineal group, comprise a category or section distinct from all other groupings in the society. Ego cannot, under exogamy, marry any member of his mother's group or his father's group but must find his spouse among people who belong to neither. Under what is known as the four-section system, a given community or society consists of two patrimoieties, let us say Perry and Polk, and two matrimoieties, which we will refer to as Miller and Morgan. If Ego belongs to the Perry patrimoiety and the Miller matrimoiety, we may call him a Perry-Miller. The other three categories would be Perry-Morgan, Polk-Miller, and Polk-Morgan. (These hyphenated English names are used only to aid in the understanding of the system; the category names used by nonliterates having such groupings may consist of a single term.) Ego would not be able to marry a Perry-Morgan because he belongs to the Perry patrimoiety. He would not be able to marry a Polk-Miller because he belongs to the Miller matrimoiety. He could marry only a Polk-Morgan. If Ego is a male marrying a Polk-Morgan woman, the children will belong to the Perry-Morgan category, that is, the Perry patrimoiety to which their father belongs and the Morgan matrimoiety of their mother. If Ego is a female marrying a Polk-Morgan man, the children will be Polk-Miller. The explanation has gone far enough for the reader to trace the rest of the relationships for himself (see Figure 6).

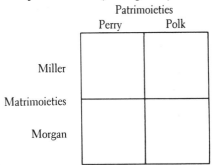

Figure 6 — Double Descent Categories

A few groups have six marriage categories, which result from having two matrilineal groups and three patrilineal groups. Even twelve-section systems have been found (Layard, 1942: 143ff.). The four-section system is strongly consonant with sister exchange and cross-cousin marriage.

Mixed descent groups are composed of some persons linked through males and others through females. Among the Mundugumor of New Guinea such groups are formed by the operation of *cross-sex descent*; that is, a boy is assigned to his mother's father's group, and a girl is affiliated with her father's mother's group (Mead, 1935: 176). This kind of group is referred to as a *rope* in anthropological literature and has been reported only for some New Guinea cultures.

COMPROMISE KINSHIP GROUPS

The composition and functions of the pure unilineal descent group have been discussed first because understanding them provides a basis for examining another kind of kinship group. This we will refer to as the *compromise kinship group*, because it compromises the unilineal principle with residence (Murdock, 1949: 66). One kind of compromise group consists of a core of men who are patrilineally related to one another; unmarried women who are patrilineally related to the men and to one another; and those women who, according to the patrilocal residence rule, have married men in the group in question. Figure 7 shows the membership of such a unit. The men are born into and remain members of the unit throughout life, but women remain members of the compromise group into which they were born only until they marry; and at that time they change to the compromise group of the husband.

Another compromise kinship group results from the operation of matrilineal descent and matrilocal residence. It consists of a core of women who are matrilineally related to one another; unmarried men who are matrilineally related to the women as well as to one another; and those men who have entered the group by marrying female members of it. A female is born into the group and remains a member throughout her life, but a male remains a member of the group into which he was born only until he marries, at which time he transfers his membership to his wife's group.

A third kind of compromise arrangement results from the compromise of matrilineal descent and avunculocal residence, whereby a married couple takes up residence with the man's maternal uncle. The resulting group consists of matrilineally related males and their wives and unmarried children.

George P. Murdock, a leading student of social organization, has called attention to the frequency with which these groups are found among nonliterate peoples (1949: 71). They may exist in the same societies in which pure unilineal descent groups are found. In a patrilineal society this means that a married woman belongs to the consanguineal group of her brothers and the compromise group of her husband.

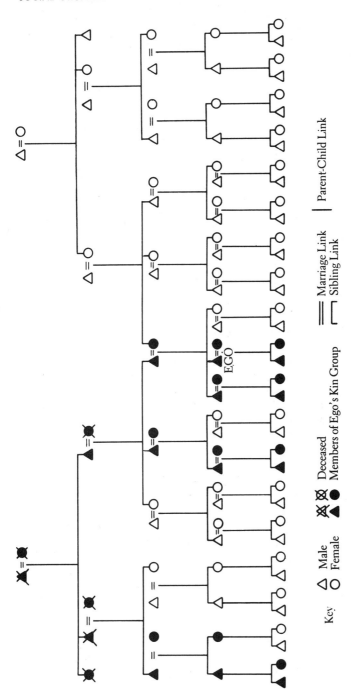

Key: △ Male   ⊠ ⊠ ● Deceased
       ○ Female   ▲ ▲ Members of Ego's Kin Group

≡ Marriage Link   │ Parent-Child Link
⌐ Sibling Link

Figure 7 — Compromise Kin Group
Based on Patrilineal Descent
and Patrilocal Residence

She retains membership in the consanguineal group throughout life and changes compromise group membership at marriage. If the descent rule is matrilineal, a married man belongs to his sister's consanguineal group and his wife's compromise group.

Murdock suggests that the functions of the compromise kinship group tend to differ from those of the pure unilineal descent group (1949: 72ff.). The compromise group generally is more important in the economic, recreational, political, and military aspects of life. Being a residence group, it is the everyday, face-to-face socio-economic group and often, in fact, is the community. The members of this unit work together in the production of food and fiber and, accordingly, they own land and other forms of tangible property. When anthropologists refer to "localized" unilineal descent groups they probably are talking about what Murdock calls the compromise kinship group.

By comparison with the compromise group the pure unilineal descent group seems more apt to be associated with marriage regulation, blood vengeance, ceremonial activities, and ownership of intangible and other ceremonial property.

THE TERMINOLOGY OF UNILINEAL
AND COMPROMISE GROUPS

The descriptive term, unilineal descent group, has been used so far due to the fact that anthropologists have been unable to agree on special terms for the various kinds known. There is best agreement as to the lineage. This is the relatively small unilineal group, either patrilineal or matrilineal, within which all the members are able to trace their relationships to one another and back to a known common ancestor. It is possible for a society to have only lineages and no larger kind of unilineal group; or it may have both lineages and the larger groups, or no lineages and only the large groups. The greatest disagreement pertains to these larger groups. The membership of such units, we have noted earlier, may consist of several hundred people who regard themselves as descendents from a common ancestor through links of one sex only but who have forgotten and therefore cannot trace all their relationships to one another. Many anthropologists, following the suggestion of Robert Lowie, refer to such unilineal groups as *sibs* (1920: 111). The large matrilineal group sometimes is referred to as a *matrisib* and the large patrilineal group as a *patrisib*. The use of the word *sib* for this type of group is of sufficient currency that the user of anthropological literature should be familiar with it. Many other anthropologists over the years have employed the word *clan* for large matrilineal and patrilineal groups, and much of the literature and many textbooks still use the term in this way. In the older literature of American anthropology readers will find that clan was used for matrilineal descent groups and *gens* for patrilineal groups.

Murdock has proposed that the term *sib* be reserved for the purely consanguineal unilineal group and that clan be applied to the compromise kinship group (1949: 67). A number of anthropologists have followed his recommendation, but many have not. Under the circumstances the only course to follow when one comes across the words *sib* or *clan* is to examine the writer's description to determine whether he is referring to the pure unilineal descent group, the compromise kinship group, or both.

KINSHIP GROUPS IN BILATERAL SOCIETIES

A unilineal culture is one with a rule which affiliates each person with groups whose members are related through either female links only or male links only. Bilateral cultures are those which affiliate the individual with relatives of both parents and, accordingly, through both male and female links. The family, including the extended family, is not most usefully viewed as a unilineal group, for it contains persons not unilineally related to one another and an explicit unilineal rule is lacking. This is the case, for example, with the extended families found in some remote rural areas of the United States.

Since both male and female links are utilized in reckoning the membership of bilateral groups, the membership may overlap. The use of all male and female links requires that a group's membership be defined in terms of genetic relationships to an Ego. The resulting group includes many people who, though genetically related to Ego, are not genetically related to one another. Therefore, it is not a purely consanguineal group. Full siblings will have the same persons in their bilateral kinship group, but their parents, their children, their cousins, and other relatives will have in their bilateral groups some persons in common with Ego's group and others who are not in Ego's group.

The *omnilateral group*, as Bohannan designates it, consists of people consanguineally related to a contemporary Ego through all male and female links (1963: 122). Figure 8 shows the membership of two such units, one for each of two individuals. An examination of the chart reveals how the membership of such groups overlaps and that many of its members are not consanguineally related to one another. It should be noted that there are degrees of kinship to Ego. His parents, his children, and his brothers and sisters are the most closely related consanguines. His grandparents, his uncles and aunts, and his grandchildren are a degree more remote, and his cousins, great grandparents, descendents of siblings of grandparents, and great grandparents, for example, are even further removed. Cultures vary from one another in regard to the scope of such bilateral groups. The Anglo-Saxons had such a unit, which included Ego's sixth cousins but excluded the seventh cousins and more remote relatives.

Any person, of course, has relatives of these kinds. The crucial question is whether or not these relatives function in some way in rela-

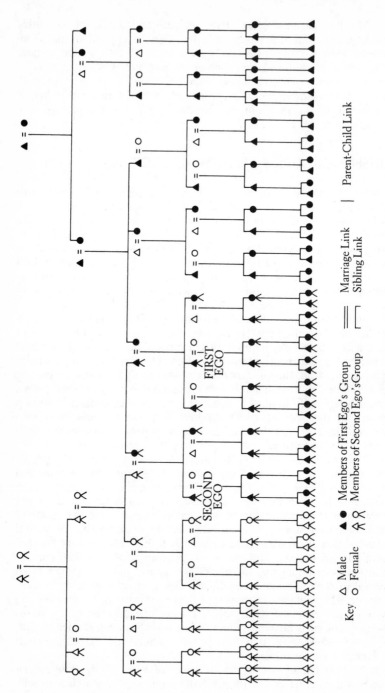

Figure 8 — Omnilateral Groups of Two Egos

FIRST EGO

SECOND EGO

Key   △ Male
       ○ Female

▲ Members of First Ego's Group
● Members of First Ego's Group
⋀⋀ Members of Second Ego's Group

| Marriage Link
⊔ Sibling Link

| Parent-Child Link

tion to Ego. If so, the unit may have to do with blood vengeance, helping Ego raise goods or money for bride wealth, or other specific functions. Another qualification is that only certain bilateral relatives may actually function as members of this Ego-oriented group; for example, one of Ego's maternal uncles may choose to involve himself with Ego and another maternal uncle may refuse to have anything to do with him. Thus, nonkinship factors may affect the composition of the actually functional unit.

In American society relatives linked to one another through both males and females tend to assemble for occasions such as weddings, christenings, funerals, holiday celebrations, and the like. They visit one another and aid one another to varying degrees. Some anthropologists have referred to this group as the kindred. It appears to be different from the omnilateral group, though it includes people who interact because they are linked to one another through the same Ego. It clearly is a bilateral group, since both male and female links are involved, but, unlike the omnilateral group, it does not appear to be defined by the members in terms of only one Ego. As a youngster you may have been a member of a functioning group of relatives who visited in one another's homes, who appeared at your high school graduation, or who assembled for summer picnics and holiday dinners. The group was not defined in terms of you only, however, for the same people might attend the graduation ceremonies, baptisms, and the like of your cousins and other persons to whom they were related. This group, understood as a functional unit, seems to form and operate on the basis of several criteria. It consists of people closely related through both sexes, but only those who are interested in one another and who live close enough to one another to function as group members. Apparently it is a loosely defined friendship and mutual aid group in which bilateral descent links are significant. Such groups probably are widely distributed among the world's cultures.

Another type of bilateral group differs from those described above in that membership is reckoned from a common ancestor or founder, all descendents of that person through both male and female links being counted as members or potential members. As with the omnilateral group and other bilateral groups defined in terms of a single Ego, the membership of different groups overlaps, as Figure 9 shows. Bohannan has referred to this type of unit as the omnilineal group (1963: 129).

Some such groups are unrestricted in membership, that is, all lineal descendents of the common ancestor must be counted as members. But other factors can operate to exclude some descendants, producing groups of somewhat different membership. Ward Goodenough found that the Gilbert Islanders had the unrestricted descent group, but they also had groups limited by additional factors (1955: 73ff.). One such group consists of all those who have descended through female or male links from an ancestor who first held a seat in the community meeting house, and who have inherited land which once belonged to that ancestor. Not all members of the unrestricted group have inherited such lands and are

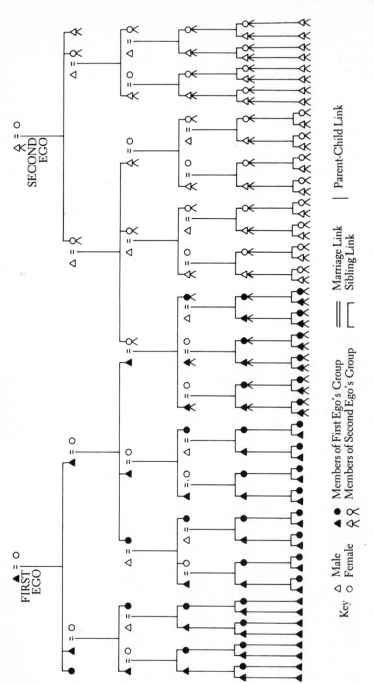

Figure 9 — Omnilineal Groups of Two Egos

thereby excluded from the smaller group. A third unit among the Gilbertese is limited by an additional criterion, that of residence. Only those whose parents have lived on the land inherited from the common ancestor are counted as members of this group.

Murdock has called attention to still another type of bilateral group, which he refers to as the *deme* (1949: 62ff.). It is a local group the members of which are genetically related to all or nearly all of the rest of the group. Ideally, then, it can be a purely consanguineal group. The people making it up are related to one another through both male and female links, but since it is a territorial group, those genetic relatives who live elsewhere are excluded. Some demes are endogamous, but they also may be exogamous and patrilocal or exogamous and matrilocal. Whether exogamous or endogamous the result is a bilateral group composed of persons most of whom are genetically related to one another and who think of themselves as a consanguineal unit. The territorial subdivisions of the Aztec city of Tenochtitlán apparently were endogamous demes (Driver, 1961: 306). Demes commonly are political units, and they may also own property and assume ceremonial or other specific functions.

The various kinds of bilateral kinship groups have not been well studied by anthropologists. They either went unrecognized by many ethnographers or they were confused with unilineal descent groups. While the paucity of data makes it difficult to generalize about the frequency and distribution of such groups, the knowledge we have adds to our understanding of the possible range and variety of ways in which people can organize themselves into functioning units on the basis of kinship.

KINSHIP TERMINOLOGY

Something of the range and variety of ways in which relatives may be formed into groups has been explored. The peoples of the world also classify relatives into terminological categories in a variety of ways. Some kinship terms differentiate between relatives on the basis of sex, whereas others lump under the same term individuals of both sexes. In some cultures an Ego uses one term to refer to an older relative and a different term for a younger relative of the same kind. A number of groups have separate terms for older brother and younger brother. It also may make a difference whether the speaker is a male or a female, as when a son uses one term for his father and the daughter uses a different term. Whether the relative referred to is dead or alive also may be a criterion of distinction.

Setting aside consideration of the above factors for the time being, it is possible to distinguish several kinds of kinship arrangements on the basis of three criteria. Some terms are limited to persons of the same generation, and others include relatives of two or more generation levels. There are some cultures in which relatives linked to one another through intermediate relatives of the same sex are distinguished from those who are linked by intermediate relatives of different sex. The former are *parallel relatives*, and the latter are *cross relatives*. Thirdly, some terms differentiate relatives who are in the same line of descent as Ego from those who are in a different line of descent. The former are called *lineal relatives* and the latter, *collateral relatives*. Parents, grandparents, children, grandchildren, and—for present purposes at least—siblings are among one's lineal relatives; whereas uncles, aunts, and cousins are collateral relatives. Terminological systems commonly are distinguished on the basis of how Ego refers to near relatives of his own generation, in other words, how he classifies his siblings and his cousins (Murdock, 1949: 223f.). This, as we will see later, may be consonant with the terminology in adjacent generations.

Some societies use *Hawaiian* terminology. In this system there is no distinction between lineal and collateral relatives and no differentiation between cross and parallel relatives. Ego refers to his siblings and his cousins all by the same set of terms, "my brother" or "my sister."

In contrast to Hawaiian terms, *Sudanese* terminology distinguishes between lineal and collateral relatives and between cross relatives and parallel relatives. This means that Ego refers to his siblings as "my brother" or "my sister," but cousins are referred to by other terms. However, parallel cousins are called by terms different from those for cross cousins. Thus, three sets of terms are necessary for Ego to refer to those of his generation, one for his siblings, one for his parallel cousins, and another for his cross cousins.

The terminology used in the United States commonly is called the *Eskimo* system. Lineal relatives are terminologically distinguished from collateral relatives, but there is no distinction made between parallel relatives and cross relatives. This means that he uses one set of terms for his siblings but uses separate terms for cousins, not distinguishing parallel cousins from cross cousins.

In many unilineal cultures we find the *Iroquois* system. Here lineal and collateral relatives are not distinguished, but parallel relatives and cross relatives are distinguished. This means that Ego refers to his siblings and to his parallel cousins by the same set of terms, "my brother" or "my sister." Cross cousins, however, are referred to by different terms.

The *Omaha* kinship system and the *Crow* kinship terms are similar to the Iroquois system in that they lump parallel cousins with siblings and employ separate terms for cross cousins. They differ in that for both the patrilateral and matrilateral cross cousins they employ terms which are also used in other generations. In other words, they lump relatives of different generation levels under one term. In the Omaha system a male matrilateral cross cousin is referred to by the same term as that for Ego's mother's brother, and a female, matrilateral cross cousin is referred to by the same term as that for Ego's mother's sister. On the patrilateral side the terms used for Ego's cross cousins are the same ones that he uses for his sister's children. In the Crow system the oppo-

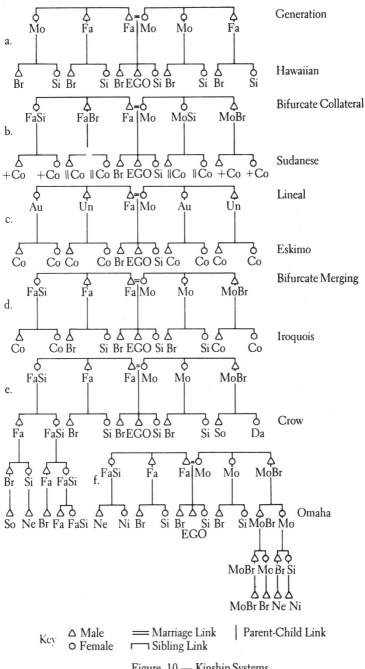

Figure 10 — Kinship Systems

site is true. Ego uses the same term for his patrilateral cross cousins as he does for his father's sister and his father's brother; and he employs the same terms for his matrilateral cross cousins as he does for his brother's children. This description of the Omaha and Crow systems gives an unfortunately truncated view of the total kinship arrangements existing in societies which utilize such terminologies, but we will return to this matter later.

These alternative systems of contemporary generation terms often are reflected in the first ascending generation. Hawaiian terms for the contemporary generation harmonize with *generation* terms for the parental generation. In a generation system Ego lumps his parents together with their siblings on both sides of the family. It is as though Ego refers to his father, his father's brother, and his mother's brother all as "my father," and his mother, his mother's sister, and his father's sister as "my mother." The actual terms used by a society may not mean "my father" and "my mother." They are more apt to mean "male of my parental generation" and "female of my parental generation."

Sudanese terms for Ego's generation may be reflected in the parental generation as *bifurcate collateral* terms. In a bifurcate collateral system there are separate terms for parents, for the mother's siblings, and for the father's siblings. This means that each kind of relative in the parental generation is referred to by a separate term. Descriptively they would be "my father," "my mother," "my father's brother," "my father's sister," "my mother's brother," and "my mother's sister."

Eskimo terms for the contemporary generation are consonant with *lineal* terms for the parental generation. In a lineal system Ego refers to his parents by specific terms, "my mother" and "my father." The siblings of his parents are lumped together with no distinction between parallel and cross relatives. Our terms "uncle" and "aunt" are examples.

Iroquois terms correspond with *bifurcate merging* terms for the parental generation. In such a system the father's brother is called by the same term as the father, and the mother's sister by the same term as the mother; while the mother's brother and the father's sister are referred to by different terms.

It is apparent that by utilizing three criteria of distinction, namely, the differences between cross relatives and parallel relatives, lineal and collateral relatives, and different generations, six basic kinds of kinship terminologies for Ego's generation and four for the parental generation can be recognized. As applied to the total kinship terminologies of given peoples a number of combinations of these systems are possible. Ego's generation may not harmonize terminologically with his parental generation, and one system may be used for patrilateral relatives and another for matrilateral relatives.

Though the Omaha and Crow systems are ordinarily defined in terms of Ego's generation only, such an approach, as noted previously, fails to provide a satisfactory appreciation of the larger picture. In the Omaha system, for example, not only is Ego's mother's brother's son referred to as "my mother's brother," so also are all of the male descendants of the mother's brother through male links only, regardless of generation. Moreover, if Ego's mother's sister is called "my mother," so also is the daughter of Ego's mother's brother and, in fact, any daughter of anyone Ego calls "my mother's brother." What this amounts to is that all members of Ego's mother's patrilineal descent group (from the parental generation inclusive and on down) are referred to by only one set of terms, a term for females and one for males. This is shown in (f) of Figure 10. In societies which utilize such a system Ego's mother's patrilineal group means less to him than his own, yet as a group they may all be considered in a sense as mothers to him (Beattie, 1968: 50). In some systems, in fact, the word used for the mother's brothers may be translated as "male mother." Omaha systems occur in patrilineal societies and Crow systems in matrilineal societies. Both are common. There is much more that can be said about the Omaha and Crow systems, but this will have to suffice for this presentation.

In spite of the way it may seem to those who come from terminologically simpler societies, kinship systems do make sense functionally if the cultural contexts in which they operate are fully understood. There is a relationship between what terms are used to refer to relatives and the socially standardized behavior toward those relatives; or to put it another way, kinship terms designate statuses with which culturally defined roles are associated. This has been explored somewhat already in the discussion of the Omaha system, in which there is a connection between terminology and a person's relationships with members of his mother's patrilineal descent group. In those systems in which Ego refers to his mother's sisters as his mothers, it often will be found that these women will behave toward Ego in some of the same ways as his biological mother does, and Ego may well think of them as second mothers in some respects. If one refers to a cousin as "my sister" he may not marry her, since this would be defined as incest.

Among the Hopi Indians a boy's father is a teacher and older companion. The father instructs the boy in farming and herding and may help the boy get started with animals and land. When the father becomes incapacitated with age, it is the adult son who looks after him. Since the Hopi kinship system is a Crow system, the term "my father" is used not only for the biological father but for the father's brothers and all male offspring of father's sisters regardless of generation (see Figure 10). These fathers are all members of Ego's biological father's matrilineal descent group; and, in harmony with the fact that they are all fathers, Ego's relationships with some of them may take on something of the same flavor as his relationships with his biological father. Under some circumstances one of these other fathers may take special interest in a classificatory son, and the boy responds by assuming the obligations of a son to his father. Since generation is disregarded in the father category, some of them may be much younger than Ego. This is handled simply by reversing the nature of the interaction in keeping with the relative ages, but without changing the terms (Eggan, 1950: 31f.).

The ethnographic literature is replete with examples of correspondence between interaction patterns and kinship statuses. It was noted earlier that terminology is one of the less sensitive kinds of cultural data to gather; consequently, the genealogical method is a good avenue to clues as to the behavior patterns of the society with which the ethnographer is working.

FICTIVE KINSHIP

There are various arrangements found among nonliterate peoples whereby individuals not related to one another may enter formally into a relationship which partakes of the nature of kinship ties. A relationship sometimes known as *institutionalized friendship* may bind together unrelated members of the same sex for life. Two men, for example, may pledge themselves to life-long comradeship and mutual support. Cree Indian boys might form an attachment which involved calling one another by a term which means "he with whom I go about" (Mandelbaum, 1940: 244). They address one another's parents as father and mother, and if one of the boys dies, the other goes to live in his home for a time and, from then on, thinks of it as his own. Such relationships, varying in their specific content, have been reported from several parts of the world.

The *compadrazgo* system of Latin America is another well-known fictive kinship arrangement. On occasions such as baptism or confirmation the parents select godparents for their children, thus forming for life a special relationship between the godparent and child and between the parent and the godparent. Godparents take an interest in the development and welfare of their godchildren, and the latter are expected to show respect for their godparents. The parents and godparents refer to one another as *compadres*, and all parties to the relationship are supposed to stand together in times of difficulty or need.

ASSOCIATIONS

Kinship and coresidence have been the main factors involved in the formation of the groups discussed so far. Associations, however, are basically nonkin groups formed because of some interest or function shared by the members. This kind of unit is abundant in modern civilized communities, in which kinship as a factor in group formation is so much less important than in nonliterate cultures. This is consonant with the fact that one of the main kinds of groups studied by sociologists is the *voluntary association*. Two basic functions of voluntary associations commonly are recognized—*instrumental functions*, which have to do with bringing about or preventing some cultural change (correcting a social problem, for example) and *expressive functions*, which have to do with the pursuit of some hobby or other personal interest the members hold in common (Gordon and Babchuk, 1959: 25f.). Many associations strongly emphasize one or the other of these two functions.

Nonliterate peoples generally are little concerned about controlling cultural change, and they lack the variety of expressive interests manifested in civilized communities. They do have several kinds of associations, however. One type is what may be called a *tribal fraternity*, a club composed of all the adult men of the community. These vary from culture to culture in respect to specific purpose and activities. Not uncommonly this tribal club has a clubhouse. Here the men may work together on crafts, eat, tell stories, conduct ceremonies, hold councils, play games, and the like. Initiation may be required for a boy to join the club. Frequently, such groups are set in opposition to the women; the club's activities are kept secret from the women and children, and women may be rigidly excluded from the clubhouse. A somewhat similar group is what might be called a bachelor's club, which is for unmarried men only.

Male *secret societies* with limited membership are found also in a number of groups. West Africa is noted for secret societies which exercise a good deal of political power.

Age associations, usually for men but sometimes for women, are occasionally found. In some nonliterate communities there are special organizations for the young men or the young women. These groups may render special services to the community, and they may have educational and social functions. The Inca had such groups for both young men and young women, who served the monarch in administrative matters, crafts, and some other areas as well (Rowe, 1946: 268f). The Samoans have groups which provide leadership and group planning education for the boys and ceremonial training for the women (Mead, 1928: 55ff.). Often the members of such associations live in dormitories, some of which are occupied by both sexes. A few peoples have included both sexes in a single youth association.

A special kind of age association is found in several places as a part of what is commonly referred to as an *age class system*. Such systems are usually for men only. In the most clearly developed age class system the life cycle will be divided into well defined *grades* or levels for which there are culturally prescribed customs. The men are divided into associations or *sets*, one for each age grade. Only one set occupies a grade at a time, each beginning at the lowest age grade and, every few years moving to the next grade as it is vacated by the next oldest association. The set is formed from among the boys of a certain age range, who, as a group, are initiated into the lowest grade and remain together as a group throughout their lives as they pass through the various grades. Among the Galla of Ethiopia there are five grades, the members of each set changing grades every eighth year. The class of men occupying the next to the highest grade exercises political power and responsibility, and those in the highest grade serve as advisers. They are retired from the system at the same time their sons enter the lowest grade (Prins, 1953: 24f., 61).

Such a neat arrangement is not found in all cultures with age class systems. Among the Hidatsa Indians of the Northern Plains each set of males had to buy the rights and paraphernalia of the set occupying the grade which they wished to enter. Adolescent boys joined forces and with the help of their families assembled the goods necessary to purchase entrance into the Kit Fox age grade. When the club occupying the Kit Fox grade sold out, they were without any organization until they managed to buy their way into the Half-shaved Head age grade, which in turn had to purchase from the Dogs, and so on until the old men entered the Bull Club (Lowie, 1913: 294ff.).

Among the Zulu of South Africa all boys of roughly the same age were initiated to form a set occupying the lowest grade, and while in this grade they served as soldiers, police, and tribute collectors. After about ten years the men of the association retired as a group to become elders. As such they married, raised families, and assumed community leadership. In the neighborhood of age sixty, still as a corporate social group, they retired from active community responsibilities and became "ancestors" (Krige, 1936: 36ff.).

One of the most unique age class systems is the age village arrangement of the Nyakyusa of what is now Tanzania. All of the boys of about ten or eleven years of age leave their parents' village and establish a new one a quarter of a mile or so away. There they sleep and spend their spare time, though they return to their mothers' huts for meals. For a few years additional boys join the new village until, when the first members are about 15 or 16, admission to the group is closed. The residence unit so formed continues throughout life. When the boys marry they bring their wives to the village, and when the last member dies, the village dies (Wilson, 1951: 32, 158ff.).

The other kinds of associations found among nonliterate peoples are diverse in purpose. There are military societies, curing societies, dancing societies, cooperative work societies, and many others. These are more common for men than for women, for men are less burdened by sustained activities such as caring for children and preparing food. There are some groups, such as many of the tribes of the arid Great Basin of the American West, who lack associations completely.

RANKED CATEGORIES AND GROUPS

Differentiation in prestige among individuals and/or groups within a community or larger unit is a universal of human culture, but many cultures lack well-defined groups of different rank. These groups take various forms in those societies which have them. A secret society, a society of healers, or an age set of prestigious old men are examples of high prestige groups. There are a few communities which divide all members of the society into prestige groups called *social classes*, which are differentiated from one another with various degrees of sharpness. Membership in such groupings may be mainly on an individual basis. For example, the Kwakiutl Indians of the British Columbia coast distinguished nobles from commoners, but one man might be a noble and his brother a commoner, depending on whether he had inherited a chiefly title (Boas, 1895: 338 f.). In other societies rank may be more of a family matter, as it is in the United States, where all members of the same family ordinarily are of the same class level. Many sociologists believe that there are five or six classes in most American communities, with the main criteria of differentiation being occupation and wealth. Here as in many other societies, however, it is difficult to classify many families. There is enough movement among the classes so that many families are transitional or intermediate. In those societies in which mobility between classes is rare, perhaps theoretically impossible, the term *caste* is ordinarily used. The caste system of India is well known, and some American communities have Negro and white castes.

LOCAL AND OTHER TERRITORIAL GROUPS

It is usual for more than one factor in group formation to be involved in a particular group. Many discussed so far have emphasized kinship; others have emphasized age or sex or some common purpose. An important factor always is proximity, which may involve residing either under the same roof or near one another, usually within a community. The groups to be discussed now are somewhat larger territorial units which are spatially more remote from other such groups. The basic territorial unit is the *community*. It is identifiable as a territorial unit distinct from other such units and is that group in which the member individuals and families can carry out most of the activities regarded as important and necessary for daily living, whether technological, economic, social, political, religious, recreational, or aesthetic. Another way of saying this is that a community has a *relatively complete culture*.

The type of community characteristic of hunting and collecting and, also, herding cultures is the *band* or *horde*. The band is a nomadic group of several families moving about within some territory, which may or may not exclude other bands. Bands may be very small, consisting of no more than two or three families, and they appear to average around fifty persons. The *village* is a sedentary community, the families occupying a cluster of dwellings, commonly near the ecological center of an exploited area. Villages are characteristic of farming groups, and Murdock suggests that they average around 300 persons (1949: 81). Another kind of sedentary unit is the *neighborhood*, which has its families scattered in semi-isolated homesteads. Neighborhoods generally are somewhat smaller in population than villages and are less often found, most of the agricultural peoples of the world preferring to live in villages. A number of parts of the world, of course, have what are known as towns and cities. The size at which it is appropriate to speak of a town or city rather than a village is problematical. The 2,500 figure utilized in the United States is arbitrary, as any figure must be. Some writers emphasize regular face-to-face interaction as an essential characteristic of the true community and suggest a population of 1000 to 1200 as being the largest number of people who can maintain such interaction. For population clusters larger than this they would not use the term community. Another important functional distinction would be between villages or communities which are simply clusters of farmers living together and those which are characterized by the occupational diversity typical of the urban way of life. A few nonliterate peoples have developed such urban centers.

Tribe is a term used to refer to a number of culturally similar communities within a given territory, the members of which think of themselves as belonging to the same social unit (Mandelbaum, 1956: 295f.). Often they have a name which distinguishes them as a unit, and this name frequently means "people." The tribe may or may not be politically organized.

POLITICAL ORGANIZATION

Anthropologists have been unable to agree fully as to whether all cultures have government or political organization. The answer depends in part on how such terms are defined, and they have been defined in many ways. It may be helpful to one wading through the writing on this subject to remember that a distinction can be made between government, political organization, or administration as some kind of process and a government, a political unit, or an administration as a unit of society which specializes in carrying out the process. It is clear that some nonliterate groups lack full time specialists in ordering group affairs and, in that sense perhaps, can be said to lack a government. It seems more useful, however, to define government as the administration, however informally, of the affairs of a territorially based social unit, such as a band, village, city, compromise kinship group, or tribe. The administrative process involves making decisions for the group, putting the decisions into action, and appraising current circumstances and the results of previous actions as the basis for future decisions (Litchfield, 1956: 12f.). Put this way, it appears that nearly every people known exhibits government, either over the tribe or over smaller territorial units within the tribe.

Many tribes are not politically organized as such; that is, government for the tribe as a unit does not exist. This was true of the Hopi Indians of Northern Arizona. To say that the tribe lacks government, however, does not mean that the members of the tribe are not subject to political regulation. The Hopi, as is true of virtually all peoples who lack tribal government, have government at the community level. By contrast, many other American Indian groups, the Cheyenne for example, had true tribal government.

We cannot be sure that government as defined above exists in every culture. Lauriston Sharp has alleged that the Yir Yoront of Australia are "people without politics," partly on the grounds that there is no social group among them which is identifiable with a territory (Sharp, 1958: 1ff.). They apparently lack communities and they do not constitute a tribe distinguishable from other tribes of the area. It is impossible to locate Yoront country or a body of Yoront customs. Yir Yoront simply refers to Yoront speech and those who use it. The only landholding units are the clans, but the lands of each are composed of a number of small tracts scattered about the region occupied by the Yir Yoront and two other language groups. If we stick to the definition of government as administration over the people of a territorial unit, perhaps the Yir Yoront are among the few nonliterate peoples of the world without government.

There are many groups which have little in the way of territorial organization beyond the residential family group. Many of these manifest multi-family assemblages only for certain occasions or seasons. In such groups, nevertheless, it is not simply every man and family for himself. There are persons who, because of their experience and their success in terms of culturally defined standards, are looked to for advice more often than others and are granted informal administrative responsibilities. The Western Shoshone and many of the Paiute groups of the Great Basin of Nevada and Utah had few permanent residential units larger than nuclear and polygamous families. In the summers these groups wandered independently in search of food, the most experienced male exercising the most influence. In winter two to ten families would assemble to form temporary villages. In the larger villages a recognized leader called a "talker" appeared, who gave periodic speeches in which he exhorted the people to live right, advised them as to where plant foods might be ripening, and assigned each family a locality in which to seek food. His authority remained weak, however, and a family could ignore his instructions without fear of enforcement (Steward, 1938: 246f.). In groups at this political level there may be other figures who assume limited and temporary authority for specific purposes. The Great Basin peoples had antelope shamans, who were thought to have special supernatural power to attract antelopes and who directed several villages at their annual assembly for the antelope drive.

In still other societies, in which the family groups were larger and had more frequent contact with one another, most decisions affecting the group as a whole would be made by a number of experienced old men. This kind of government is sometimes called gerontocracy.

Such informal administrative mechanisms are apt to be found among hunting, collecting and fishing peoples who spend much of their time moving about in very small groups. Among those who have larger bands and who assemble in substantial population units fre-

quently or for relatively long periods of time, administrative arrangements are apt to be more complex. The same is true of herding peoples
and, also, of farming peoples with their sedentary communities. In such
larger groups there are apt to be large extended families or, perhaps,
unilineal or compromise kinship groups which have leaders, and one or
more of these may become recognized leaders of the territorial group.

Administrative leaders are those who have been granted influence
over group affairs because of various personal qualifications such as age,
experience, wealth, bravery, supernatural ability, or generosity—different
groups emphasizing different combinations of qualities. Leadership often
is inherited as well, but frequently whether a man is permitted to assume
and retain an inherited administrative position will depend on whether
he exhibits the required qualifications. When assumption of band or
village authority depends exclusively on personal characteristics and
there is more than one person about equally qualified, governmental
leadership may be shared, or there may be competition or conflict for a
position. In some societies, the village or band leader, often called
the *headman*, is the senior leader of one of the extended families or
unilineal kin groups. Some communities, it already has been noted,
have a kinship group which has the recognized function of supplying
the headman or chief.

One question of significance at this point is whether the administrator exercises his influence in the course of carrying out the same
activities as his fellows or whether he is given time off to act as a part
time or full time administrator. There is no question but that most
nonliterate societies lack full time political leaders. Yet many have
officials who are granted some time off for making and executing decisions or who because of their wealth can afford to spend time on such
matters. It is in such communities and tribes that administrative structures set up and maintained explicitly for governmental purposes may
appear. These structures are apt to be more complex in large communities and in tribally organized groups than in small communities because
of the problem of maintaining order in large populations. There is apt
to be a hierarchy of officials with more specialized functions. Some
Indian tribes of the Great Plains, for example, had one or more principal
tribal chiefs and a tribal council of chiefs of the various bands composing
the tribe. There were also officials with responsibilities of a ceremonial
nature. This civil government shared political power with the military
societies, which were consulted frequently in the decision-making process
and which often acted as police to carry out decisions. Among the
Arapaho, as among some groups elsewhere in the world, the main political leaders were drawn from a particular age grade, and lesser political
leaders came from a lower grade (Kroeber, 1902: 153, 157). The American Indians as a whole were rather highly democratic. The chiefs of the
Great Plains tribes were hardly dictators; they often were elected, and
they often exerted pressure more by persuasion than by force.

Perhaps the most complex and highly centralized governments
among nonliterate peoples were found among some African Negroes,

who had political systems about as complex as can be achieved without writing. Here were true monarchs heading confederacies consisting of territorial subunits, each of which had its own political structure. Some of the African rulers had large numbers of ministers and retinues of major and minor officials of many kinds. They commonly made extensive use of symbols of authority such as palaces, escorts, and special clothing. Many African governments used force rather extensively to maintain order, though there was a good deal of local authority democratically exercised. Rulers were identified symbolically with the kingdoms and empires over which they presided and were accorded a great deal of respect; but seldom were they able to do as they wished without consulting their ministers and members of councils, which commonly were the chiefs or headmen of the component territorial units. These African nations conducted wars of conquest by which they overcame and incorporated other states, thus forming true empires.

Some kind of centralized government seems necessary for the largest tribal groups, but tribes of tens of thousands of persons can function politically without centralized government. Such "nations without rulers" are found in parts of Africa. They consist of politically equivalent segments and sub-segments which recognize that they are mutually interrelated with one another and control not only their internal affairs but relationships with other tribes. There is here a hierarchy of segmented relations. Starting at the bottom, lineages may be viewed as the smallest segments. When a member of a lineage has trouble with a member of another lineage, the lineage of each man supports him against the other. However, lineages are grouped to form larger units of about equal size, and if a lineage in one of these larger segments has a feud with a lineage in another segment, all of the other lineages within that segment must come to its aid. These segments in turn are grouped into larger units, and so on up through a hierarchy of groups until the tribal level is reached; and the principle of each unit supporting the other units within its segment against other segments of equivalent size applies at each level. On the tribal level this means that the largest divisions of the tribe will aid one another when one is threatened by an alien tribe. Within the tribe, when one segment defeats another, it does not establish political dominance. The whole unit maintains itself as a set of segments and subsegments which exert approximately equivalent force upon one another to maintain political equilibrium. The maintenance of unity is aided by the fact that the segments are exogamous kinship groups which have members scattered among a number of communities. Such an arrangement is often called a *segmentary lineage system*.

It is apparent that political arrangements among nonliterate peoples vary widely in degree of complexity. They also differ in the degree of centralization and in respect to whether they operate democratically. It is safe to say that headmen, chiefs, and other rulers among nonliterate peoples seldom have the dictatorial authority Euroamericans so commonly have attributed to them. Beyond these ways in which nonliterate political systems vary it must be said that the great range of specific structures and mechanisms has not begun to be indicated in this brief presentation.

DIPLOMACY AND WARFARE

Relations between political units, whether communities or tribes, are regulated either by peaceful means, that is, *diplomacy*, or by *warfare*. Governments of nonliterate societies do conduct diplomatic relations, but anthropologists have paid so little attention to this that little is known about them. The League of the Iroquois in North America and a number of African kingdoms are known to have sent ambassadors to other tribes.

Anthropologists commonly use the term *war* to refer to any kind of intergroup combat, but little of such activity among nonliterate peoples is of the kind carried out by modern nations. Some prefer to define war more narrowly, restricting it to the sustained and well organized combat conducted by formally organized governments. This kind of fighting was uncommon among nonliterate groups, but it was found among the more highly developed nonliterate nations, such as the Zulu, Ashanti, and other African states, as well as the states in Peru and Mexico during pre-Columbian times.

Intergroup combat in the form of feuds and raids was common in many nonliterate groups and was carried on for a variety of reasons. Among the North American Indians participation in raids was a common way of obtaining prestige, and, in some groups, it was the only way one could become a man. Trophies such as scalps, heads, or other body parts often were taken, either as a way of gaining prestige or for supernatural or ceremonial reasons. Fighting between relatively small groups often takes place because of competition over land or other resources. Some peoples raid others to secure goods which they do not produce, as the Navaho and other Athapaskan speaking nomads raided the agricultural Pueblo tribes. In a number of cultures violence may be undertaken with the purpose of forcing the other group to alter or restrain its behavior.

Though common, intergroup combat is not universal in human culture, which demonstrates that it is not a necessary aspect of human nature. Among the peoples which haven't utilized intergroup violence are a number of Eskimo groups and European societies during early Neolithic times.

SOCIAL CONTROL

The maintenance of order and the restraint of socially disapproved behavior is accomplished within a community or tribe by a number of means, sometimes as a function of the political system and sometimes more informally. One form of social control, *law*, is ordinarily thought of by Euroamericans as consisting of written regulations produced and enforced by specialized branches of governments. From this point of view one can say that nonliterate peoples lack law, but anthropologists generally prefer a broader definition which recognizes the functional similarity between the systems of social control of civilized and non-literate peoples. This approach recognizes that no matter whether regulations are written or not, or whether they are produced and enforced by specialized governmental agencies or not, they can properly be called laws or legal norms if their violation brings about community sanctioned exercise of force or the threat of force to punish the violator or bring him into line. It is well to be aware that law has a double meaning; that is, the legal norms which are backed by community sanctioned force may be called laws, or the process of applying force may be called law (Hoebel, 1954: 28).

The notion that legal norms may originate from sources other than special legislative bodies has precedent in Euroamerican cultures, in which there is recognition of what is called *common law*. This consists of customary and legally enforceable norms which are of remote or unknown origin, and such are many of the laws of nonliterate cultures. On the other hand, the origin of legal norms in some nonliterate groups has been observed. In the very process of resolving interpersonal and intergroup disputes, headmen, chiefs, monarchs, and councils may propose and pronounce norms which thenceforth are applicable to and sanctioned by the whole community. The Indians of the Plains developed legal norms to cope with the problem of horse theft, which emerged as the result of the adoption of horses by Plains societies (Hoebel, 1960: 55). Thus it is seen that traditional legal norms of unknown origin and laws produced by agencies recognized as having the right to legislate exist in both civilized and nonliterate groups.

It has been indicated that the enforcement of laws is not always the responsibility of special agencies. Such responsibility is found in some nonliterate cultures, but in many the informal leaders or even victims may apply force against the violator. The Eskimo commonly are cited as an illustration of this. They lack courts and police, but when a man violates the norm there is recourse supported by the community. If one's rights are violated and there is no other way, the violator may be killed; and the rest of the members of the community will support the defender of his rights. If a man kills repeatedly, however, and without good reason, other members of the community may cooperate to dispose of him—this action being understood and approved by the community as a whole (Hoebel, 1954: 88). This is law enforcement just as surely as if carried out by police and courts. The Eskimo also utilize the singing of insulting songs to one another and regulated athletic contests to settle disputes.

African cultures are noted for their highly developed legal systems. Some of the Bantu-speaking groups of southern and central Africa have indigenous courts composed of twenty or more chiefs representing different elements of the society. The parties to the dispute present their cases before these courts, and statements of witnesses are taken. When this is completed the judges consider the matter and render their decision. In some other African societies these courts are more modest in size and less formally operated, but there is no question but that the judges are applying, in behalf of the community, a complex set of well standardized legal principles with which they must be intimately familiar.

By virtue of the very fact that cultures differ from one another it follows that they vary in the content of their legal norms and the relative severity of the sanctions applied to violators. In some societies premarital intercourse is a serious violation, whereas in other groups it is looked on with tolerance as long as the incest rules are observed. Personal property may be taken without permission in some cultures as long as the borrower in some way identifies himself, but in other cultures this would be theft. This does not mean that there are not basic similarities among cultures in what behaviors they define as crime. No society lacks legal regulations concerning the taking of human life, the use of material objects, or sexual activity. The point is that they differ in how much and what kinds of behaviors are permitted in these areas as well as how severely they are punished. There is a great diversity of precise prescriptions and proscriptions among nonliterate and peasant cultures.

All cultures have law, but there are a number of other ways of maintaining conformity to the social norms. Among the major elements of social control in all societies is *reciprocity*, which may be viewed positively or negatively. The basic idea is that the individual is prompted to conform, that is, to abide by what others expect of him because he realizes that by so doing he can expect them to observe his rights. That is the positive side. Negatively, reciprocity is withheld when someone does not conform, and it is the realization that one may find himself cut off from the support and daily cooperation of his fellows if he does not behave that keeps many a person in line.

Another extensively used means of social control is the bringing of *shame* upon the violator. Through education and other aspects of socialization the individual is conditioned to feel embarrassed and chagrined when it is known to his fellows that he has violated the accepted norms. The technique is to let the violator know by ridicule or some other such means that his behavior is disapproved, this for the purpose of stimulating a sense of shame. This operates, of course, only if the members of the society in question have been conditioned to feel ashamed under such circumstances.

Some people feel ashamed of violating a norm whether found out or not or whether or not there is any expression of disapproval. In fact, some writers have distinguished those cultures which condition people to feel guilty about violations and so control their own behavior without external disapproval from those cultures which condition people to feel embarrassed or ashamed only when they are found out (Benedict, 1934: 222ff.). In either case exposure or condemnation will invoke or intensify feelings of shame.

The specific techniques of invoking shame are variable. Ridicule and gossip are among the most common. Avoidance, public insult, self deprivation, and even suicide also are among them. In some South Pacific cultures one who has been offended or who has had his rights violated may threaten suicide to bring shame on the violator, and the threat may be carried out. Actual physical violence also may be included as one of the specific means by which shame may be stimulated.

Affective reinforcement may be considered as a separate means of social control, though it is related to the stimulation of shame as its positive converse. If people can secure conformity by invoking shame they also can do so by invoking a sense of pride by the expression of approval. This is particularly applicable to the person who goes beyond what is prescribed or who abides by the cultural prescriptions with unusually high frequency. He may be rewarded by being honored publicly, by being given positions of prestige-bearing responsibility, or by being provided with physically and psychologically gratifying experiences of a number of kinds. Not only does this encourage the rewarded individual to abide by the norms; it presumably has a motivational and educational effect upon those who honor him, admire him, or witness his reward and honor.

Another technique of social control is what has been called *logic* (Honigmann, 1959: 500). A person is reminded, directly or indirectly, that violation or contemplated violation of the norms is incompatible with a belief that he shares with his fellows. There may be argument about the issue, and a person of much influence may pressure one of lesser position to accept his point of view (Wilson and Wilson, 1945: 56). Among the Yurok Indians of northern California there was a good deal of concern with justice, and the way to maintain justice was to insist on retribution through fines when a violation had been committed. A Yurok who failed to take immediate steps against a violator of his rights to the flippers from any sea lion taken by another person along his stretch of the coast was reminded that his behavior was inconsistent with one of the beliefs he shared with the rest of the Yurok; that is, that justice and good social relations cannot be maintained without careful adherence to the principle of quick retribution for any offender (Spott and Kroeber, 1943: 198f.).

These are only a few of the significant means by which violations of cultural norms may be kept at a minimum and the consequent disorganization of social relations avoided. When such violations are so frequent that members of a society cannot predict and therefore count on the behavior of their fellows, it becomes difficult if not impossible for the people to accomplish the culturally defined goals of life, a state which sociologists sometimes refer to as *social disorganization*. Anthropologists have not given nearly so much study to nonlegal means of social control as sociologists, and further investigation of this area in nonliterate and peasant cultures should yield a better picture of the range and variety of social control customs than we now have.

11

RITUAL

Ritual is of much functional significance in every aspect of life and occurs in much more of daily activity than is usually recognized. Much ritual is religious, but a great deal occurs in technological, economic, kinship, political and other activities. The subject is treated in a chapter of its own as a way of emphasizing this point.

Any society's members have culturally defined feelings about all kinds of things, and people of all cultures are inclined to symbolize these feelings in standardized ways. Ritual behavior is an economical means of expressing or reinforcing important sentiments. Political leaders, for example, are recognized as functionally important persons who must maintain some degree of authority and respect if they are to be effective. This feeling is expressed in behavior which emphasizes this, such as the playing of special music when a president arrives on the scene, a genuflection executed before approaching a monarch, and the many other specifics that occur on occasions of contact between a political leader and his people. In another context, the employer who removes his tie and dons his old clothes to labor for a time alongside his workmen may be engaging in ritual affirmation of equality and commonality. Exchange of gifts, already discussed in other contexts, may be a ritual declaration of a friendship bond. Honigmann has suggested that ritual is ". . . the symbolic expression of the sentiments which are attached to a given situation." (1959: 509). It is defined here as the symbolic affirmation of values by means of culturally standardized utterances and actions. A ritual may be considered as a unit of such symbolic expression and a *ceremony* as a given complex of rituals associated with a specific occasion or kind of occasion.

The techniques and objects employed in ritual are highly diverse. Manipulation of the body is frequent, and nearly any bodily movement or physiological activity may have ritual significance. Among these are the folding of the hands to show reverence for God, weeping to express solidarity, spitting to show contempt, clapping the hands to show approval, and bowing to manifest subordination. Various dance movements also are used to express sentiments. Cultures vary in respect to the meanings of ritual actions. Placing the palms together indicates an attitude of prayer in some places, but in others it is a gesture of respect. In some groups weeping is more explicitly utilized to symbolize solidarity than it is in Euroamerican and many other cultures. Some rituals are verbal or actional or both without the involvement of objects, and when objects are of ritual significance they may be either manipulated or simply present as a part of the desired ritual setting. Cultures differ in the substances and materials employed for ritual and in the frequency of their use. Cattle, for example, are much more extensively employed in ceremonies in East Africa than they are in a number of other groups which raise them, and tobacco is of great ritual significance in many American Indian cultures. The meanings of bodily movements, musical and other sounds, utterances, and materials commonly are so well standardized that their employment not only expresses but also stimulates the feelings which are supposed to be experienced on given ritual occasions.

Anthropologists have given greatest attention to two major categories of ritual—*rites of passage* and *rites of intensification* (Chapple and Coon, 1942: 485). Rites of passage are those which occur when individuals or groups move from one status to another. Naming ceremonies, baptisms, initiation rites, graduation exercises, investiture ceremonies, and funerals are examples. Intensification rituals sometimes are called calendrical rites, since they are associated with events which occur repeatedly in the society in question, perhaps annually, seasonally, monthly, or weekly. The Aztecs and other Mesoamerican groups performed world renewal ceremonies every 52 years, since it took that much time for the 365-day calendar and the 260-day calendar to return to the point at which the first day for each would coincide. Some Euroamerican communities have centennial rituals, which consist of observing the hundredth anniversary of some important event. Rites of intensification may occur also at irregular intervals, for example, in those tribes which stage renewal ceremonies whenever they feel they are needed.

It is clear that passage and intensification rituals are not the only kinds, but anthropologists have not had notable success in developing mutually exclusive and comprehensive ritual categories. Accordingly, we will turn our attention to the functions of rituals.

Validation and reinforcement of values is one of the most obvious functions; in fact, this is indicated in the definition of ritual. It is on ceremonial occasions, such as Independence Day, the investiture of political officials, or weddings, that speeches may be delivered which allude to group values in conventional kinds of statements, reminding the people of what they are supposed to be committed to and, perhaps, even praising them for their correct attitudes and behaviors. In this sense, ritual has a social control function.

Ritual also *provides reassurance* and feelings of security in the face of the psychological disturbances of everyday life. Magical rituals comfort the person in that he feels that he is doing something to overcome his problems, and the praying person who has put his problems in God's hands feels comforted and renewed. Many ritual activities reassure one by providing him with a sense of having conformed to the requirements of powers beyond him and a consequent feeling that all will be well. Much religious worship is of this kind. Ritual also may be viewed as providing reassurance in the sense that it is a ready-made solution to problems which may be poorly understood and difficult of solution. In the face of danger and uncertainty it is comforting to be able to cross one's self, utter a standardized prayer, or sing a song with the group.

Much ritual, obviously, is conducted in group situations. Simply the enjoyment of doing things together provides the participant with a sense of belonging. Beyond this the ritual may be designed specifically to express and reinforce group ties. Whichever way it works, ritual has the consequence of *unifying the group*.

Ritual also *aids status change*. Passage rituals, particularly, may be concerned with acquainting the person with the roles he is to perform in his new status and motivating him to perform them well. Political leaders assuming office and young people entering married life often are adjured to acquit themselves well and advised as to how they are to behave. Initiation into tribal fraternities often involves extensive education to the secrets of manhood.

One of the more significant functions of ritual is the *relief of psychological tensions*, many of which are culturally induced. Often simple participation in meaningful ritual serves to relieve emotional strain, but of particular interest are what Gluckman has called "rites of reversal," by which people are permitted to do the opposite of what is culturally prescribed, and by such ritual license the prescriptions actually are strengthened (Gluckman, 1955: 109). Among some African groups in which the monarch enjoys great power, there are occasions when the king's subjects are allowed to insult him to his face. Many groups have times when sexual relations which ordinarily are proscribed are permitted.

Some have suggested that rituals exist as ways of restabilizing patterns of interaction which have been disturbed by crisis (Chapple and Coon, 1942: 398). It seems that most, if not all, of the functions just reviewed may be interpreted in terms of either maintaining stability in the face of potential disturbance or adjustment to such disturbances. Many intensification rites strengthen the group for dealing with all kinds of crises by reinforcing the sense of commitment to cultural values, draining off tensions which might threaten social stability, bolstering feelings of confidence and security, or providing a stronger sense of unity. Rites of passage occur at those points in the life cycle where physiological and other changes have disturbed the stable patterns of adjustment to which people are accustomed. Birth and death, growth changes, sexual maturity, and the decrepitude of old age inevitably upset established and satisfying modes of interaction. Rituals function to maintain and restore at such emotionally disturbing times.

Ritual seems to have negative functions, too, judging by the fact that some people find ceremonies wearisome and wonder why they exist. Thus it is that ritual may cause tension as well as reduce it. Some groups, in fact, utilize clowns to provide release in the midst of boring ceremonies. But it is not only the tedium of long ceremonies that causes difficulties. Some rituals are difficult to execute, and if precise performance is required for the success of magical or other instrumental rites, the strain on both performer and concerned observer can cause difficulty. Yet, the fact that ritual customs are so common and continue to be observed is evidence that, generally, positive functions override undesired consequences.

12

RELIGION

Anthropologists have devoted much attention to the study of religion, and they agree that religious customs are found in all cultures. In many, in fact, religious beliefs and practices may play the major role in integrating a way of life into a functional unity. It is true, of course, that the religious beliefs and practices of a number of cultures differ greatly from those to which the reader is accustomed, but all are alike in that they have to do with the supernatural and perform similar functions. Anthropologists usually define religion as beliefs and practices having to do with the concept of the supernatural.

This does not mean that it is a simple matter to distinguish religious from nonreligious customs, and various writers are by no means agreed on the best criteria for defining religion. Some emphasize emotional commitment to something above and beyond one's self, whether it be a supernatural person or an ideological cause. Others emphasize a sense of awe. The position taken here is that most phenomena which have been called religion have to do with what is called the supernatural and that it is most useful to limit religious phenomena to these. There remains, then, the problem of defining what is meant by the supernatural. Many nonliterate groups lack any word for religion, and many things which we would label as religious or superstitious are not distinguished from things we think of as purely natural. The Nyoro of Africa, for example, make no such distinction between the act of setting fire to a man's house with a match and the practice of placing some magical medicine in the roof of an enemy's house in order to damage him (Beattie, 1960: 73). What Euroamerican students of other religions do is to apply the term supernatural to those things which Euroamerican logic and science have not been able to demonstrate the existence of. Some Euroamericans may use logic to argue for the reality of a supernatural order, and they may interpret empirical phenomena as evidence of its existence, but the supernatural remains beyond proof by reason and the senses and is embraced as a matter of faith. What the anthropologist does is to classify as religious customs those elements of nonliterate cultures which have to do with the kind of things which, by Euroamerican standards, are classified as supernaturalistic.

RELIGIOUS BELIEFS

Anthropologists sometimes have distinguished two major kinds of religious belief; one a belief in supernatural persons, and the other belief in impersonal supernatural entities or power. Belief in supernatural persons is called *animism*, and it has as the objects of belief, souls, personal spirits, and gods. These are supernatural in the sense that they ordinarily are thought of as completely or mostly nonmaterial, and, of course, their existence has not been demonstrated by modern science. They are persons in that they have the attributes of people; they are conscious, they have will and intention, and they experience emotions which human persons experience.

There is no well-standardized term for belief in impersonal supernatural power or entities corresponding to animism, but the word *animatism* comes closest. R. R. Marett used the word to apply to the supernatural character of things which are not persons (Marett, 1912: 23ff.). Anthropologists have made wide use of a term which designates the object of the belief called animatism, namely, *mana*. Mana is an Oceanic term used to designate a kind of impersonal potency which permeates the universe but may be concentrated in persons or objects. It is rather like electricity—a kind of voltage which is in many things and is spiritual or nonmaterial and powerful but, nevertheless, impersonal. To say that it is impersonal does not mean that the people consciously think of it as impersonal. They may, but sometimes it is simply a matter of not thinking of the power as personal. To summarize the two religious beliefs mentioned, animism is belief in supernatural spirit-persons, and animatism is belief in mana.

It is important to remember that in practice it is not always possible to distinguish these kinds of belief and that they may be combined. The *manitou* of the Algonkian-speaking Indians of North America, for example, is sometimes thought of as sheer spiritual force and sometimes as a supernatural person, the Great Spirit. When a nonliterate regards a power as resident in an object it may be quite impossible for him to be explicit about whether a supernatural person resides in the object or simply power. It seems best to regard the distinction between animism and animatism as one useful to the anthropologist in classifying religious phenomena which, in fact, intergrade.

The variety of specific kinds of supernatural entities is so great that it is not surprising to find it difficult to classify them. Describing a *soul*, for example, is no simple matter, since souls come in a variety of natures. Some souls have definite personal qualities; others seem rather impersonal. Some are completely invisible, and others may not be. Some souls outlive the body and some don't. In fact, many peoples believe that they have more than one soul. Whatever the nature of the soul, this concept of some kind of immaterial entity existing within and fundamental to the life of the body is universal. Functionally, soul concepts are used to explain death and illness and dreams. Illness may be due to partial or temporary loss of the soul, and death may occur when it is completely and permanently separated from the body. Dreams are accounted for as the travels and experiences of the soul while one is asleep.

Souls of the dead may become *ghosts*, which may be involved in a variety of forms and functions. They may take up residence in some abode of the souls of the dead and live there in some kind of immaterial or semi-material state similar to that of life on earth or, sometimes, the reverse of it. After a short period of wandering or frequenting the grave or various places its former owner frequented during life the ghost may cease to exist entirely. Nonliterate peoples have a number of customs concerning belief in souls of the dead, including conversations with them and making offerings to them. Such a complex of customs sometimes has been referred to as the *cult of the dead*. In some cases some souls of the dead, particularly those of deceased kinsmen, may possess enough interest in and power over human affairs that they may be regarded as deities, and the associated religious complex has been referred to as *ancestor worship*.

The world's cultures manifest a great variety of other kinds of spirits which are not disembodied souls or ghosts. They manifest a great diversity of forms and functions, but all are alike in that they are modeled after the personal attributes of people. Many of these spirits roam the countryside rather than indwelling something, though they may be found in greater numbers in some places than in others. Objects, particularly portable ones, which are indwelt by personal spirits sometimes are called *fetishes*. Mountains, trees, waterfalls, mysterious-looking places, and other natural features also may be indwelt by one or more personal spirits, though the word fetish is not so commonly applied to them. A personal spirit may also indwell a human and still not be thought of as a soul. Spirit possession would be a case in point. Many cultures include a kind of *guardian spirit* concept, whereby the person develops a special relationship with a spirit, who gives him power and knowledge of specific kinds and acts as his guide and protector, perhaps throughout the rest of his life. The quest for a guardian spirit is a significant element in the religion of many North American Indian cultures. Cultures differ from one another in regard to whether the personal spirits are more often good or more often bad. A number of religions are characterized by belief in an abundance of evil spirits.

The distinction between an ordinary personal spirit and a god is somewhat difficult to make, and it perhaps is most useful to think of a god as a supernatural person of greater power than most spirits. In nonliterate cultures the god commonly is a local personage. He may be either good, bad, both, or neither. Those religions which are characterized by a number of gods commonly are referred to as *polytheism*. If there is only one such being the familiar term *monotheism* is used, though true monotheism is extremely rare. By this definition Christianity is not truly monotheistic, since it incorporates belief in an evil deity, Satan. Those cultures whose religions manifest belief in a deity of much greater power than other deities and spirits often are said to have a *high god* or *supreme being*. The Roman Catholic anthropologist, Father Wilhelm Schmidt, saw such occurrences as survivals of an original monotheism, but this is not demonstrable. It has been pointed out that these high gods often do not resemble the Christian God as closely as has been alleged.

There is a special kind of supernatural common in nonliterate religions which is difficult to classify. These beings are much more material than most supernaturals and may be quite visible, though they may be material sometimes and not at other times. The most distinctive thing about them, perhaps, is that they take various grotesque forms, and possibly they can be referred to as *monsters*. They commonly are identified with certain places, such as a pool, a wood, a glen, or a well, and they usually are thought of as being malevolent or, at least, tricksters.

RELIGIOUS PRACTICES

Ways of responding to or influencing supernaturals depend to some degree on their nature. Prayer is conversation addressed to a supernatural, and it is most appropriately applied to those which are regarded as persons. Euroamericans generally associate prayer with supplication and praise, but any verbal communication is included in prayer by the anthropologist. Personal spirits who aren't very intelligent may be made victims of deceit. One may lie to them and get away with it, or he may make a false promise in order to get the god or spirit to do something for him. It is also possible to get a supernatural to act in one's behalf by flattering him, threatening him, or even commanding him. It depends on what kind of person he is. The point is that any verbal communication which one may use with a fellow human may be used with a supernatural person, and this is prayer. Prayer, of course, is not the only way of dealing with supernatural persons, as will be seen later.

Many students of religion have contrasted prayer as a technique with magic. It appears that magic may be used on supernatural persons, but it seems most frequently associated with animatism or, at least, uncertainty or lack of attention to the kind of power being manipulated. The key thing in magic is the observance of some specifically prescribed procedure which is assumed to have a predictable result. The magician utters a verbal formula, performs an action, perhaps through the use of some supernaturally powerful substance; and if he has done these things properly and there is no interference, the result is assured. It should be apparent that what Euroamericans call prayer is sometimes highly magical in nature.

It is common to recognize two forms of magic. *Imitative magic* involves some procedure similar to that which one desires to happen. Placing slivers or pins in an image of one's enemy to cause him to sicken and die is an example. The Upper Palaeolithic practice of painting realistic pictures of a bleeding animal, perhaps with an arrow through his heart, is thought to be a case of imitative hunting magic. Ritual sexual intercourse at the time the crops are planted is also a kind of imitative magic, since a parallel between human fertility and the fertility of the seed is involved. *Contagious magic* is done by working with something which has been in contact with whatever the magician wishes to influence. A hair from an enemy's head may be stamped upon, submerged under water, or burned in the supposition that its former owner may be damaged thereby. Magical acts of this kind, because they are attempts to do evil, may be called *sorcery* or *black magic*. *Taboo* sometimes is viewed as a sort of negative magic; that is, one avoids certain consequences by refraining from some act. Substances and objects which are used in magic sometimes are called *medicines*, and nonliterate peoples do not always distinguish them from substances of actual medicinal value. Objects which attract supernatural aid may be called *charms*, and those which ward off evil supernatural influences, *amulets*. Both charms and amulets sometimes are included as *fetishes*.

Witchcraft is not always distinguished from sorcery, because sorcery often is practiced by persons called witches. Anyone can perform an act of sorcery, but a witch can do evil as a kind of psychic act, without the performance of any mechanical procedure and without having to learn his craft. Among the Azande of Africa witch power comes from a kind of substance which is found in the bellies of certain people, and they are able to injure others simply by their bad feelings (Evans-Pritchard, 1937: 21f.). It is common, also, for witches to have familiars, and they often are thought to appear in the form of an animal. In some cultures witchcraft and sorcery are major explanations for illness, and students of nonliterate religions believe that witchcraft also functions as a way of draining off frustration and the consequent hostility. People can blame their troubles on witches rather than on each other, and in some groups there is much talk of witchcraft even when no one deliberately practices it and few, if any, can identify any specific person as a witch. Witches, incidentally, may be either male or female.

Divination, the practice of ascertaining the unknown through supernatural means, is an important element in nonliterate religions, particularly in the determination of the causes of illnesses. It is so important that part time specialists in divination are common among nonliterate peoples. The variety of specific means employed is great, but many of them are magical in nature and ordinarily require the use of equipment which is independent of the diviner. A rather different kind of divination which is common is direct contact and communication with a personal spirit, who gives the diviner the desired information or, perhaps, possesses him and speaks through him.

RELIGIOUS PERSONNEL

Many of the religious techniques mentioned may be practiced by an ordinary person, but in every group there is some degree of specialization. The commonest kind of religious personage among hunting, fishing, and collecting groups is the *shaman*. Shaman is a Tungus word, the Tungus being a major tribalistic group of Siberia, a region well known for the high development of shamanism. A shaman is a religious specialist who has individual ability to communicate and deal with the supernaturals and who applies this ability primarily as an individual rather than as a representative of a group. Other terms in use for this type of person are *medicine man* and *witch doctor*. The major function of most shamans is dealing with illness in terms of both divination and healing. Some of them employ magic in part and utilize herbal preparations of actual medicinal value. One of the most common healing techniques is sucking from the body the intrusive foreign object or substance which is believed to have caused the sickness.

The shamanism of Siberia is sometimes called *inspirational shamanism*, which refers to the fact that the shaman acquires his supernatural power by some direct personal religious experience—a vision, dream, or some such revelation. Generally he has familiar spirits which give him the powers he possesses and which he deals with in the application of his powers. The Siberian shaman puts on an exhibition of dealing with them. He wears special clothing and sings and drums. As the spirits approach, various supernaturalistic sounds are heard and different voices speaking. The tent may shake. The spirits leave their message, and the shaman may end up unconscious, exhausted by his successful efforts to contact the spirits. A particularly interesting kind of shamanistic performance is found in some parts of the world in which the shamans engage in public contests to see who can perform the most impressive supernaturalistic acts or who can overcome the other shamans.

Though healing commonly is associated with shamanism, shamans may have other abilities as well and, in fact, may specialize in them. The antelope shaman of the Great Basin cultures had special powers to attract antelope and presided over antelope drives.

The other main kind of religious personage found in nonliterate societies is the *priest*, who is a specialist in group ritual. Priests may have special personal ability to deal with the supernatural, but this is not relevant to the definition. It merely recognizes that it is possible for the same person to be both priest and shaman. The key thing is that the priest is a ceremonialist who operates as a representative of the group and in its behalf. While not absent in all hunting, fishing, and collecting societies, priests are found more commonly in larger societies with fairly elaborate cultures and organized religious cults with theological doctrines and standardized rituals.

RELIGIOUS FUNCTIONS

During the last century and the early part of this century many anthropologists concerned themselves with the problem of the origin of religion. Sir Edward B. Tylor, possibly the most renowned of the nineteenth century anthropologists, felt that the concept of souls was the earliest religious belief and that it formed the basis for the evolution of other concepts, such as spirits, ancestor deities, and, eventually, monotheism (Tylor, 1889: 426ff.). The concept of souls, he felt, came about as man tried to account for the difference between a living body and a dead body or a sick person and a well person on the one hand and, on the other hand, those images which one sees in dreams. The answer was to assume the existence of spiritual entities which ordinarily dwell within the body during life and health and consciousness but which are absent during death, sickness and sleep. It has been noted already that the concept of souls does, in fact, perform these functions. The theory was abandoned not because it was demonstrated to be false but because there are other equally logical ways by which supernaturalistic concepts could have originated.

Other students propounded various theories of the origin of religion, but anthropologists generally have given up efforts to determine what the earliest religious beliefs were like in favor of trying to understand the functions of religion. When these are understood it is reasonable to suppose that they have something to do with the origin and continued existence of supernaturalism.

Certainly one of the major functions of religion is *explanation*. Psychological investigations demonstrate the propensity of humans to account for things—to make sense out of the circumstances of life. People all over the world have wondered how things got started, why people die rather than living forever, why people suffer from diseases and other troubles, and a diversity of other such questions. Non-scientific cultures lack means of getting at natural explanations for things and, given the human demand for explanations, they are left with supernaturalistic ones. A spring dries up because the spirit who lives there is displeased at not being supplied with the desired offerings. The earthquake comes because the gods are displeased over man's behavior. The mountains were formed as blobs of mud dropped from the feet of the creator as he plodded across the landscape. The severe pain in a man's chest is from a bone splinter magically sent into his body by an enemy sorcerer. Great is the diversity of specific explanations produced by man's inventive mind. Many such explanations are embodied in the universally found sacred stories known as *myths*.

A second important function of religion is *reassurance*. "Man is born to trouble" said Eliphaz the Temanite (Job 5:7), and so it is. He is faced with sickness and death, hunger, cold, pain, itches, and many other uncomfortable physical sensations. Moreover, he worries about the possibility and probability of these things for himself and those he loves, and physical discomfort is translated thereby into psychological discomfort—worry, anxiety, and fear. His friends, his relatives, and strangers don't treat him well. They fail to be friendly; they insult him and injure his ego; they threaten to do him physical injury; they cause him to fail in the pursuit of his desires. Life would be too much to endure were it not for the divination which determines what is wrong, the magic or the prayer which brings healing, the sorcery by which the enemy is vanquished without the danger or discomfort of direct confrontation. Thus religious beliefs and practices provide the comfort and reassurance that comes from having some way to explain and cope with the troubles and uncertainties of living. Some wonder why "primitives" continue to believe in magical and other supernatural approaches when they so often fail. A large part of the answer appears to be the psychological comfort derived from having something to do which holds some promise of coping successfully with the troubles of life.

A third major function of religion is *validation* of a people's customs and values. Religious beliefs are important in any culture as powerful support for the things which people believe they should and should not do and as explanations for them. Female infanticide seems a horrible custom to most Euroamericans, but if one lives in a society where it seems unlikely that there will be enough food to keep alive a newborn child and it is believed that if it is killed, its spirit will later be born into another body, the taking of the child's life may seem the right thing to do. Such practices are validated, justified, or sanctioned by a religious belief. In respect to this function, there is the question of how social order will be maintained as people abandon the belief in supernaturals who have prescribed certain standards of behavior to be violated at the risk of their displeasure and punishment.

Social integration also is an important function of religion in many cultures. This can be so only in those societies where there is a common set of religious beliefs and practices for the whole group. In such societies the solidarity of the group is enhanced by the feeling of belonging acquired from believing in and participating in the same religious rituals.

Another aspect of integration, however, is *cultural*. A culture, viewed as a functional complex of customs, may be given unity by the presence of various religious themes which indirectly link many customs. Bronislaw Malinowski, particularly, emphasized the manner in which religion penetrates all aspects of the cultures of many nonliterate groups. He has shown how magical rituals intrude into every phase of the life of the Trobriand Islanders—in their gardening, their canoe-making, their initiation ceremonies, their weddings, their recreation (1953: 73). This sort of thing is in contrast to many Euroamerican communities, in which religion is a compartment seen as having limited relevance to most aspects of everyday life.

There is little doubt that religion is much less important in modern scientifically oriented cultures than in most nonliterate groups, and there seems to be a trend toward what has been called the abolition of religion. To the extent that this is true it may be understood in terms of the functions of religion just discussed and their greatly reduced importance due to the success of science in formulating natural explanations for things and providing effective means for coping with hunger, disease, and other forms of discomfort. A personal God is no longer needed to explain many of the phenomena of the universe. Moreover, science has shown many of the supernaturalistic explanations of these phenomena to be in error, consequently reducing the confidence of people in such explanations and augmenting a growing faith that the as yet unexplained will ultimately be explained by science. When one is threatened by disease, he is justified in feeling considerable confidence that modern scientific medicine may banish it or, at least, allow him to live out his remaining days in some comfort. The suffering which comes from hunger and lack of shelter from the cold or from insect bites is banished by a scientifically based technology. Man still seems to be suffering quite a bit of psychological disturbance from his intractable fellow humans, but even now the developing psychological and social sciences are holding forth the promise of scientific resolution of interpersonal and intergroup conflict.

As the result of the cross-cultural approach, anthropologists strongly tend to see supernaturalistic beliefs and practices as man-made and having no real referents. They exist only because they have functional value and if other means can be found to perform those functions religion might cease to exist. In fact, it might be found dysfunctional. There is not complete agreement as to whether nonsupernaturalism can replace supernaturalism successfully. A number of individuals in Euroamerican society seem to have shed religiosity without maladjustment, but many others are experiencing difficulty. There is, in fact, an interesting way station between supernaturalism and frank nonsupernaturalism which insists on the retention of Christian terminology and other symbols of the Christian religion, such as salvation, the sovereignty of God, Christ as the Lord of Life, and the like, to stand for essentially nonsupernaturalistic phenomena and concepts. The sovereignty of God, for example, may become the significant fact that the total milieu of existence determines the fate of the individual. This kind of position is very possibly held because of the psychological disturbance at giving up words and concepts which have come to have some functional value, even though they are no longer believed to refer to any supernatural reality.

Many writers doubt that man is ready to abandon supernaturalistic concepts completely. They see man as requiring something which he feels is bigger than mankind to commit himself to and see those societies which abandon supernaturalism completely as suffering from secularism or other damaging commitments. Anthony F. C. Wallace has suggested that secular ideologies may produce ". . . unfortunate consequences for world peace and human welfare when directed toward people improperly perceived and toward organs of political action and cultural ideologies" (1956: 277f.). He suggests further that the abolition of religion may well be accompanied by a ". . . corresponding incidence and severity of transference neuroses, or human relationships will be increasingly contaminated by character disorders, neurotic acting out, and paranoid deification of political leaders and ideologies" (1956: 278). It is the proven functional value of religion which explains its persistence.

The British anthropologist, Raymond Firth, views religious systems in terms of means for handling the fundamental problems of social organization; ". . . for reducing uncertainty and anxiety, for increasing coherence in human relationships, for assigning meaning to human endeavor, for providing justification for moral obligation" (1951: 250). He concludes that it is impossible for human society to exist without some kind of symbolic solutions to such problems which go beyond those based on empirical evidence. The range and variety of such symbolic solutions which have been invented and found functional by man is great.

13

IDEOLOGY

All cultural traits are ideological to the degree that they are ideas. Ideology is used here to embrace several categories of beliefs and knowledge about the nature of man and the universe, time and space, animal and plant life, and how things ought to be. In these areas there is a high proportion of multi-individual notions which lack direct actional or artifactual expression and, consequently, are most often communicated verbally. It should be clear that religion, especially, but also all other aspects of culture, incorporates many customs which are ideological in this sense.

REASON AND SCIENCE

The scientific method may be viewed as consisting of two essential components, the *rational* and the *empirical*. Which one is given priority is a question as difficult as deciding whether the chicken or the egg comes first. The important thing to realize is that both are essential. That which is empirical, that is, which can be experienced by the senses or some extension of them, must be present. Contrary to what is sometimes said, however, facts do not speak for themselves. Man interprets empirical data by means of his mind. By rational processes he determines what empirical phenomena he will experience or collect and what meaning these have for him. Science began with ideas about natural phenomena derived from everyday observations. From these ideas various hypotheses or statements about the relationships among phenomena have been formulated. The setting up of hypotheses is a rational process. Once they are set up data are gathered, and then, by rational processes, it is determined whether they increase or decrease our confidence in the hypotheses. In Euroamerican culture this process has been highly formalized and named the *scientific method*, but nonscientific nonliterate peoples reason and interpret empirical data in basically the same ways that we do.

It has been suggested by some that so-called primitives have a kind of prelogical mentality or that they only feel in some mystical fashion rather than employ the same processes of reasoning as Euroamericans. There is abundant anthropological data showing that this is not true, and as near as can be ascertained, people in all cultures follow the same rules of logic as Euroamericans. This is not to say that Euroamericans and nonliterates think reasonably at all times; it is known that both may violate the rules of logic. The thing to remember is that the ideas of one culture seem unreasonable to people of another culture because different premises are employed. It certainly seems illogical to many an American to think of the past as lying in front of us and the future behind us as some groups do (Nida, 1954: 206). Americans think of themselves as moving forward into the future, and in terms of this notion it obviously is appropriate to conceive of the future as lying in front of one. If, however, one starts with the assumption that the past can be seen in the sense that what has happened is known and that the future cannot be seen in this sense and, moreover, he remembers that one's eyes are in the front rather than the back of his head, it becomes quite reasonable to speak of the future as being behind one. What seems logical or illogical is often relative to the context of culturally defined assumptions or premises.

Shifting the emphasis to the empirical approach, there is abundant evidence that nonliterates are keen observers. A detailed study of the subsistence technology of any nonliterate culture will reveal that they have apprehended the "real" nature of many phenomena and have acted logically to get results. The gardening of the Trobriand Islanders is not all magic. They understand and apply a great number of practical bits of knowledge. Malinowski reports that they possess extensive knowledge of different kinds of soil, the kinds of plants which grow best in them, and how each is best handled. They also understand the weather and the seasons well, and the plant pests, also. They act faithfully and reasonably upon all this knowledge to produce good crops (1935: 76f.). On a number of occasions Euroamericans have attributed mystical or animal-like instincts to nonliterates when the fact is that they may detect and reason about empirical clues which the cultural alien is not trained to discern. Such was the case with one event shown on American television, in which natives locate a grave in a place where, as far as the American knew, all surface traces had been destroyed by natural action. In the interests of accuracy, it is well to be careful about attributing mystical instincts to people who operate in ways which we are not culturally equipped to understand. Nonliterate people may not have formalized the processes of logic or the method of setting up hypotheses and testing them by systematically collecting empirical data; they nevertheless do think logically, and they do have notions which they check against empirical evidence. In fact, they have enough of this kind of thing that some anthropologists have used the term *ethnoscience*.

PHILOSOPHY AND WORLD VIEW

Anthropologists have given less attention than they might to explicit philosophical systems as an aspect of nonliterate cultures. In large part this may be because simpler peoples have few specialists who reflect about ultimate problems. Moreover, the premises, assumptions, tenets, and axioms about life and the universe which govern behavior tend to be more implicit than explicit for a high proportion of a society's members. There may be another reason; and that is that philosophical customs are part of the covert culture and must be transmitted verbally. Couple with this the fact that philosophical issues are rather abstract and can be communicated effectively only in the native language. These things mean that the ethnographer is not likely to learn much about philosophical ideas of the people he is studying unless they talk about them; and if the anthropologist does not speak and understand the aboriginal language very well he may not be able to apprehend their philosophical concepts. That many groups may have unsuspected philosophical systems is illustrated by what happened to a Brazilian anthropologist, Vicenzo Petrullo, while studying the technologically simple and highly nomadic Yaruro of Venezuela. He became seriously ill and largely immobilized for some time. The Yaruro remained with him and cared for him until he could leave them, and during the long conversations he had with them, he discovered that they had an elaborate philosophy concerning the nature of the universe (1939: 190ff.). Most of it was what Euroamericans would label as mythological, but the point is that they did speculate about ultimate questions and develop socially standardized notions—an explicit life and world view.

Philosophy ordinarily is thought of as having to do with rather explicit notions of the nature of things. Currently anthropologists make rather extensive use of the concept of *world view*, which includes both explicit ideas and implicit assumptions and orientations. The implicit, of course, must be inferred by the investigator from his observations of behavior, since such esotraits seldom are expressed directly and clearly by utterances. Many elements of a group's world view turn out to be pervasive cultural themes.

Anthropologists have noted that world views differ notably from culture to culture. Not only may cultures hold views and orientations contradictory to those of alien groups; but the specific elements of world views are highly various. It has been suggested that the American middle class thinks of the universe as a mechanism, which, because it is a mechanism, can be mastered by man. There also is the tendency to think of men as equal and perfectible (DuBois, 1955: 1233). The Dusun of northern Borneo are unable to share American optimism about mastering nature, for it is thought beyond man's control. Dusun, to a certain degree, can submit to and cooperate with the universe to avoid misfortune, but the notion of dominating and changing the natural world is alien to them (Williams, 1965: 90). There are nonliterate groups whose attitudes toward the possibility of manipulating the universe are similar to those of middle class Americans, but the Dusun are not among them.

Contrary to the common American view that people are equal is the feeling of the Banyarwanda of East Africa that some groups are naturally superior to others. This is expressed culturally in the presence of castes, with one's rights depending on which caste he was born into. If, for example, a member of a certain lower caste murders a person of a high caste, the king may authorize the putting to death of two persons of the lower caste (Maquet, 1954: 186). The Igbo of Nigeria seem more like Americans in regard to equality. The Igbo ideal is to provide all with equal opportunity to become successful, and this is consonant with their individualistic competitiveness and their democratic sociopolitical system (Uchendu, 1965: 19f.).

World views differ in these and many other ways. Some societies think of the universe as a dangerous place, while others regard it as friendly. It may be regarded either as highly personal, that is, animistic, or largely impersonal. Some people manifest great concern with cosmic forces, whereas others are more interested in relationships among men. Some world views are much concerned with the control of powerful sexuality, and others are not. A description of the total range and variety of world views would require the spilling of a great deal of ink. Perhaps it is among the more fascinating aspects of cross-cultural variation.

VALUES AND ETHICAL PRINCIPLES

Sometimes anthropologists single out the values and ethics of a culture for separate treatment. It is undoubtedly apparent that values already have been mentioned repeatedly. In fact, it is difficult to conceive of a cultural element which carries no overtones of either negative or positive sentiment, however weak. The very fact that a social custom is maintained may be taken as evidence that it has value for the people. This, of course, fails to negate the fact that some values are far stronger than others and that cultures differ much from one another in what is greatly valued. Ethical principles are values which concern conduct, especially in relation to one's fellow men.

Some anthropologists have been much impressed with the diversity of values and ethics, so much so that some allege that there are no universal ethical principles. Ralph Linton has suggested that, in general terms, the similarities among the ethical values of the world's cultures are significant. Among other things he mentions the rule against incest, the rejection of promiscuity, the valuation of marriage, mutual obligations of parents and children, family loyalty, private property, standards of truth, and proscriptions against killing and maiming as examples of universal principles (1952). These similarities are significant as evidence of kinds of universal human wants, but the degree to which attitudes differ and the great variety of specific forms in which such concerns are manifested also are significant. For example, standards of truth are universal, but sometimes the truth hurts. Accordingly, in some cultures the ethical principles prescribe that, in ordinary social intercourse, the thing to do is to tell people whatever they wish to hear. Personal property rights are universal, but there are cultures in which one may help himself to another's possessions as long as it is known who has taken them, and he may not have to return them until asked. Whatever one's personal standards of behavior, it is important to keep in mind the principle of cultural relativism as a way of understanding the values and ethics of culturally alien groups. It should be apparent that this is one of the more difficult areas in which to apply cultural relativism.

KNOWLEDGE

Knowledge is a term referring to rather specific ideas about relatively concrete elements of the universe. Such ideas are knowledge in the sense that they are assumed to be correct in the groups who hold them. Obviously, nonliterate peoples lack the resources for obtaining the knowledge of cosmic and other phenomena that Euroamericans have developed. As was the case in the prescientific times of Western culture, nonliterate peoples tend to regard the earth as the center of the universe and as a flat expanse covered by the sky, across which the heavenly bodies move. Also common is the idea that the earth is bounded by waters. Beyond these basic things there is a notable variety of specific ideas about the earth and the heavens. A number of peoples, for example, believe that there are several levels of worlds. The sun, the moon, or other heavenly bodies and occurrences may be personalized. Constellations are named in many cultures, but what they represent varies. Reported from India is the notion that the four stars of the big dipper are the bedposts of a bed under which a rich man has hidden his money, and the stars of the handle are thieves about ready to steal it. The Fox Indians of the American Midwest see the four stars as a bear and the other stars as hunters (Jones, 1939: 22). Culturally standardized responses to eclipses are virtually universal, many peoples regarding them as due to attacks on the sun or moon by an evil being.

Culturally standardized reactions to weather are found everywhere. Means of forecasting the weather seem to be universal, and a number of them probably enjoy some reliability. The Makah Indians of the Olympic Peninsula of Washington interpret a clear, calm night with the stars twinkling brightly as a sign of coming strong winds (Swan, 1870: 92). The Teotitlán Zapotecs say that it is going to rain when they hear the chachalacas (a kind of bird) calling repeatedly from the foothills.

Peoples living near oceans, lakes, and rivers accumulate extensive knowledge about currents, tides, water temperatures, and other such factors. The Polynesians use both knowledge of the stars and of ocean currents in navigation. Handicraft technology requires an extensive knowledge of physical and chemical properties, though, of course, exactly what happens in scientific terms is unknown. The Eskimos know that one must not blow his damp breath on the tinder when starting a fire in the cold Arctic air and that certain kinds of ice may be melted to obtain fresh water.

Nonliterates also have well formulated notions about time and space. All peoples, of course, order time according to the regular appearance and disappearance of the sun, which produces days. Periods corresponding roughly to a month, as indicated by the appearance and disappearance of the moon, also are common. Years frequently are recognized, even if it be no more than counting the number of winters since some event. It is usual for nonliterates to keep track of different times of the year according to the weather changes and variations in the position of the sun or the stars and planets. Most such observations are rather imprecise, but a number of nonliterate peoples make quite systematic observations. The Havasupai of the southwestern United States stand at a specific place at sunrise to observe the solstices (Spier, 1928: 168). Other groups note where the sun rises each morning along a ridge of hills or mountains with a distinctive outline. Such observations comprise a kind of crude calendar. Some may find it surprising that many nonliterate peoples keep track of the movements of the stars, but those groups which spend much time in the open at night may be expected to make such observations. The Bushmen of South Africa, often thought of as having one of the most primitive cultures, observe the seasonal rising of the stars, Sirius and Canopus, and keep track of their later movements as a way of reckoning the passage of winter (Leach, 1954: 116). The peoples of Middle America devised an accurate calendar based on astronomical observations of the planets. Among other things they correctly determined that it takes about 584 days for Venus to revolve around the sun. Nonliterate peoples have not developed concepts as precise as hours and minutes, though various kinds of markers for certain times of day may be utilized. Workers in the Teotitlán community of Zapotecs say it is time to return from the fields when the shadow on the mountainside assumes the shape of a man's face.

Nonliterate peoples obviously do not think in terms of great distances. On the other hand, a number of peoples move about occasionally over areas of several hundreds of miles and even make maps of the areas, some Eskimos being among them. Directions are often important to nonliterate peoples, and many of them think in terms of six rather than four, these corresponding to north, east, south, west, nadir, and zenith. Distances and dimensions commonly are measured by parts of the body, such as the length of the thumb or arm, the width of the hand, or a pace. Capacities and weights are seldom measured by nonliterates.

Ethnobotany and *ethnozoology* are terms used by anthropologists to refer to ideas about plant life and animal life respectively. Much of this knowledge is highly practical. The Tarahumara Indians of Northern Mexico boil in water the flower head of a certain herb to obtain a bright

yellow dye for coloring wool (Bennett and Zingg, 1935: 142). The Bena
of Africa know what plant root to use as an antidote for poisons affecting the heart (Culwick and Culwick, 1935: 388). Some such knowledge,
of course, is not accurate. The Eyak Indians of Alaska believed that
young people who ate bone marrow would suffer from aching bones
(Birket-Smith and De Laguna, 1938: 99). In spite of many such erroneous ideas, a thorough study of the botanical and zoological notions of
the nonliterate world provides impressive evidence of their powers of
observation. Many peoples can distinguish one sex of a game animal
from the other by the difference in gait. The Trobriand Islanders have
names for different varieties of yams and taro and know which will grow
well only if planted deeply, for example. Their discrimination of several
types of garden soil already has been mentioned. The knowledge about
inanimate objects, plants, and animals is far greater among nonliterate
peoples than most of us realize.

Some nonliterate peoples have surprisingly accurate knowledge of
man's physical structure. The Aleuts, who preserved the bodies of the
dead by drying over a fire, have uniquely accurate and detailed knowledge
of the internal organs of the body (Marsh and Laughlin, 1956: 38f.). A
number of groups have applied practical knowledge of the body and its
functions for healing purposes. The Havasupai, for example, bathe a
bleeding nose in cold water and set fractured bones (Spier, 1928: 284f.).

Most of the ideas mentioned in this discussion are of a practical
nature, though it was noted also that many of the ideas of nonliterates
are erroneous or supernaturalistic. The nonliterate, of course, does not
distinguish between those ideas which are correct and those which are
erroneous, but it seems a fair assumption that many of the ideas Euroamericans have about the nature of the physical and biological environment, even some of the scientifically derived ones, are incorrect. Undoubtedly Euroamericans have acquired a higher proportion of correct
ideas than nonliterates, but it is only a relative difference.

THE ARTS

There is no culture which fails to incorporate ideas and behaviors which provide aesthetic pleasure. It is difficult to define beauty, and it is well known that standards of beauty differ from culture to culture and, also, at different times and from one sub-group to another within the same society. Whether or not there are universal standards of taste is a problem anthropologists seldom concern themselves with, but they do emphasize that all peoples engage in activities which provide them with satisfactions beyond practical usefulness.

As a process, art may be defined as the exercise of skill in the expression or communication of sentiment or value (Honigmann, 1963: 219). This covers the sense of creativity or the aesthetic satisfaction obtained by the person exercising that skill. It also means that many kinds of activities may be considered as art. Rituals, dancing, painting and drawing, carving, horseback riding, bull fighting, story-telling, speech making, and a host of other human endeavors may be art to the degree that skill is exercised to express emotion. Many of these activities do not produce artifacts, though some result in what we may regard as objects of art. And perhaps artistic efforts of the same kind may be compared in terms of the degree of skill exercised, though it would not be possible to say that those activities involving a high degree of skill are better in any absolute sense than those requiring less skill, unless evaluators agree that this is an acceptable criterion of evaluation.

FOLKLORE

Folklore is a term commonly used to include the various stories told in any society, but it also may be extended to such things as riddles and proverbs. It is conventional to divide stories into *myths*, which have to do with supernatural characters and events, and *legends*, which are concerned with secular and supposedly historical persons and episodes. Many stories, however, are difficult to classify in one category or the other, and this often can be done only in terms of degree of emphasis. Perhaps most stories of nonliterate groups contain supernaturalistic elements.

Major regions of the world differ from one another in the prevailing kinds of folklore. In some areas, as in Polynesia, many of the myths are concerned with philosophical themes to a greater extent than in many other portions of the globe. In the Americas there is relatively little in the way of riddles and proverbs, whereas they are important in the Old World. Some areas exhibit a relatively high incidence of complex creation stories, myths about families of gods, morality stories, or myths and tales concerning animal tricksters. Differences of this kind are sufficient to make possible classification of the globe into major folklore areas and differentiation of such regions into sub-areas.

In spite of such divergence from place to place, many of the world's stories are widely distributed. Certain kinds, in fact, are found in most major regions. Flood stories are widely found, and so are obstacle–flight tales. The latter, which occur as episodes in longer stories, tell of someone pursued by an ogre, escape from which is accomplished by throwing down a series of three or four objects, such as a comb, a stone, or a bottle of oil. Each object magically becomes an obstacle which slows down the pursuer's progress, eventually enabling the hero or heroes to escape.

Even in this case, however, cultural differences are illustrated in that the story varies in its specifics from one society to another (Thompson, 1946: 440). In one place a stone thrown over the shoulder may turn into a mountain which must be climbed, but in another place it may become a ravine to be crossed. Or the ogre may be slowed down by a lake produced from a mirror in some cases or a container of oil in others. Folklore students regard the widespread occurrence of this tale to be the result of borrowing rather than independent invention because of its continuous distribution over much of the world and because of the combination of three kinds of elements—a landscape barrier due to a magical stone, a thicket or forest due to a magical comb, and a body of water due to magical liquid or a mirror (Kroeber, 1948: 545).

Folklorists have studied extensively how the elements of stories are combined and recombined as they are borrowed by different groups. The characters, the incidents, and the plot may vary independently of one another and do so from culture—and even within the same culture to a degree. Stories seem to diffuse readily from society to society, as the obstacle–flight has, and their elements are inevitably reworked to reflect the content and interests of the storyteller's culture.

Many of the functions of folklore are the same as those noted for religion and ritual. Myths are highly explanatory, and they provide validation or support for cultural behavior. Stories also are important in maintaining group solidarity. Another important function is education. Around

the fire in the evenings or during long winters, children are told or over-
hear the telling of all kinds of stories which have a lesson to them, and
the lesson may be stated explicitly before or after the telling. No less
important is the sheer enjoyment of interesting, skillfully told stories,
and from this point of view folklore may be thought of as one of the arts.
Apparently folklore also functions to reduce tension and conflict. Many
stories incorporate accounts of situations in which the characters behave
in ways which are culturally disapproved. The gods of much mythology
violate the standards of behavior by which humans must abide. Perhaps
people derive psychological release from identification with characters
who express desires which real human beings must suppress. Tension also
may be reduced by the telling and hearing of stories in which those who
exert burdensome authority and power or are otherwise the source of
trouble to others get their come-uppance. Perhaps mother-in-law jokes
perform this function for some Americans. In many stories release is
provided by accounts of solutions to the problems of life which come
far more readily than in real life.

Folklore is highly variable in specific content, but the functions are
similar in all cultures. In Euroamerican and other literate cultures, much
of the folklore has been put in writing or in moving picture form, but the
tendency to separate this completely from oral folklore must be avoided.
Social scientists have shown that magazine stories, novels, and television
soap operas perform the functions which have been reviewed here.

GRAPHIC AND PLASTIC ARTS

It is most difficult for the Euroamerican to divorce himself from the
values of his own culture in understanding the art objects of nonliterate
peoples, and it has been a definite tendency of western artists to misinterpret "primitive art" for this reason. They often have supposed that
nonliterate artists are highly original, whereas it is nearly always the case
that they conform closely to culturally established functions of the art
objects in question. Art objects which are technologically crude and,
possibly, somewhat aesthetically unappealing by Euroamerican standards
are sometimes taken as evidence of inferior ability, whereas a knowledge
of the cultural matrix might reveal that the quality of the work is considered by the artist to be irrelevant to its specific function.

Anthropologists, then, insist that art can be accurately understood
only by relating it to the cultural context within which it has been produced and within which it has meaning. A notable example is one kind
of Yoruba dance mask (Herskovits, 1948: 382). Some Euroamerican art
critics have depicted it as a conventionalization or abstraction of the
human face involving creative and skillful reworking of facial proportions
to produce the abstract, distorted version. In its cultural context, however, it is used as an accurate depiction of a face. The modification of the
features actually is related to the fact that it is worn on the top of the
head in a horizontal position, and when so viewed it provides a realistic

impression of the Negro face. Lacking knowledge of its cultural context, however, western artists customarily exhibit the mask in the vertical position and misinterpret it accordingly.

The specific function of art forms, then, may vary extensively between civilized and nonliterate cultures and from one nonliterate culture to another. The media of art differ culturally as well. Some groups, such as the Maori of New Zealand, the Indians of British Columbia, and some African groups, go in for wood carving. Various kinds of carving in the round may be highly developed, whereas painting and engraving may be neglected or inept.

Among other media are three-dimensional pottery figures; painting and engraving on the surfaces of pots; basketry materials, cloth, and hide; the carving and engraving of bone and stone; netting, lace, and other cord work; feather work; metal casting; and bodily decoration. Which are developed will depend on culturally defined interests and resources. The attempt to evaluate the abilities of nonliterates by testing them with art media to which they are not accustomed is to be avoided. To give a pencil and paper to a nonliterate artist who has never used them and expect him to draw skillfully is cross-culturally naïve. Any artist is competent only in those media in which his culture has prepared him.

Anthropological objectives do not require the evaluation of nonliterate art, but such evaluations inevitably are made as a reaction against misinterpretations of that art. If technological skill only is considered, it is apparent that many examples of nonliterate art easily qualify as highly competent work, especially when the simple tools employed are taken into consideration. And while the question of universal standards of beauty is difficult, nonliterate peoples produce many forms which are aesthetically pleasing to Euroamericans.

Many anthropologists find the greatest beauty of nonliterate art not in its appearance but in the way it expresses and is functionally integrated with religion, mythology, and other elements of the culture. One of the most outstanding features of nonliterate art is that it is part of everyday life. It is true that certain persons specialize because of greater interest or ability, but there ordinarily are no professional artists who produce for a segment of society which specializes in the appreciation and evaluation of art. In other words, there is no distinction between professional art and popular art in nonliterate cultures. Pots, baskets, tipi covers, dishes and trays, and other everyday objects are elaborated for aesthetic reasons and the pleasure gotten by the creator. Masks, totem poles, pottery figurines, useless but pleasing woodworking tools, carved wooden figures, and the like are produced to impersonate the gods and the spirits in a ceremony, proclaim ownership of a chiefly title, provide a dwelling place for a spirit, and a variety of other nonaesthetic purposes.

Just as in Euroamerican art, the art of nonliterate peoples may be either highly abstract or highly realistic. In fact, the cave art of the Upper Palaeolithic is outstandingly realistic and that, possibly, because the artist felt that accuracy would provide greater magical potency. The bronze heads produced by the Yoruba of Ife, Nigeria, are both skillfully done and of realistic appearance (Adam, 1949: 112ff.). On the other hand, many designs are so conventionalized as to communicate little or nothing beyond geometric form to the cultural alien. In some cases, the aesthetic pleasure of viewing the form is all the artist is concerned with, but in many other cases the forms have additional meaning for those who are familiar with it. The Bush Negroes of Dutch Guiana, for example, produce wooden rice-winnowing trays into the surface of which are carved circular designs which, though they are commonly aesthetically pleasing to the outsider, are meaningless to him. The Bush Negro, however, knows that these are fertility symbols and can interpret realistically the various elements in the designs (Herskovits, 1948: 383).

DRAMA

Euroamericans occasionally have difficulty perceiving anything in non-literate cultures akin to Euroamerican dramatic performances. This is partially because nonliterate cultures lack theatrical production as a specialty. Euroamerican societies include specialists who write plays which other specialists produce and perform, but the notion of a performance by a group of actors staged for the benefit of an audience of nonparticipants is foreign to most cultures. In nonliterate societies the community as a whole often participates in the development and staging of a dramatic performace.

Drama is actional expression of beliefs, values, moods, fantasies, desires, or events and conditions remote from people in time, space, or probability. It appears to be a consequence of the desire to portray actionally things which seldom, no longer, or never exist just that way in ordinary life. The spirits and gods are not seen or heard, but they authorize men to adorn themselves in costumes and masks and behave as the gods behave. Highly valued historical or mythological events are depicted to remind the people of their heritage and reinforce their commitment to significant ideals. Circumstances which people wish for or hope for, but which are not realized in real life, are symbolically acted out and vicarious satisfaction achieved thereby.

Drama is so intimately linked into other aspects of life that anthropologists only occasionally grant it separate treatment. Frequently, dramatic activities are described in connection with religious ritual, for ritual is essentially dramatic and frequently religious. Dancing also is dramatic in nature. Dramatic events commonly occur as a part of everyday life, the performance of a brief magical act during the building of a house or the gathering of plants being an example. Yet, nonliterate peoples also stage dramatic performances as special occasions distinguishable from the routine of daily life. In fact, such occasions often involve the planned accumulation of supplies, costumes, and other paraphernalia. Such special dramatic events are not just unorganized happenings but manifest structure just as surely as Euroamerican dramas. It is his lack of familiarity with them which accounts for the cultural alien's failure to detect sequence, climax, or plot in nonliterate dramatic productions.

Among nonliterate cultures, then, dramatic occurrences vary in complexity and duration from the brief ritual or magical act to highly intricate pageants lasting many days and, in a few cases, performed by specialists. The ritual dramas of the Indians of the southwestern United States are well known for their complexity, their long duration, and their beauty and dramatic impact. These spectacles, which go on for days at a time, serve to maintain proper relationships with the supernaturals, thus insuring the benefits they can award. In addition, of course, they provide aesthetic pleasure and the enjoyment of participation in a social event. A few Pacific island groups had voluntary associations which specialized in producing drama and related forms of entertainment. They travelled from community to community and are reported to have been very popular with the people.

Some Euroamerican dramas involve minimal use of the various aesthetic forms whereas others make extensive use of dancing, singing, instrumental music, and objects of art. Nonliterate performances also vary in this respect, but the general tendency is toward intimate integration of drama with the other arts and with ritual and mythological concerns.

DANCING

Dancing already has been mentioned in several other contexts. It may be considered as an art form, an amusement, or a kind of ritual activity. One or another function may be emphasized in a particular dance complex, or all three may be combined.

Dance forms and the arrangements governing dancing occasions are highly variable among nonliterate cultures. Some involve vigorous physical movement and high excitement; others involve rather slight movement, perhaps only a swaying of the body with little or no foot movement. The variety of postures, movements, and combinations of movements which can be made by the human body is great, and the cross-cultural variation is considerable. Actions in imitation of game animals are common in the dances of hunting groups, which serves to illustrate that artistic activities are linked to non-aesthetic elements. Arrangements vary from performances by a single dancer to those in which all join. Sometimes only one sex dances at a time, but in some societies there are dances in which the opposite sexes not only perform at the same time but move in relation to one another and touch one another. Those peoples which prescribe separation of the sexes in dancing often find American ballroom dancing highly offensive. Ballroom dancing seems to be uniquely Euroamerican.

MUSIC

Ethnomusicology is the term sometimes applied to the cross-cultural study of music. It is not a highly developed branch of anthropology, partly because its pursuit requires special interests and knowledge and partly because scientific study in this area had to wait on the coming of high quality recording equipment. It is a significant area, however, and the rate of its development appears to be increasing. Now that excellent recordings of nonwestern music are readily available, the cross-cultural study of music is one of the most effective ways of elucidating the significance of cultural differences.

As was seen regarding art, one's understanding of music of other cultures is distorted by his cultural background. Hearing is thought of ordinarily as a purely physiological process, but it is a culturally conditioned psychological process as well. Thus, music of nonliterate cultures contains richness which we do not hear because we have not been conditioned to hear it. One who attempts to reproduce a melody from an alien culture inevitably alters it to fit the musical patterns with which he is familiar. This is why recording devices are essential to this kind of study.

One of the ways in which the music of nonliterate peoples differs from Western music is that it is seldom tonally polyphonic (Nettl, 1956: 77). This applies both to singing and to instrumental music. Singers sing in unison, and those instruments which play in groups most commonly play the same notes. A limited amount of polyphony and singing of harmony is found in a few widely scattered nonliterate cultures. In the many which lack it, however, the people either do not hear the parts in band, orchestra, or choir music, or it is nothing but a jumble of confusing, unattractive noises. One investigator, convinced that the tribespeople he was studying should hear some of Beethoven's music, played it for them on his phonograph. He reports that the people stopped all that they were doing and, after a moment of stunned silence, fled into the forest.

Another common characteristic of nonliterate music is the lack of emphasis on exact pitch. Euroamericans utilize exactly tuned instruments, and musical training emphasizes the ability to recognize particular tones, deviation from which is a source of distress. Our singing, of course, follows this instrumentally dominated standard. In most nonliterate groups singing ordinarily is not in a fixed key. Repetitions of a song will manifest relatively the same intervals between tones, but not absolutely.

Neither is there anything inevitable about the Euroamerican seven-tone scale. In fact, the kind most widely found is the pentatonic scale, not only among nonliterate peoples, but among peasants and literate Oriental groups (Nettl, 1956: 48). More infrequently found are scales of two, three, four, or six tones. It should be remembered, however, that scales also differ from one another in range between highest and lowest tones and the intervals between adjacent tones. Accordingly, there is a considerable variety of scales in the world's cultures, though certain of them are much more common than others.

Song melodies are distinguished in a variety of ways not explored here. Suffice it to say that melodies which either descend or move about equally in both directions are far more frequent than ascending melodies. It also has been noted that most nonliterate groups sing with much greater tension of the vocal cords than Euroamericans find acceptable. This may be accompanied by a good deal of ornamentation in the form of trills, grace notes, and similar devices (Nettl, 1956: 57f.). There is no denying that many of the melodies of other cultures fail to please the ear of the Euroamerican. At the same time it is significant that an understanding of a given composition's functions and meanings as well as its musical characteristics, along with repeated listening sessions, can result in greater appreciation of the selection. Not only does the listener become aware of some of the value of the song in its cultural context, he also learns to hear musical qualities not detected at first.

Of course, the lack of tonal polyphony and exact tone intervals makes impossible the kind of manipulation of tunes and combinations of tunes which is so pleasing to Euroamericans, but it is significant that music among exotic groups may achieve great richness through the utilization of various rhythm combinations uncommon or lacking in Euroamerican music. The music of nonliterate groups often emphasizes rhythm instead of tunes; and the rhythmic complexity of their music ranges from that which is very simple in all respects to combinations more intricate than anything found in Euroamerican music. In several parts of the world, specifically Negro Africa, portions of Central Asia, and Melanesia ethnomusicologists have found true rhythmic polyphony, that is, the blending of parts having different stress patterns or metric units (Nettl, 1956: 68). The uncontrolled abandon which western observers often find in so-called primitive dancing and music actually may seem so only because the observers are not culturally prepared to detect and appreciate the complex texture of rhythms involved.

As one might expect, percussion instruments dominate in nonliterate cultures. A wide variety of kinds of drums are found, some of which utilize membranes over one or both ends of a frame or cylindrical body and others of which lack membranes. Some drums are adjustable for tone variation. Xylophones and many kinds of rattles are found. Wind instruments include a variety of kinds of flutes, trumpets, flageolets, and panpipes made from a variety of materials. The commonest stringed instrument is the musical bow, which, when plucked, produces such a low sound that it often is played for the sole enjoyment of the instrumentalist. There is a fair variety of instruments produced and used in nonliterate cultures, but they are not technologically of the sort which stimulates the development of the tonally polyphonic music so valued by many Euroamericans. Nonliterate music, nevertheless, possesses a richness unexpected by the cultural alien, and as previously indicated, it is possible to condition oneself to detect and appreciate this richness.

GAMES AND OTHER PASTIMES

Story telling, dancing and music, and the production of art objects all have an element of play involved. Some anthropologists, in fact, have been impressed with the mammalian play impulse as the motivation for vast areas of human culture. Kroeber has suggested that if our ancestors had not possessed the trait of playfulness we probably would have many fewer aesthetic and intellectual developments (1948: 29).

If the range and variety of aesthetic pursuits testifies to the power of the human traits of experimentation and play, so does the variety of games. Games requiring vigorous physical activity, which might be called sports, are found in all parts of the world of nonliterate and peasant cultures. In terms of the pleasure gotten from participation in and observation of skilled control of bodily movements this kind of game certainly has its aesthetic element. Ball games of a variety of kinds are widely found, some of them being quite elaborate. A number of other athletic contests using equipment other than balls occur, such as the hoop and pole games of the American Indians and some other groups. In these a shaft of some sort is thrown through a rolling hoop. Racing of many kinds is found. Some groups have long distance foot races. Horse racing was found among the Plains Indians as well as among the Kazaks and other peoples of interior Asia. Stilt races are staged in several places. Groups living by bodies of water may have swimming races, boat races, or diving contests. Other athletic contests include tree climbing, high and broad jumping, and pulling or lifting. Athletic contests in which opponents attempt to physically overcome one another are also common among nonliterate peoples. Wrestling is virtually universal, but boxing is only occasionally found. Fencing of a kind also occurs in a few folk groups, as do kicking bouts and a number of other forms of athletic combat. Even familiar types of contests vary culturally more than one might realize. Wrestling stances and holds are not the same for all groups, nor is boxing always limited to males.

A diversity of other contests and exercises involve varying degrees of physical strength and bodily control. Archery competition and throwing spears or other objects at targets require both dexterity and strength. Still others require much finger or arm control, such as the nearly universal cat's cradle, which is a string figure game, and the cup and pin game which is so widely found in North America. The latter involves impaling a swinging object on the point of a pin.

There are many other games which emphasize intellectual ability rather than strength or dexterity. A number of games of the general nature of checkers and chess are found in all parts of the world.

Games of chance come in an astonishing variety. A seemingly endless variety of guessing games are found. Widespread in North America are games involving the guessing of which hand of a member of an opposing team contains an object. Among the California Indians some games of this type might continue for more than a day without a break. A variety of card games, dice games, and lotteries occur. Games of this sort are universally used for gambling, and when they are the stakes may be high. The games are played in great earnest, and non-literates have been known to gamble away their dearest possessions, including members of the immediate family.

Children's pastimes consist of many kinds of play, which often are educative in that they imitate adult labor. Just as small girls in American society may play at ironing clothes, in some agricultural groups a girl may have her toy grinding stone. In some places boys shoot at beetles or other small life forms with their small bows and arrows. Toys for amusement alone are common, too. Dolls, noisemakers, tops and the like, sometimes made by the children themselves, are found in all parts of the world. Beyond play with objects, however, children everywhere go in for a great variety of exuberant activities such as jumping games, swinging on trees or other objects, hide and seek, chasing rabbits, playing leapfrog, sliding, and rolling. Organized team games for children are lacking or unimportant in many nonliterate communities.

Games are not just pastimes in all cases. Children's play already has been noted to have educative functions, and many games are related to supernaturalism and legal procedure. Some North American Indian groups played a game in which the ball was filled with seeds. If the players managed to break the ball early in the game and the seeds were well scattered, the supernaturals were expected to send an early and abundant harvest. The Eskimos of the Hudson's Bay region played the cat's cradle in the fall so as to catch the sun in its meshes and delay its disappearance (Boas, 1907: 151). Games sometimes are employed to determine whether or not an accused person is guilty. The rationale is that the supernaturals will see that the test indicates the guilt or innocence of the defendant.

15

LIFE CYCLE CUSTOMS

Biological factors can be among the most demanding in the cultural field. Some, of course, are more productive of cultural responses than others; and among them are the physiological changes and states of the human life cycle. Every culture includes customary responses to pregnancy, the birth of children, pubertal changes, the biological vigor of young adulthood, sexual capacity, the decrepitude of old age, and death. Direct cultural responses to these are the main concern of the following discussion.

PREGNANCY

The physiological changes which come with the development of a new human within a woman can hardly be ignored. Enlargement of the abdomen eventually must become obvious, but other symptoms, most frequently the failure to menstruate, are ordinarily taken as first signs of pregnancy. Some peoples reckon the date of birth by counting from the first missed menstrual period. Breast enlargement, nausea, laziness, and loss of appetite are among other pregnancy symptoms reported for some cultures (Ford, 1945: 43).

The occurrence of pregnancy symptoms in women, followed by the birth of a child, has precipitated cultural responses in all groups. In accounting for such developments most peoples recognize that sexual intercourse is involved, which indicates that the biological realities provide a tendency for this cultural belief to occur. A few groups, however, have been reported as ignorant of the father's role. The Australian aborigines have the notion that a woman conceives as an ancestral soul enters her when she passes near places where the ancient totem ancestors entered the ground; in fact, one who wishes to avoid pregnancy should avoid such places. Some anthropologists suggest that the Australians and such groups actually do know the necessity of intercourse but that they merely place the emphasis on other explanations. This notion receives support in that a number of nonliterate groups think that intercourse plus other circumstances must occur to bring about a pregnancy. Soul reincarnation is one of these, but the moon, fertility deities, and the consumption of juices may be involved (Ford, 1945: 35f.). As Ford points out, the fact that given sexual unions often fail to result in pregnancy is not overlooked by nonliterate peoples, and the notion that it occurs only when supplemented by other factors is a logical reaction. This also may explain why a number of groups think that repeated intercourse is necessary. The Alorese of Indonesia, for example, emphasize the repetition of intercourse for the development of the fetus (DuBois, 1944: 106).

In spite of the nearly universal belief that intercourse and conception are related, nonliterate peoples lack a scientific understanding of the processes of conception and fetal development. Apparently, most believe that the germ of the fetus comes from the man only and that he places it within the female. A few believe that both male and female substances have a part. The people of the Indonesian island of Alor believe that a fetus results from the accumulation within the mother of the man's semen and the woman's menstrual fluid and that the child is in liquid form for the first weeks of life (DuBois, 1944: 106).

Sometimes nonliterates are interested in avoiding conception, and this is most commonly done by avoidance of intercourse. Cheyenne spouses sometimes avoided intercourse for several years after the birth of a child so that the father's energy would contribute exclusively to the growth of that child rather than being dissipated in sexual acts (Hoebel, 1960: 84). In many other groups children are nursed for over two years, and intercourse is avoided so that the lactation period will not be interrupted by the arrival of another child. In addition to intercourse avoidance, magical means of contraception are fairly common, and some groups utilize physical techniques such as withdrawal and interfemoral coitus.

For some couples, of course, the problem may not be avoiding conception so much as how to bring it about. Barrenness commonly is a source of concern and shame, and a diversity of means of preventing or overcoming it have been developed. Usually the husband is considered innocent, and the woman without offspring may be the object of pity, contempt, or derision and is sometimes divorced (Ford, 1945: 36).

When measures for avoiding conception fail or are not employed, abortion may be used, though the practice is highly repugnant to many nonliterate groups. Both medicinal and mechanical means have been recorded.

Cultures vary notably in the amount of response to a fully accomplished pregnancy, but some kind of restriction is nearly universal during this period. Most commonly, certain foods which are thought to be harmful to the fetus are prohibited, and restrictions on intercourse are common. Occasionally there are proscriptions against heavy exertion, though there are groups in which the mother works until the time of delivery. A variety of behavioral taboos of a magical nature may be imposed, sometimes upon the father as well as the mother. The principle of sympathy seems to operate here, as the parent's acts may be thought to affect the unborn child. In some cultures the husband may become ill or weak during his wife's pregnancy, possibly out of jealousy over the deprivation he will suffer with the coming of the new one.

CHILDBIRTH CUSTOMS

Nonliterate women not uncommonly engage in normal physical activity up until birth, but they nearly always have assistance at the time of delivery. Elderly women usually serve as midwives, with all others being excluded. The husband may be present in only a few societies, and a priest or shaman will be on the scene only when supernatural aid is thought to be necessary. The most common position for childbirth is sitting, though kneeling is fairly frequent (Ford, 1945: 58). Less common are squatting and reclining. It is usual for the woman to hang onto something during childbirth or to be supported by someone.

The notion that childbirth is inevitably simple and easy for non-literate women is false. There is a good deal of variation on this point from group to group, just as there is from community to community and person to person in Euroamerican society. It is of interest to note that birth also may be difficult for the husband. In some societies he takes to his bed during and after his wife's parturition, and even imitates her labor. This practice is known as the *couvade*.

When the birth is accomplished, the umbilical cord is cut and disposed of, often in some magically significant fashion. Also, all groups appear to exercise care in the disposal of the afterbirth. Newborn infants usually are bathed immediately. Most peoples require the mother and child to remain secluded for a period of time, thus avoiding the spread of infection and giving opportunity for recovery. Among some peasant and nonliterate peoples the recovery period is of many weeks duration. Mothers of Tepoztlán in Mexico, for example, are expected to remain in bed thirty or forty days if possible (Lewis, 1951: 361). In those cultures having the couvade, however, the mother may be up and around within a short time, while the father remains abed to recover from the effects of his difficult experience. In most groups intercourse is avoided for a period of time which varies from culture to culture.

If a child was unwanted and abortion was not attempted or accomplished, infanticide may occur. This tends to be practiced by hunters or collectors whose subsistence systems are not adequate for the support of large families. Some peoples kill deformed children or one or both twins. It must be understood, however, that nonliterate peoples ordinarily desire children, and that the act of infanticide is usually not undertaken out of cruelty or lack of feeling.

CARE AND REARING OF CHILDREN

Infants manifest two major characteristics to which there must be cultural responses; they are unable to care for themselves physically and they are culturally inexperienced. Accordingly, any culture must incorporate a large number of socially standardized ways of keeping infants and children alive and healthy as well as provide them with experiences which will enable them to become full-fledged participants in and contributors to the adult culture. At birth the child is virtually lacking in both areas, but the balance gradually changes as he develops the ability to care for himself and learns more of the culture. The two areas are interrelated in that the relatively long period of dependence as contrasted with the situation among other mammals provides the culturally sophisticated members of the society, that is, the child's parents and other adults and older children, with the opportunity to impose upon him the necessary learning experiences.

The ways of caring for and training children are standardized for a community. This means that children in different families have similar experiences and logically may be expected to develop similar personalities. On the other hand, cultures differ from one another in the specific customs of caring for and training their children, so that different cultures may be expected to produce different kinds of adult personalities. The response of the anthropological subculture to this notion has been the attempt to correlate certain customs for dealing with children with certain adult personality traits.

The process by which a person is influenced and learns to participate in his group's customs is sometimes referred to as *enculturation* (Herskovits, 1948: 39). From the anthropological view all people who, as the result of these experiences, have become able to practice their way of life are "cultured." While most of this enculturation goes on during the earlier years of life, it remains a lifetime process. In even the simplest culture there is always more that one may learn about his way of life.

It is important that the context of the enculturation process be understood. It always involves interaction between individuals, with the result that the esotraits of a culturally inexperienced person become similar to those of the more experienced members of his society. Picture a group of persons having a set of multi-individual ideas and other esotraits; that is, a culture. The individuals comprising the society regularly express the esotraits through utterances and actions and the artifacts which are produced by some actions. Unless they made their esotraits objective in these ways the neophyte could hardly know of their existence, since, barring parapsychological processes, ideas do not move directly from the mind of one person to that of another. A culturally experienced person who objectifies an esotrait by an utterance or an action suitably may be referred to as an *objectifier*. When he makes an esotrait objective, the resulting utterance, action, or artifact may be experienced empirically by a child or other person who does not possess a similar esotrait. This culturally inexperienced person may be called a *respondent*, for he will react either by ignoring the experience, forming an esotrait very unlike the objectifier's, or developing one closely similar to it. When the latter occurs and the esotrait to which he reacts is multi-individual, the respondent has been enculturated in respect to the custom in question. This is what happens when a child learns from a parent, an older sibling, a teacher, or other objectifier how to tie a shoe; that the world is round; what to call his mother's sister; or any other cultural trait. Enculturation may be described as the ongoing process by which culturally inexperienced persons respond to esotrait objectifications so as to become similar in their personality traits to the culturally experienced members of their group.

Culturally inexperienced respondents may intentionally become like the other members of their society; that is, they imitate. But they also may become like them without intending it. For a respondent, then, enculturation may be either intentional or unintentional. Also, an objectifier may intend to influence the respondent to develop personality traits similar to those of the culturally experienced members of the group. In other cases he may influence the respondent in this way without intending to. Much of what one acquires during enculturation is probably unintentional for the objectifier or for the respondent or for both. It is common for Euroamericans to assume that family personality traits are genetically inherited, whereas they may have been passed from person to person unintentionally, with no awareness that the younger family members were learning the personality traits of their elders.

Cultures differ from one another not only in the content of what they objectify but also in the means employed in influencing culturally naïve persons. Some groups are permissive and some are not. Some nurse infants on demand, and some don't. Some permit children great freedom physically; others restrict them. Some treat them consistently; others inconsistently. Many are the ways in which the culturally inexperienced may be handled, and these are socially standardized. Undoubtedly they produce different types of personalities, and it has been assumed that each culture consequently has its distinctive *modal personality, basic personality structure,* or, if the idea has validity on the national level, *national character.*

Nonliterate cultures are relatively lacking in the formal schooling, particularly by specialists, which we refer to as education. It is not too uncommon for grandparents and other elders to take special responsibility in a child's enculturation, and sometimes there are special periods of training, perhaps in isolation from the community, for one or both sexes about the time they are initiated into adult society. The Negroes of West Africa have arrangements of this sort which have been called "bush schools," and the Australians and a number of other peoples give special instruction in supernaturalistic concepts and rituals to boys. Nowhere, however, is education divorced from everyday life as a special experience to the degree that it is in Euroamerican communities.

ADOLESCENCE AND ADULTHOOD

When puberty arrives the person enters a period during which, in most cultures, he is expected to take on more adult roles. Often it is only shortly after puberty that marriage is expected to occur and the young person is recognized as an adult. Boys may be initiated into the tribal fraternity at about this time. This, of course, is in contrast to most Euroamerican communities, in which adolescence is culturally prolonged beyond the point of biological maturity and the young person kept in a dependent position. In the United States it is commonly thought natural for adolescence to be a period of awkwardness, rebellion, conflict, and stress, but anthropological evidence indicates that in many cultures this does not happen.

Menstruation is such as to require some kind of cultural response in all groups. Many cultures include ceremonies at this time, though not all do. It may be a time for pride and celebration, or it may be an occasion of danger and consequent seclusion. In hunting cultures, especially, it is common for menstruating women to be isolated or tabooed in various ways throughout their lives. Menstrual fluid commonly is regarded as dangerous.

Sexual reactions are culturally standardized to a high degree. Erotic arousal is a biological fact in all groups, but there is great cultural variation in the frequency of arousal and in what is defined as having erotic significance. In American culture nudity is erotically interpreted, but as was noted in the discussion of clothing, this is not so in a number of other cultures. In some societies there is much preoccupation with sexual stimulation and the acquisition of sexual experience, and in others there is considerably less. Some groups define sexual behavior as desirable or good in many ways, whereas others regard it as wrong or generally undesirable in most situations. No culture is free of restrictions on sexual behavior, which seems to reflect the fact that complete sexual freedom would disrupt social relationships seriously. Premarital sexual activity is permitted to some degree in many cultures, possibly in the majority, and those which permit it vary in the restrictions imposed. A relatively small proportion require only that the incest taboos be observed. Though adultery is common, it is much more widely proscribed than premarital relations. A number of cultures explicitly provide for some extramarital experience, wife-lending being an example.

Cultures also differ in regard to the nature of intercourse. In some much sexual foreplay is expected, whereas in others there is little. Postures considered normal in one culture are regarded as aberrant or abhorrent in another. Of the several most commonly used positions, available evidence indicates that no one of them is preferred in more than a minority of the world's cultures (Kluckhohn, 1948: 97).

Adulthood begins with marriage in most cultures. In fact, it is usual to regard marriage as the normal adult state. In a few cultures adulthood may be marked by distinctive clothing or ornamentation. Assumption of new responsibilities characterizes adulthood in all cultures, and adults usually enjoy greater prestige than sub-adults.

OLD AGE

The age at which one is considered elderly differs from culture to culture. In some places people in their late thirties are thought of as elderly, whereas in some Euroamerican nations there is now a tendency to postpone use of such a designation until one has reached sixty-five or seventy. Retirement from an age class system, having grandchildren, and passage of the menopause are among the several criteria of old age which have been utilized in various cultures.

In some societies old age is culturally defined as a time of cheerless resignation or even despair. The aged are most secure, of course, where they are granted high prestige. Respect for the elderly is sometimes high in slowly changing cultures, for it is of advantage to others to be able to draw on their great cultural experience. Respect also may be high where the aged control inheritable wealth or where the ancestors are thought to exercise much influence over the living. In rapidly changing communities old people often are thought of as out-of-date old fogies. Prestige also may be low for the aged among food gatherers, for the poor food supply may make anyone who cannot engage in his share of food getting a serious burden to the community. Old age also may be a better time for one sex than the other. Elderly males, especially, often find forced retirement from a vigorous, challenging and prestigeful life rather devastating.

DISEASE AND DEATH

Disease may strike at any point in the life cycle. Infant mortality is especially high among nonliterate and peasant peoples, and fatal sickness attacks frequently enough during all phases to reduce the life expectancy of some groups to a level two or three decades below that of some Euroamerican communities. Moreover, disease, as the word itself indicates, is uncomfortable. Such threats require cultural responses, and explanations for sickness as well as healing practices are universal. The two main kinds of disease theory are the notion that something alien has entered the body, perhaps an evil spirit or an object or substance sent by a sorcerer, and the concept of soul loss. Curing methods, then, may center on extracting the alien object or spirit or recovering the soul. Shamans, as previously indicated, ordinarily specialize in divining the specific causes of illnesses and curing.

Death is a significant event in any community. There always is the problem of separating the corpse from the living. There is the disturbing reminder that death will be the fate of each survivor, and there is the psychological disturbance from the new vacancy in a network of valued interaction patterns. Every culture manifests a complex of customary responses to a death.

The corpse commonly is washed and clothed or wrapped in preparation for disposal. It may be interred immediately or after several days. The body may be buried, placed in a cave or tomb, left in the open, placed on a platform, tower, or in a tree, or cremated. If buried, it may be placed in a flexed position oriented in one of several ways, or arranged in a seated, squatting, or extended position. Some peoples retain a part of the body for ceremonial or magical purposes, or all portions of the body may be exhumed and used for one of these purposes or secondarily interred. Mummification is known in only a few places. A number of peoples inter objects with the dead, either for use in the next world or because it may not be considered suitable for the living to use them.

Anthropologists have found that a major function of funeral ceremonies is to permanently separate the ghost of the dead person from the survivors. The ghost often is thought to be reluctant to leave, and special rituals are conducted to insure its permanent departure. Another major function of the funeral ceremonies is thought to be the reestablishment of social solidarity in the face of its breach by the death of a loved one.

16

CULTURAL
STABILITY
AND CHANGE

One of the most important subdivisions of cultural anthropology is *cultural dynamics*, which is concerned with processes and conditions of cultural stability and change. Anthropologists have found that all cultures are resistant to rapid change, and they investigate the reasons for this stability. Popular and semi-popular ideas to the contrary, however, no culture stands still; all cultures always are in process of changing. Some have pictured so-called primitive cultures as completely stagnant and as having exactly the same ways of life that they had hundreds and thousands of years ago. It still is common to encounter statements to this effect in non-anthropological articles and books. Anthropologists have not been able to confirm such a lack of change; in fact, they feel that they have evidence of regular, unceasing change. Archaeologists inevitably find that the objects made by various societies differ from one time level to the next. Historical accounts provide evidence of change. In every society there are some cultural differences between the generations, with the older generation expressing its displeasure over the tendency of the young people to ignore some of the traditions and substitute new ones and the younger generation regarding the old people as too conservative. Moreover, in all parts of the world large areas can be found in which there is gradual variability from one culture to another within the area. The cultures are different from one another, but they are too similar to one another to assume that independent invention accounts for the variability. The inescapable conclusion is that they have borrowed from one another and the slight differences are due to cultural change (Herskovits, 1948: 481). Cultural change, thus, is a constant of culture, and anthropologists are much interested in understanding the processes involved.

ORIGINATION, SOCIAL ACCEPTANCE,
AND ACCULTURATION

Inasmuch as cultural traits are multi-individual customs, it should be remembered that any trait ultimately is brought into being by a given person. The process of bringing into being an esotrait which may become a part of a culture may be called *origination*. This is essentially a psychological process in which the individual perceives a new relationship between two or more pre-existing ideas or portions of them, which he combines into a new idea. H. G. Barnett has probed the nature of this process in depth. There seems to be good reason for viewing the basic process as the same in all situations, only the content varying from one context to another. In all cases, in harmony with the notion that cultural traits are essentially esotraits, origination involves the manipulation of mental configurations. As noted in the discussion of the scope of a cultural trait, such configurations can be viewed as units or analyzed into parts. What happens in origination is that the individual substitutes a part of one mental configuration for a part of another mental configuration, thereby bringing into being something psychologically new to him. This, Barnett suggests, is made possible by the analysis of configurations into their elements and the identification of one of the elements in a familiar configuration with one in a different configuration (Barnett, 1953: 188ff.). The identification is possible because the originator experiences the elements of the analyzed configurations as similar to one another in some respect. A simple example would be the origination on the part of some individual of the notion that socialism is atheistic. One of the traits of American culture is the belief that Russian communism is atheistic. Let us say that an American familiar with and committed to this belief studies about socialism and thereby acquires the notion that both socialists and Russian communists advocate government ownership of industry. This feature in common enables him to identify socialism and Russian communism and substitute socialism for Russian communism to form the belief configuration new to his mind, namely, that socialism is atheistic. Turning to an example with artifacts as referents, people in the United States were familiar with the use of internal combustion engines in combination with four-wheeled vehicles, these being known as automobiles. Anyone who sensed or thought of four-wheeled vehicles as being similar to two-wheeled vehicles would thereby be enabled to substitute two-wheeled for four-wheeled vehicles in the configuration, four-wheeled vehicle with internal combustion engine, to arrive at the notion of a motor powered bicycle.

An origination is not a part of the culture, in the view of most anthropologists, until it is multi-individual. Other people than the originator must accept the new custom. There is no doubt that many originations, perhaps the vast majority, do not spread to other members of the society. They remain unique and personal. And many of those which do spread are not accepted by enough other persons to become very significant. Anthropologists seldom have focused attention on this problem of what happens to inventions, but it is clear that the issues are similar to those involved in the acceptance by a person of one culture of a custom from an alien culture. In both cases some individual must accept or reject the custom of another person. The issues are the same in both cases, and will be considered later.

Anthropologists have been interested especially in how and why customs spread or diffuse from one culture to another. The situation in which a culture is being modified by the borrowing of customs from one or more other cultures is called *acculturation*, an important and widely used anthropological term. This term is also applied frequently to the reciprocal diffusion of customs between cultures. An alternative term, not widely used, seems to be somewhat more descriptive, namely *interculturation*.

In regard both to social acceptance and to the diffusion which takes place in acculturation it is important to remember that two kinds of persons are involved. There are at least one *objectifier* and one *respondent*. The problem is to determine why a respondent accepts or rejects a custom objectified by someone else and to understand what he does by way of reinterpreting a custom he accepts. In a sense these are psychological problems, but they also are cultural and, therefore, anthropological, because the respondent's reaction is determined in significant measure by the multi-individual esotraits he shares with other members of his society.

It also is significant that origination, unintentional and often unnoticed, takes place during enculturation. The individual customs which make up the multi-individual esotraits called cultural traits never are identical; and the personal traits formed by a culturally inexperienced respondent as a consequence of his experience with the utterances, actions, and artifacts of objectifiers are always slightly different from those of the objectifier. This is one of the major sources of cultural change and the cultural differences found between the generations in all societies.

CULTURAL CONDITIONS FOR ORIGINATION AND CHANGE[1]

Cultures vary from one another in respect to a number of factors which either facilitate or restrain origination and acceptance. There is a good deal to be learned yet about the many variables involved and how they relate to one another. It should be understood that cultures vary from

[1] Based on Barnett, 1953: Chapters 2 and 3.

one another in these conditions not only from society to society, but also from one time level to another in the same society.

No one has succeeded in making a complete inventory of any known culture, but it is clear that cultures differ in sheer volume of content. This is significant for change in that members of societies whose cultures contain many multi-individual ideas have much more available to think about than members of culturally simple societies. Before an origination can occur the prerequisite esotraits must be available, and most elements employed by inventors are drawn from their culture. Other things being equal, a complex culture should change more rapidly than a simple one.

It should be kept in mind, however, that the presence of the necessary ideas in a culture does not of itself guarantee that the origination will occur. Individuals originate, not cultures as such; and if there is no one in the society who has the prerequisite elements concentrated in his mind, the origination cannot take place.

On the other hand, there may be more than one member of the society with the same or similar ideas concentrated in their minds. This is true particularly if there are many opportunities for collaboration provided by the culture, that is, opportunities for originators to exchange ideas or to draw on the same sources of information. The result of such a situation is the development of *simultaneous inventions*. Charles Darwin and Alfred Wallace came up with the idea of natural selection about the same time. Wallace deferred to Darwin, and, consequently, it is Darwin's name that we know so well. Alexander Bell beat a man by the name of Gray to the patent office by only a few hours. If he had not, we might be using "Gray Telephones." The eminent anthropologist, Alfred L. Kroeber, has compiled a long list of such simultaneous inventions (1948: 341ff.). They are to be accounted for by the fact that the necessary building blocks are part of the cultural inventory and have become concentrated in the minds of more than one member of the society. Moreover, the individuals involved share the same cultural goals and interests, with the result that more than one person is thinking about the same problems at the same time. It is important to avoid the supposition that inventors pluck their new ideas out of the blue. Studies have shown that originators are persons with a wide range of knowledge.

Cultures also vary a good deal in respect to the degree of contact with alien cultural esotraits. Those societies in marginal geographic areas, such as the Australians, the Bushmen of the Kalahari desert, the Shoshones of the arid Great Basin, and a number of others, until recently have had little opportunity for contact with peoples very different from them culturally. This seems to be one reason why their cultures have changed more slowly than less isolated groups. By contrast the areas where the world's most complex civilizations were originated are those in which many peoples of a variety of cultural backgrounds came into contact with one another, stimulating a ferment of change. This happened in the region around the eastern end of the Mediterranean Sea; it happened in the river valleys of the subcontinent of India and Pakistan and, also, in Middle America and the adjacent portion of South America. No such concatenation of cultures occurred in sub-Saharan Africa, which is one possible reason why no Negro society developed a complex literate civilization. The fundamental reason that culture contact increases the rate of change is that originators have available to them not only the ideas of their own culture but those of other cultures; and the possibility of new combinations is increased many times. It is worth noting, too, that contact with alien ideas provides a challenge to think about and either question or defend the ideas, values, and behaviors of one's own culture, thereby precipitating origination. Much of the seminal thought of ancient Greece seems to have been stimulated by just such challenge and rethinking. Plato, for example, reacted against what he felt to be the fallacious teachings of aliens moving into the area. Much of his thought seems to have resulted from attempts to discredit foreign ideas, and in the process he appears to have originated some new mental configurations which incorporated parts of culturally alien thoughtways.

One of the most common results of intersocietal contact and the resulting conjunction of cultural differences is what has been called *syncretism*. This, in fact, may be an appropriate name for some systems of ancient Greek thought. Syncretism is a term applied to those culture complexes which are known to be a blend of elements of different cultures. Many of the component complexes of present day Indian cultures of Latin American are intentional blends of pre-Columbian Indian and Spanish customs. The same is true of the cultures of the New World Negroes. Herskovits has identified the Dahomean ancestor religion elements and the Catholic features in the Vodun cult of the West Indies (Herskovits, 1937: 635ff.). It is both interesting and significant that a syncretism often consists of many linkages between overt forms borrowed from other cultures and the more covert meanings and functions already existing in the borrowing culture. Thus, many a Christian Saint in the religions of modern Latin American Indian communities functions in the same way as indigenous pre-Columbian deities (Madsen, 1960: 29).

The conditions mentioned so far—large cultural inventory, concentration of ideas, means of collaboration, and intersocietal contact—are not the only ones which may precipitate origination and change. In fact, all of these may be present hypothetically in equal degrees in two cultures and one change slowly while the other changes rapidly. A partial reason may be that one society is oriented toward change and the other not. American culture is one in which change is expected and desired in a number of aspects, particularly technology. The Navaho Indians are another group who expect and welcome change. Apparently they originated from a group which spawned both Navaho and Apache. These people moved into the American Southwest at least four or five centuries ago, bringing with them a hunting way of life of the kind which prevailed in the Western Subarctic. Since then they have adjusted their culture to, first, incorporate many Pueblo Indian traits; then Spanish elements; and, finally, American customs. The Pueblo tribes among whom they live, by contrast, resolutely oppose change and tend to fare rather badly when forced to change. Anthropologists have written much about this difference between the two kinds of cultures of the Southwest.

Cultures also differ from one another in the amount of freedom allowed for individual inquiry and creativity. Totalitarian political units often suppress or limit individualistic thought in areas in which they fear that new ideas will undermine the system. All cultures appear to have some areas in which authority and power are exercised to limit novelty. This has been true to some extent, for example, in medicine as an aspect of Euroamerican cultures. During periods of social and political disorganization, however, many authoritarian controls are broken and emphasis may be placed upon the resourcefulness and initiative necessary to readjustment.

Competition, either between groups quite different culturally or among subgroups of the same society, varies in extent and intensity from one society to another. Origination may occur in the development of means of besting one's competitors; or one group may borrow something from the rival society in order to compete with them on more equal terms. The invention of advertising slogans illustrates the former; and the acceptance of guns by the American Indians is an example of the latter.

Another condition stimulating change is deprivation, which is defined by Barnett as the elimination of something to which people feel they have a right. War and such threats to security are generally known to precipitate originative activity. The launching of the Russian Sputnik in 1947 was perceived as such a great threat that it stimulated a flurry of inventive effort in the American space program as well as a reevaluation of our entire system of formal education. One of the most widespread consequences of acculturation has been the felt deprivation of subordinate groups, which in turn, has prompted the cultural reactions sometimes known as *nativistic movements*. These emphasize the restoration or perpetuation of certain cultural elements highly symbolic of valued lifeways. Those movements emphasizing a return to former ways have been referred to by Linton as *revivalistic movements*, and those which attempt to preserve the status quo as *perpetuative movements* (1943: 231). One of the best examples of revivalistic nativism is the Ghost Dance religion which swept through the western tribes during the last decades of the nineteenth century. The Indians had reached an acute stage of frustration and despair as the result of the exterminative wars against some tribes and the attempts to confine all tribes to reservations and civilize them. The major prophet of the Ghost Dance predicted exclusion of the whites and called for a return to ceremonial aspects of the old way of life. The widespread acceptance of his doctrines testifies to the appeal of his program.

Deprivation may result also in acquisitive reactions when what the subordinate group wants is more of certain things which only the dominant group can supply. In many parts of the world so-called *Cargo Cults* have sprung up, calling for the provision of goods and services for which the people have acquired tastes as the result of contact. The reason this type of reaction is called a Cargo Cult is that a common element in the acculturative responses of New Guinea tribes is the prediction that a ship will arrive bearing the desired goods. One of the latest reported New Guinea cults included the notion that President Johnson was sending just such a ship. In 1812 a shaman of the Chipewyan near Hudson's Bay predicted that the world would be changed in such a way as to bring the Indians more of the items they wanted from the traders. Either the whites there at the time would become subservient to the Indians, or they would be replaced by others who would supply what the Indians wanted (Oswalt, 1966: 42, 60).

Among the most common conditions making for cultural change is the modification of some element of the culture, or of its field, which is interdependent with various other traits. Barnett calls such an element the *dominate correlate*, dominance being understood in terms of the trait being the first modified in the situation in question. The description in Chapter Three of the changes in the culture of the Shoshone Indians due to the introduction of horse riding illustrates well the chain of reactions which may result from such a modification. Change in the natural habitat also may have cultural repercussions, whether it be due to indigenous activity, contact with a culturally alien group, or independent of cultural activity. The Eskimo of Smith Sound in Northern Greenland were completely isolated from other Eskimos by ice and cliffs, with the result that their culture retained no clear knowledge of the existence of other humans or of kayaks. The absence of kayaks seems due to the lack of driftwood with which to make the kayak frames. Kayaks did not reappear among this group until an Eskimo from Baffinland joined them and taught them how to make kayaks from the wood newly available to them through contact with the outside world (Kroeber, 1948: 375f.).

The extent of functional repercussions from the modification of a dominant correlate depends on the number and strength of the linkages. It is significant that much mischief has resulted from this source. Many an agent of change has failed to foresee the results of an introduction. In fact, the significance of this principle seems to be among the notions most difficult to put across to people who are trying to change other cultures.

INCENTIVES TO ORIGINATION AND CHANGE[2]

Since individuals are the ones who originate and who accept alien customs, the question of their motivation is always of concern. All of the foregoing conditions for change have relevance to motivation, but a brief specific treatment is in order. Many people institute or accept change because they want the credit or prestige that may accrue. Often a novel esotrait results from random movement such as doodling, fiddling with objects, and other tension-reducing activities which are

[2] Based on Barnett, 1953: Chapters 4-6.

engaged in either consciously or unconsciously. Such activities may be recognized by the actor or an observer as having value and become standardized. Many other originations come about as the result of efforts by the individual to maintain satisfying definitions of himself as a person and in relation to the total milieu in which he exists. Accordingly, each person constantly selects and reinterprets the stimuli to which he is exposed in conformity with his concept of himself and the environment he values. All of these incentives, whether the desire for prestige, the release of tension, or the maintenance and protection of the ego, have in common the desire for maintenance or reinforcement of the self.

Still other incentives develop as a consequence of attempts to satisfy other needs or wants. For example, two or more wants may converge accidentally. An individual may be in process of satisfying one desire and accidentally come upon the solution for another felt need; or he may find that the satisfaction of one desire conflicts with the satisfaction of another, and a compromise origination may result. In many cases the individual invents in compensation for some goal he is unable to reach by available means. He either modifies his goal, develops means of attacking that which blocks him, or originates a new means of reaching his objective.

The incentives mentioned above are not oriented specifically toward change as such; and any changes which result are byproducts of a felt need for something else. Among the incentives oriented toward change is the satisfaction of creating new things and new ideas—the desire to create, in other words. In other cases originators may want to change things in order to secure relief from or avoid physical or mental distress, whether it be desire for relief from boredom and monotony, release from restraint, release fom pain, or the reduction of intellectual dilemmas. Finally, change may be sought because of a desire to modify quantity. The originator may want more money, more time, more space, greater efficiency, more accuracy, greater duration, or greater immediacy of effect.

CULTURAL DRIFT

Students of change have long noted that cultures alter gradually and cumulatively in certain directions, with the result that the changes involved may be either unnoticed or only dimly sensed while they are going on. They may be detected as significant only when one looks back over the years and, comparing past cultures with that of the present, realization comes that a change of some magnitude has taken place. A pertinent problem is why these changes are directional. In this connection it is well to note that change takes place as the proportion of members of a society participating in a given custom either increases or decreases. Two customs of American culture are wearing a hat out-of-doors and going hatless out-of-doors. The proportion of men going hatless may increase as, one by one, individual Americans stop wearing hats. It is also possible for large numbers of persons, perhaps most of those who will change from wearing hats to going hatless, to simultaneously and gradually reduce the frequency with which they put on a hat when they go outside. In either case the change would be both directional and so gradual as to be little noticed.

Such directional and gradual change can be understood in terms of culturally standardized goals or incentives which affect the responses of individuals to the stimuli they encounter day by day (Herskovits, 1964: 150). Let us suppose that the members of a society come to share the notion that it is a mark of good grooming and a matter of acceptance to display well-combed, well-groomed hair on all possible occasions. Sharing this goal, many men over the years may select with gradually increasing frequency those habits, including going hatless, which make this goal possible. A number of the incentives mentioned in the previous section may become culturally standardized as goals which govern the direction of cultural drift.

ACCEPTANCE AND REJECTION[3]

Since cultures change as members of the society either accept or reject the customs of their fellows or those of culturally alien persons, a crucial question for the anthropologist is what it is about the trait itself, about the person who practices or advocates it, or about the potential acceptor which determines the custom's fate. There is a great deal more to be learned about the many variables involved and how they relate to one another. One of the major tasks facing cultural anthropologists is identification of such factors and the development of effective means for assessing their relative effects. A few of the factors which have been explored are noted here.

1. *Objectification* is a necessary prerequisite to acceptance, for a custom cannot be accepted by a respondent who has not observed an action, artifact, or utterance which expresses the custom.

2. *Advocacy* may also be a determining factor. Many customs are not borrowed or diffused because no one is advocating that anyone accept it, and no effort is made to convince a respondent of its desirability. There is some evidence that negative attitudes toward advocacy may be culturally standardized in some societies, thereby inhibiting the rate of social acceptance and, consequently, affecting the over-all rate of change (Taylor, 1966: 119ff.).

3. *Personality* is often of great importance. Many a custom has been rejected because the respondent found the objectifier's personality offensive, even in cases when the respondent was actually attracted to

---

[3] Based on Barnett, 1953: pp. 293-295 of Chapter 10; and Chapters 11 and 13.

the custom. In other cases respondents have accepted customs they were not especially interested in because of the force of the advocate's personality.

4. *Personal relations* comprise another variable which is often of importance. It refers particularly to friendship and kinship. Many respondents will accept a custom advocated by a friend or relative and reject it if it is proposed by a stranger.

5. *Majority affiliation* is for many respondents a recommendation for acceptance. Many people accept a new idea because "everyone else" is doing so. Majorities tend to be intimidating.

6. *Compatability* is a cultural factor of considerable importance in understanding a respondent's reaction. Often an alien custom is simply out of harmony with the respondent's culture, and the proposed trait simply can't co-exist with present items in his way of life. Women of the Yurok tribe of Northern California were unable to accept women's hats with feathers on them because, by aboriginal definition, only Yurok men could wear feathers on their heads. There are many examples of incompatability in the anthropological literature. Compatability, of course, may constitute a recommendation for acceptance.

7. *Efficiency* frequently is a factor recommending acceptance. The issue is whether the proposed custom does the job it is alleged to do and how well it does it.

8. *Cost* is one of the commonest deterrents to acceptance. Many an item has been rejected because it requires too much money or the draining off of too many other valued resources in order to put the custom into effect.

9. *Penalty*, if it is a necessary concomitant of acceptance, may influence the respondent to reject a custom. Commoners on the island of Palau in the Western Pacific failed to accept American sun-helmets because the Palauan chiefs threatened reprisal on any who wore them.

10. *Advantage* is another factor of widespread significance. Some customs are accepted simply because they provide the respondent with some sort of gain which cannot be obtained otherwise. Some peoples have accepted Christianity overtly in order to acquire the material benefits available from the missionaries.

11. *Mastery* of a custom is a significant determinant of a respondent's reaction. His talents and cultural background may be such as to provide little or no satisfactory basis for learning the custom. To some it simply may not be worth the effort. Some of the Indians of northeastern Oregon found it pretty much beyond them to learn the use of a plow. Many peoples of the world do not use complex mechanical devices, such as cameras, because they find their use too difficult to master.

12. *Functional repercussions* may result in rejection. Cultures, it has been emphasized in this volume, are not composed of discrete elements but are systems composed of traits which are functionally linked to one another; and a change in one custom may result in a chain reac-

tion in other parts of the culture. If the respondent is unwilling to undergo the secondary changes he may reject the custom which would precipitate them. Some Americans will not accept the custom of smoking because it is linked in their minds with irreligion. Acceptance of smoking to them would imply a change in their ethics. The Yir Yoront of Australia accepted steel axes, but if they had known the changes which would result, they might have rejected them. Since men maintained their dominance over their families by providing stone axes for them, the newly acquired independence of their wives and other women due to their possession of easily obtainable steel axes went far toward the destruction of the Yir Yoront family (Sharp, 1952: 84).

These are only a few of the factors which may be considered by students of culture change.

PRINCIPLES OF DIRECTED CHANGE

The discussion of some of the principles of cultural change should suggest that anthropologists are qualified to make predictions about change. As a matter of fact anthropologists are now rather frequently called upon to predict in the increasing number of cases in which efforts are being made to persuade or force people to accept new ideas. Such effort is called *directed change*. On the basis of what has been learned about cultural processes and about the content of the cultures to be modified, the anthropologist is able to answer questions concerning whether proposed changes can be accomplished and the possible or probable effects upon a given culture. The notion that social scientists can predict human behavior seems strange to some, but it should not in view of the fact that men predict one another's behaviors daily and govern their own actions and reactions accordingly. Drivers in the United States can predict with a useful degree of certainty that other drivers will leave the right lane of a roadway only under culturally specified circumstances. Waitresses are able to predict that people entering a restaurant will order food, and they govern their behavior accordingly. No individual can exist normally without such prediction of his fellows' behaviors on the basis of what he has learned during enculturation. Anthropologists can predict the behavior of people of other cultures by studying those cultures; and since the processes of human thought and behavior are basically similar in all societies, he has an additional basis from which to predict. This does not mean that anthropologists and other social scientists have learned enough about human behavior to predict consistently. The wise anthropologist limits his predictions to those he can make with some degree of certainty, and he qualifies them in terms of the estimated degree of certainty.

This, of course, is in some contrast to the tendency of many people to attempt prediction and control of cultural change on the basis of common sense knowledge only. Specialized training and licenses are not required of such persons, in spite of the fact that the consequences of their efforts may affect the well-being and biological survival of hundreds, thousands, or even millions (Spicer, 1952: 13). Edward Spicer has cited several sources of difficulty which appear over and over again as agents of change, trained and untrained, pursue their craft.[4]

1. One of the most elementary principles of change, but one which seems to be difficult to get across to many change agents, is the fact that the customs which comprise a culture are linked to one another and to elements of the cultural field. The fact that cultures are systems, and that modification of parts of a culture may have repercussions which are destructive either to the goals of the change agent or those of the people undergoing change often goes unappreciated until serious mischief is done. This has been illustrated adequately in the preceding pages. It is a principle which merits a good deal of repetition because of its importance and the frequent failures to observe it.

2. Social scientists have found that one of the most effective ways of securing agreement to a desired change is to work through the proper social units. Frequently this is not done. In a South American village the people refused to use the water from the wells drilled for them by the national government; this in spite of the fact that the water was wanted desperately. The source of the problem was that the directors of the project failed to secure the cooperation and approval of the large landowners and the priest, who were the people of power and prestige in that community.

3. The nature of the relationships between objectifiers and respondents has been found to be one of the most relevant issues of all. Administrators of the Relocation Centers during World War II often had difficulty securing cooperation from the Japanese inmates because of their insistence on treating them as inferior and untrustworthy. The Japanese reacted by rejection of attempts to get them to participate in organizational, economic, and other projects. The wife of the director of a government cultural mission established to improve the agricultural, sanitation and other practices in a remote Latin-American community insisted on wearing slacks because of their practicality. This was offensive to the people, and they were inclined to reject many things because of the consequently poor relationships with the director's wife.

4. Misinterpretation of the customs of culturally different groups because of ethnocentrism, that is, viewing customs in terms of one's own culture, is an exceedingly common source of trouble. Missionaries and Indian agents to the Pawnee Indians planned to break up Pawnee villages and place individual families on separate plots of farmland in conformity with white cultural values, which were not shared by the Pawnee. Americans attempting to secure the cooperation of Pacific Islanders assumed that those persons identified by them as "chiefs" could influence their subjects to do what they wanted. They were puzzled and angered by their inability to do so. Cultural relativism as

---

[4] Based on Spicer, 1952: p. 281.

an approach would have enabled the Americans to learn that islanders of senior rank do not possess such authority and do not consider themselves responsible for the actions of their followers.

5. Finally, a common source of difficulty is the failure of change agents to bring the members of the respondent's society into the planning and carrying out of a program. It has been found that people often do not like to have ideas imposed on them from outside but want to feel that they have participated in the formulation and execution of whatever changes they accept. Effective agents of change often encourage people to make their own decisions with minimum possible guidance, and many a change has been rejected because of failure to do this. Indian Bureau administrators carefully refrained from ordering the Acoma people of New Mexico to adopt the government's plan for saving their grazing lands. They planted the ideas and gave the people the time and latitude to decide for themselves whether or not they would take the action and how. Soil conservation efforts failed on one Indian Reservation when outside experts drafted a program for the people. Only when they were consulted about how to deal with the problem and some of their suggestions accepted were they willing to go along with a conservation program.

Anthropology learns about human nature through the study of the total range and variety of human characteristics and the common processes which underly this variety. Consequently, this youngest of the major social sciences finds itself in a position to contribute richly to the understanding and solution of human problems.

Appendix A

ETHNOGRAPHIES

Cultural Ways probably is used most effectively as preparation for the study of several brief ethnographies during the course of a semester or quarter. Student understanding and remembrance of anthropological concepts is greatly augmented by having them learn to recognize examples in ethnographic literature. *Cultural Ways* is brief enough to complete within the first weeks of a course, making it possible to spend the bulk of the time studying the ethnographies.

The following annotated list includes only brief, low-priced works of the kind most effective at the introductory level. At the time of this compilation (Spring, 1968) the majority were $1.95, and none cost more than $2.50.

The list is meant to be suggestive rather than exhaustive. There are other low-priced ethnographies of several hundred pages and accounts of folk groups in popularized style which are not included. Also, there is no question but that the immediate future will see the publication of a number of additional ethnographies in paperback format.

BARNETT, H. G., 1960. *Being a Palauan* (85 pages). A study of an island culture of the western Pacific having a fishing and root crop technology. Effective for illustrating linkages between unilineal kinship and other aspects of the culture.

BEALS, ALAN R., 1962. *Gopalpur: A South Indian Village* (97 pages). The way of life of a rural Telegu-speaking hamlet told from the point of view of individual villagers. Good exposition of the caste system. A peasant farming group.

BEATTIE, JOHN, 1960. *Bunyoro: An African Kingdom* (83 pages). Depicts the culture of the Bantu-speaking Nyoro of East Africa. Sets forth typical features of an African feudal, monarchical society. Contains a good description of an Omaha kinship system and its relationships to social behavior.

BOAS, FRANZ, 1964. *The Central Eskimo* (250 pages). A study of the culture of the Baffin Island Eskimos, first published in 1888. Extensive description of technology. An outstanding picture of the relationships between a culture and its natural habitat. Sea-mammal hunters with relatively simple sociopolitical organization.

CHANCE, NORMAN A., 1966. *The Eskimo of North Alaska* (102 pages). Describes a modern Eskimo community whose culture is a blend of the traditional and the Western. Sea mammal and caribou hunters with relatively simple sociopolitical organization.

COHEN, RONALD, 1967. *The Kanuri of Bornu* (112 pages). Shows how the various aspects of a culture of northern Nigeria are interrelated and built upon the household, much of the description being from the point of view of specific persons. A society of farmers and craftsmen living in hamlets, villages, and towns.

DOWNS, JAMES F., 1966. *The Two Worlds of the Washo* (110 pages). Description of the Washo Indians of California and Nevada as they once were and as changed by contacts with Euroamerican culture. A hunting, fishing, and gathering group with relatively simple sociopolitical organization.

DOZIER, EDWARD P., 1966. *Hano: A Tewa Indian Community in Arizona* (99 pages). Describes the culture and history of a Tewa Indian village in Hopi country and the relationships between the Hopi and Tewa. A farming group with a matrilineal kinship organization. Author born in the Tewa town of Santa Clara, New Mexico.

DOZIER, EDWARD P., 1967. *The Kalinga of Northern Luzon, Philippines* (99 pages). Describes the culture of a group of rice cultivators and former headhunters. Emphasis is on kinship, ritual, and ceremonial aspects of the life cycle and religion.

DUNN, STEPHEN P. and ETHEL DUNN, 1967. *The Peasants of Central Russia* (132 pages). The only authoritative ethnography of Russian peasant life, based on the writings of Soviet ethnographers. Provides a balanced description of the culture, beginning with pre-revolutionary times and tracing the effects of Soviet political and industrial forces.

FRASER, THOMAS M., JR., 1966. *Fishermen of South Thailand* (105 pages). An analysis of the culture of a peasant fishing village. Emphasis on the ways in which intracultural linkages are related to the culture's adaptation to change.

FRIEDL, ERNESTINE, 1962. *Vasilika: A Village in Modern Greece* (106 pages). A balanced description of the way of life of a peasant community.

HART, C. W. M. and ARNOLD R. PILLING, 1960. *The Tiwi of North Australia* (113 pages). Analyzes the culture of a gathering and hunting group isolated on Melville and Bathurst Islands off the Australian coast. Emphasizes how men compete for influence and power through the acquisition of multiple wives.

HENRY, JULES, 1964. *Jungle People* (152 pages). Describes a nomadic hunting culture in a difficult jungle habitat in Brazil. Analyzes the internal forces causing the group to commit social suicide. Fifty-six pages of appended information on material culture, body paints and kinship, rituals, songs, and language.

HITCHCOCK, JOHN T., 1966. *The Magars of Banyan Hill* (109 pages). Presents a well-integrated view of the culture of a Magar hamlet of tribal Nepal. A completely sedentary community of rice growers.

HOEBEL, E. ADAMSON, 1960. *The Cheyennes: Indians of the Great Plains* (99 pages). Describes the culture of a group similar in many ways to other buffalo hunting societies of the American plains. An effective presentation of the integrating rituals and themes of Cheyenne culture.

HOGBIN, IAN, 1964. *A Guadalcanal Society: The Kaoka Speakers* (98 pages). Analyzes a gardening and fishing culture of Melanesia. A clear presentation of matrilineal and other social groups and their interrelationships.

HOROWITZ, MICHAEL, 1967. *Morne-Paysan: Peasant Village in Martinique* (108 pages). Analyzes the culture of an agricultural village on an island in the West Indies. The people of Morne-Paysan are descendents of Negro slaves.

KUPER, HILDA, 1963. *The Swazi: A South African Kingdom* (84 pages). Describes the culture of a Negro society manifesting complex unilineal arrangements and a highly centralized, monarchical state. The Swazi are farmers and raisers of livestock as well as hunters and gatherers.

LESSA, WILLIAM A., 1966. *Ulithi: A Micronesian Design for Living* (114 pages). Describes the culture of Ulithi in the Western Pacific. Includes good treatment of religion and magic and the social and legal linkages of sexual behavior. Subsistence mainly by gardening and fishing.

LEVINE, ROBERT A. and BARBARA L. LEVINE, 1966. *Nyansongo: A Gusii Community in Kenya* (200 pages, 111 pages constituting a balanced ethnography and the remainder on child training). Negro farmers and cattle herders with patrilineal kinship and non-centralized political organization.

LEWIS, OSCAR, 1960. *Tepoztlan: Village in Mexico* (103 pages). Depicts the way of life of a contemporary Nahuatl-speaking peasant village not too far from Mexico City.

MADSEN, WILLIAM, 1964. *Mexican-Americans of South Texas* (110 pages). Describes four Mexican-American communities in Hidalgo County, Texas, ranging from a rural group to a bicultural urban group. Emphases include relationships with Anglo-Americans and the system of folk medicine.

MARETZKI, THOMAS W. and HATSUMI MARETZKI, 1966. *Taira: An Okinawan Village* (173 pages, 87 pages constituting an ethnographic summary and the remainder being on child training).

MIDDLETON, JOHN, 1964. *The Lugbara of Uganda* (92 pages). Analyzes the culture of a tribe of cultivators who, unlike many African groups, lack centralized government. Emphasizes interdependence of cultural aspects.

MINTURN, LEIGH and JOHN T. HITCHCOCK, 1966. *The Rājpūts of Khalapur, India* (154 pages, 93 constituting an ethnographic summary and the remainder being on child training). Deals with a land-owning caste of a village in northern India.

NEWMAN, PHILIP L., 1965. *Knowing the Gururumba* (105 pages). Describes the culture of a gardening and pig raising group in eastern New Guinea. Emphasizes the ritual significance of social behavior.

NORBECK, EDWARD, 1965. *Changing Japan* (79 pages). Compares the lifeways of a rural and an urban family as a way of focusing on cultural variation and change in modern Japan.

NYDEGGER, WILLIAM F. and CORINNE NYDEGGER, 1966. *Tarong: An Ilocos Barrio in the Philippines* (177 pages, 104 constituting an ethnographic summary and the remainder being on child training). Describes the culture of wet rice producers in a district consisting of six hamlets.

PIERCE, JOE E., 1964. *Life in a Turkish Village* (101 pages). Describes the culture of peasant cultivators and herders in rural Turkey, first from the point of view of a small boy and then in more conventional general terms.

POSPISIL, LEOPOLD, 1963. *The Kapauku Papuans of West New Guinea* (95 pages). Analyzes the culture of a tribe of gardeners and pig raisers. Culture unchanged by contact with Euroamericans when first studied. Stresses the individualistic, capitalistic orientation of the culture.

REDFIELD, ROBERT and ALFONSO VILLA ROJAS, 1962. *Chan Kom: A Maya Village* (230 pages). Describes in detail a peasant village in Yucatan. A well known study first published in 1934.

ROMNEY, KIMBALL and ROMAINE ROMNEY, 1966. *The Mixtecans of Juxtlahuaca, Mexico* (146 pages, 84 constituting an ethnographic summary, the balance being on child training). Describes the culture of a Mixtec Indian district in a town in southern Mexico.

UCHENDU, VICTOR C., 1965. *The Igbo of Southeast Nigeria* (105 pages). Provides an inside view of the culture by an Igbo who is also a professionally trained anthropologist.

WILLIAMS, THOMAS RHYS, 1965. *The Dusun: A North Borneo Society* (93 pages). Depicts the relatively complex culture of a Dusun village of rice farmers and hunters and gatherers. Strong emphasis on world view and religious ritual.

YANG, M. K., 1966. *A Chinese Village: Taitou, Shantung Province* (249 pages). Describes a pre-communist farming village. Author born and reared there. First published in 1945.

Appendix B

TOPICAL SELECTIONS

The brevity of *Cultural Ways* permits assignment of selections from books of readings. Since a number are available in paperback, it is possible to require students to purchase one or two to accompany this text. After reading a portion of *Cultural Ways*, perhaps a chapter or more or a portion of one, the student can move to relevant articles from a book of readings. The annotated list of selections found in the several books available in paperback format may aid in selecting books or making assignments from them.

BOOKS OF READINGS

DUNDES, ALAN, 1968. *Every Man His Way*
FRIED, MORTON H., 1968. *Readings in Anthropology*, Second Edition, Volume I.
FRIED, MORTON H., 1968. *Readings in Anthropology*, Second Edition, Volume II.
GOLDSCHMIDT, WALTER, 1960. *Exploring the Ways of Mankind*
HAMMOND, PETER B., 1964. *Cultural and Social Anthropology: Selected Readings*
JENNINGS, JESSE D. and E. ADAMSON HOEBEL, 1966. *Readings in Anthropology*, 2d edition.
SHAPIRO, HARRY L., 1960. *Man, Culture, and Society*

Chapter I

DUNDES
Edwin T. Hall, Jr., "The Anthropology of Manners," 511-517—Gives examples of the application of anthropology to the improvement of international relations.

FRIED, VOL. I
Alfred L. Kroeber, "The Subject Matter of Anthropology," 3-5—Sets forth the nature of anthropology as a synthesis of diverse fields.
William C. Sturtevant, "The Fields of Anthropology," 6-14—An excellent statement of the several divisions of anthropology.
Christopher Hawkes, "Archeological Theory and Method: Some Suggestions from

the Old World," 434-449–Discusses the problems of archaeological inference in relation to anthropological and historical data.

FRIED, VOL. II.

Edward Burnett Tylor, "The Science of Culture" 1-18–A statement on the nature of culture by the man who did the most to establish the concept in anthropology.

John Gulick, "Urban Anthropology: Its Present and Future," 552-564–Explores the role of anthropology in the study of cities.

Gerald D. Berreman, "Is Anthropology Alive?" 845-857–Discusses the social responsibility of cultural anthropology.

William C. Sturtevant, "Anthropology as a Career," 858-867–Discusses preparation for an anthropological career and the kinds of positions taken by anthropologists.

GOLDSCHMIDT

Edward B. Tylor, "The Science of Culture," 21-23–A statement on the nature of culture by the man who did the most to establish the concept in anthropology.

Walter Goldschmidt, "Anthropology and the Modern World," 663-673–States the potential of anthropology in respect to the solution of modern problems.

HAMMOND

Fred Eggan, "Social Anthropology and the Method of Controlled Comparison," 465-480–Explores the contributions of British social anthropology, actual and potential, to the field of anthropology.

Walter Goldschmidt, "Anthropology and the Modern World," 480-488–States the potential of anthropology in respect to the solution of modern problems.

JENNINGS AND HOEBEL

Margaret Mead, "Anthropology and an Education for the Future," 3-5–Discusses the contribution anthropological study can make to a liberal education.

George Gaylord Simpson, "The World into which Darwin Led Us," 6-13–Analyzes the role of the idea of evolution in the study of human behavior.

Sherwood L. Washburn, "The New Physical Anthropology," 75-81–Reviews how physical anthropology has shifted from concern with description to the study of process.

Sol Tax, "The Uses of Anthropology," 417-421–Sets forth the practical implications of the field.

SHAPIRO

Griffin, James B., "The Study of Early Cultures," 22-48–Summarizes the problems and methods of prehistoric archaeology.

Chapter 2

DUNDES

Clyde Kluckhohn and William H. Kelley, "The Concept of Culture," 188-211–An exploration of the culture concept through a dramatized discussion among persons from a variety of professional fields.

FRIED, VOL. II.

Morris E. Opler, "The Human Being in Culture Theory, 19-42–Reviews and evaluates the notion that man is subordinate to the superorganic and advocates an appreciation of the importance of the individual.

Leslie A. White, "Man's Control over Civilization: An Anthropocentric Illusion," 43-61–A superorganicist argues that man can do nothing to influence his culture.

David Kaplan, "The Superorganic: Science or Metaphysics?" 62-81–Argues that it is methodologically sound to study culture as though it were an autonomous level of reality.

GOLDSCHMIDT

Alfred L. Kroeber, "Culture and the Levels of Knowledge," 39-51–Favorably evaluates the superorganic approach to the study of human behavior.

Leslie A. White, "Symbol, the Basis of Language and Culture," 70-77–Affirms the uniquely symbolic nature of human language and culture.

HAMMOND

Leslie A. White, "The Evolution of Culture," 406-426–A leading superorganicist and cultural evolutionist sets forth his view of the nature of culture, the influence of technology on other aspects of culture, and the nature of cultural change.

JENNINGS AND HOEBEL

Leslie A. White, "The Symbol: The Origin and Basis of Human Behavior," 287-293–Emphasizes the uniquely symbolic nature of linguistic and cultural behavior.

A. L. Kroeber, "The Superorganic," 293-317–The classic statement of the super-organic nature of cultural phenomena.

SHAPIRO

E. Adamson Hoebel, "The Nature of Culture," 168-181–A conventional review of the culture concept.

Chapter 3

DUNDES

Ruth Benedict, "The Science of Custom," 180-188–Reviews the anthropological concept of culture.

Regina G. Twala, "Beads as Regulating the Social Life of the Zulu and Swazi," 364-379–Reviews the cultural linkages of beads among the Zulu and Swazi of South Africa.

GOLDSCHMIDT

Ruth Benedict, "Central Elements in Kwakiutl Culture," 24-30–Indicates the main features of the culture of the Kwakiutl of British Columbia.

Robert S. Lynd, "Elements of the American Culture," 30-39–Sets forth some of the characteristic emphases of the American way of life.

Edward Sapir, "Culture, Genuine and Spurious," 51-61–A classic paper. Suggests that cultures differ in the degree of integrative or harmonious patterning.

Alexis de Tocqueville, "American Individualism in Historical Perspective," 261-263–Comments on the effects of individualism in American life.

Robert Redfield, "How Human Society Operates," 635-653–Reviews the aspects of human culture and their functions.

HAMMOND

Leslie A. White, "Tools, Techniques, and Energy," 26-43–Relates the level of cultural development to the amount of energy harnessed and this, in turn, to the technological level.

SHAPIRO

Robert Redfield, "How Human Society Operates," 345-368–Reviews the aspects of human culture and their functions.

Chapter 4

DUNDES

Alan Dundes, "The Number Three in American Culture," 401-424–Suggests that trichotomy is a pervading pattern of American culture and analyzes its influence in the academic disciplines.

Ruth Benedict, "Continuities and Discontinuities in Cultural Conditioning," 424-433–Throws into relief some rather highly implicit elements of the American educational process by comparing them with those of other cultures.

Horace Miner, "Body Ritual Among the Nacirema," 433-439–An ironical exploration of some magical implications of American behavior.

Chapter 5

DUNDES

Bronislaw Malinowski, "On the Methods and Aims of Ethnographic Fieldwork," 119-137–An internationally known anthropologist describes the principles of good field work, drawing on his experiences in the Trobriand Islands to illustrate them.

Alex Atkinson, "At Home With Aborigines," 150-155–A parody setting forth some of the problems of anthropological field work.

Dorothy Lee, "Codifications of Reality: Lineal and Nonlineal," 329-343–Shows how the biases acquired from one's cultural background may affect his observation of another culture.

FRIED, VOL. II

Charles O. Frake, "The Ethnographic Study of Cognitive Systems," 85-95–An advocate of the new ethnography sets forth the analysis of terminological systems as a way of studying society's cognitive world.

Harold C. Conklin, "Comment on 'The Ethnographic Study of Cognitive Systems,'" 96-101–Sets forth some of the factors to be kept in mind as better ethnographic techniques for the study of cognition are developed.

Marvin Harris, "'Emics,' 'Etics,' and the 'New Ethnography,'" 102-134–Discusses and evaluates two contrasting approaches to studying alien cultures.

Allan R. Holmberg, "Among the Siriono, Nomads of the Long Bow," 136-141–An anthropologist describes his difficulties in contacting and living with a jungle group of Bolivia.

Raymond Firth, "Studying and Restudying Tikopia," 142-157–An anthropologist tells of two widely spaced field trips to the South Pacific island of Tikopia.

JENNINGS AND HOEBEL

Cornelius Osgood, "Ethnological Field Techniques," 15-18–Describes an anthropologist's experiences with an unusually good Ingalik Indian informant.

Chapter 6

DUNDES

Katherine George, "A Study in Ethnocentrism," 22-35–Analyzes some ethnocentric interpretations of African cultures.

Charles Darwin, "The Tierra del Fuegians," 36-47–An ethnocentric view of the Tierra del Fuegians by Charles Darwin.

Frank Hives, "Ibo Punishments for Adultery," 48-51–An ethnocentric description of adultery punishments among the Ibo of Nigeria.

George Peter Murdock, "An Outline of Cultural Materials," 160-179–Lists cultural categories from the system of classification used by the Human Relations Area Files.

John M. Cooper, "The Cree Witiko Psychosis," 288-292–Describes a culturally defined mental illness among the Cree Indians.

Ralph Linton, "One Hundred Percent American," 383-385–Demonstrates the alien origin of many customs thought to be distinctively American.

Prajuab Tirabutana, "Recollections from a Siamese Girlhood," 454-464–Provides insights into Thai culture as well as Thai attitudes toward Western culture.

Burt W. Aginsky, "A Pomo's Soliloquy," 465-467–An example of ethnocentrism in a Pomo Indian.

David Livingstone, "Conversation on Rain-making," 472-477–Reconstruction of a typical debate between a missionary doctor and an African magician.

Laura Bohannan, "Shakespeare in the Bush," 477-486–Ethnocentric reactions to Hamlet by some Tiv of West Africa.

FRIED, VOL. II

Julian H. Steward, "The Concept and Method of Cultural Ecology," 159-171–A general statement of problems in the study of relationships between cultures and the natural habitat.

Karl August Wittfogel, "The Theory of Oriental Society," 179-198–Compares the cultural consequences of irrigation agriculture with those of rainfall agriculture.

Julian H. Steward, "Levels of Sociocultural Integration," 479-496–Advocates classification of cultures by level of internal organization as a basis for making cross-cultural generalizations.

Robert Redfield, "The Folk Society," 497-517–Defines and describes the folk society and compares it with urban societies. The classic statement of the folk-urban concept.

GOLDSCHMIDT

Horace Miner, "Magical Practices among the Nacirema," 520-526–An ironic exploration of some of the magical implications of American behavior.

George Peter Murdock, "Universal Aspects of Culture," 653-662–Explores the reasons for similarities among the world's cultures.

HAMMOND

Walter Goldschmidt, "The Biological Constant," 2-9–Examines the biological conditions for cultural behavior in man.

John W. Bennett and Melvin M. Tumin, "Some Cultural Imperatives," 9-21–Discusses six major functions which all cultures must perform if the group is to survive.

Julian H. Steward, "The Concept and Method of Cultural Ecology," 427-436–A general statement of problems in the study of the relationships between cultures and natural habitat.

JENNINGS AND HOEBEL

George P. Murdock, "Universals of Culture," 13-14–Sets forth the reasons for the similarities among human cultures.

John P. Gillin, "Custom and Range of Human Response," 81-88–Indicates the range and variety of cultural responses to the potential of muscular activity and to the hunger drive.

J. N. Spuhler, "Somatic Paths to Culture," 104-108–Discusses the biological factors which make human culture possible.

Ralph Linton, "One Hundred Percent American," 253-255–Demonstrates the alien origin of many customs thought to be distinctively American.

Alexander Goldenweiser, "Limited Possibilities in Culture," 319-321–States the principle of limited possibilities as an explanation for cross cultural similarities.

Morris Freilich, "The Natural Experiment, Ecology and Culture," 404-413–Explores the possibility of investigating anthropological problems where variables are in a state of natural control and illustrates the possibility using data from the British West Indies.

Chapter 7

DUNDES

Benjamin Lee Whorf, "Science and Linguistics," 318-329–One of the advocates of the notion that language affects perception states his position.

FRIED, VOL. I

Leslie A. White, "The Origin and Nature of Speech," 314-322–Stresses the uniquely symbolic nature of human communication.

Charles F. Hockett and Robert Ascher, "The Human Revolution," 323-346–Discusses the question of the origin of language within the context of total human evolution.

Joseph H. Greenberg, "The Science of Linguistics," 346-363–Surveys the contents, methods and trends of development in linguistics.

Paul M. Postal, "Underlying and Superficial Linguistic Structure," 364-383–Outlines some of the problems and implications of constructing a generative grammar.

Morris Swadesh, "Glottochronology," 384-403–The main originator of glottochronology comments on its use as a means of studying prehistoric relationships among languages.

Harry Hoijer, "The Sapir-Whorf Hypothesis," 404-417–An evaluation of the main assumptions of ethnolinguistics and a proposal for testing them.

Joseph H. Greenberg, "Language and Evolutionary Theory," 418-429–Explores some evolutionary principles relevant to the problem of the origin and development of languages.

FRIED, VOL. II

Ward H. Goodenough, "Componential Analysis," 315-330–An explanation of semantic analysis as a means of studying cultures, using Lapp kinship terms to illustrate.

GOLDSCHMIDT

Harry Hoijer, "The Nature of Language," 77-89–A general review of the problems of origin, antiquity, structure and change.

Clarence R. Carpenter, "Communication among the Lower Primates," 90-95–Describes the communication systems of apes and monkeys and notes their functions.

Dorothy Lee, "Language and Perception of the World," 95-103–Indicates how the grammar of the language of the Trobriand Islanders relates to their perceptions and behaviors.

Benjamin L. Whorf, "Language, Thought and Reality," 103-107–One of the advocates of the notion that language affects perception states his case.

Walton W. Hamilton and Douglas Adair, "Language, Time, and the Law," 108-113–Shows how a change in the meaning of a single word can affect human events.

HAMMOND

Joseph H. Greenberg, "Current Trends in Linguistics," 369-378–Reviews the subject matter, methods, and trends of development in linguistics.

Paul Henle, "Language, Thought, and Culture," 378-392–Careful evaluation of the hypothesis that language affects thought, perception and culture.

Morris Swadesh, "Lexico-statistics," 392-404–Discusses the various ways in which linguistic procedures can contribute to the study of prehistory.

JENNINGS AND HOEBEL

Dorothy Lee, "Being and Value in a Primitive Culture," 261-270–Indicates how the grammar of the language of the Trobriand Islanders relates to their perceptions and behaviors.

Charles E. Dibble, "The Aztec Writing System," 270-277–Employs illustrations in describing Aztec writing.

Clyde Kluckhohn and Dorothea Leighton, "By Their Speech Shall Ye Know Them," 278-284–Compares certain features of Navaho with English to illustrate how grammar relates to perception and behavior.

SHAPIRO

Harry Hoijer, "Language and Writing," 196-223–General review of nature of language and writing.

Chapter 8

GOLDSCHMIDT

Kenneth P. Oakley, "Skill as a Human Possession," 126-130–Compares human tool-making with that of animals.

Erland Nordenskiöld, "Primitive Man as Inventor," 130-137–A recital of some of the significant and ingenious technological originations of nonliterate peoples.

V. Gordon Childe, "The Accumulation of Technological Knowledge," 137-148–Reviews the cumulative effects of technological development on subsequent cultural advances as seen during prehistoric times.

Edward M. Weyer, Jr., "Eskimo Ingenuity," 148-151–Illustrates the practical knowledge of the Eskimo.

Lewis Mumford, "The Clock and Technological Development," 152-157–Indicates the many linkages of the clock in modern cultures.

HAMMOND

Julian H. Steward and Leslie C. Faron, "Nomadic Hunters and Gatherers: The Chono, Alacaluf, and Others," 43-53–Describes the cultural characteristics of several groups with simple subsistence technologies.

Robert F. Murphy, "The Mundurucú: Tropical Forest Cultivators," 53-62–Describes technological and economic characteristics of an Amazonian tribe.

JENNINGS AND HOEBEL

Kenneth P. Oakley, "The Making of Stone Implements," 159-162–Describes the techniques of working stone.

Alice Marriott, "The First Tipi," 162-167–Recounts a newly married Kiowa Indian woman's experience in making her first tipi.

SHAPIRO

Leslie Spier, "Inventions and Human Society," 224-246–Deals with clothing, structures, pottery, weaving, the plow, the wheel, power devices, and time reckoning.

Chapter 9

DUNDES

Raymond W. Firth, "Work and Wealth of Primitive Communities," 238-252–A general review of economic organization in nonliterate cultures.

FRIED, VOL. II

Andrew P. Vayda, "Economic Systems in Ecological Perspective: The Case of the Northwest Coast," 172-178–An interpretation of the potlatch system among the Indians of the Northwest Coast of North America.

Melville J. Herskovits, "Before the Machine," 201-214–Compares industrial with nonindustrial cultures.

Karl Polanyi, "Anthropology and Economic Theory," 215-238–Suggests reciprocity and redistribution as the integrative principles of nonliterate cultures and argues that modern economic theory is applicable only to cultures dominated by the market principle.

Scott Cook, "The Obsolete 'Anti-Market' Mentality: A Critique of the Substantive Approach to Economic Anthropology," 239-261–Attacks the notion that modern economic theory is applicable only to cultures dominated by the market principle.

GOLDSCHMIDT

Melville J. Herskovits, "The Work Group in Dahomey," 302-307–Describes the organization and activities of the cooperative work group among the Dahomeans of West Africa.

F. J. Roethlisberger and William J. Dickson, "The Work Group in a Modern Factory," 307-313–Describes the methods by which a factory work group controlled the behavior of its members.

HAMMOND

Fredrik Barth, "Herdsmen of Southwest Asia," 63-84–Emphasizes the adaptation of a culture to a pastoral nomadic mode of subsistence.

George Dalton, "Economic Theory and Primitive Society," 96-114–Compares Western and nonliterate economic systems and suggests that modern economic theory is not applicable to folk systems.

Stanley H. Udy, Jr., "Preindustrial Forms of Organized Work," 115-124–Compares the organization of production in industrial and nonindustrial cultures.

Walter C. Neale, "Reciprocity and Redistribution," 124-136–Explores the operation of two modes of exchange in village India.

Paul Bohannan, "The Impact of Money on an African Subsistence Economy," 136-144–Describes the modes of exchange among the Tiv of Nigeria before their economic system was modified by contact and traces the effects of the introduction of general purpose money.

JENNINGS AND HOEBEL

Max Gluckman, "How the Bemba Make Their Living," 167-174–Describes subsistence production in a Central African group and its linkages to the social organization.

George Dalton, "Primitive Money," 371-383–Explores the nature and functions of money in different kinds of economies.

Manning Nash, "The Organization of Economic Life," 384-389–A full review of the main features of peasant and nonliterate economic systems.

Paul Bohannan, "The Impact of Money on an African Subsistence Economy," 389-396–Describes the modes of exchange among the Tiv of Nigeria before their economic system was modified by contact and traces the effects of the introduction of general purpose money.

Robbins Burling, "Maximization Theories and the Study of Economic Anthropology," 396-402–Sets forth a definition of economic behavior and explores maximization as one implication of the definition.

SHAPIRO

Daryll Forde in collaboration with Mary Douglas, "Primitive Economics," 330-344–A general view.

Chapter 10

DUNDES

Edward B. Tylor, "On a Method of Investigating the Development of Institutions," 54-79–Classic exposition of some aspects of social organization by a famous anthropologist of the last century.

Melville J. Herskovits and Frances S. Herskovits, "Parents and Children," 214-218–Conversation with natives of Dutch Guiana illustrates the operation of classificatory kinship terms.

Alfred L. Kroeber, "Classificatory Systems of Relationship," 218-226–A classic statement of the terminological criteria by which relatives are classified.

Janheinz Jahn, "A Yoruba Market-Woman's Life," 226-237–Illustrates attitudes toward polygyny through a life history of a woman of the Yoruba of West Africa.

Max Gluckman, "The Reasonable Man in Barotse Law," 252-275–Describes and analyzes several legal cases among the Barotse of Rhodesian Africa.

David M. Schneider and George C. Homans, "Kinship Terminology and the American Kinship System," 385-401–Analyzes American kinship terms and explores their functions.

FRIED, VOL. II

Marshall Sahlins, "The Social Life of Monkeys, Apes, and Primitive Men," 263-276–Compares the social organization of nonhuman primates with the simplest human social systems.

Ralph Linton, "The Natural History of the Family," 277-295–Surveys the main principles of family organization and notes some consequences of the various kinds of family groupings.

George P. Murdock, "Family Stability in Non-European Cultures," 296-305–Introduces the Human Relations Area Files as a research instrument and compares divorce rates in the United States with those in forty non-European societies.

Alfred L. Kroeber, "Classificatory Systems of Relationship," 306-314–Sets forth and discusses the criteria by which the world's peoples distinguish terminologically among relatives.

Elman R. Service, "Kinship Terminology and Evolution," 331-349–Discusses the problem of relating kinship terminology to evolutionary levels of human culture.

Robert F. Murphy, "Social Distance and the Veil," 350-369–Suggests that the veil worn by men among the Tuareg of North Africa functions to symbolize social distance.

Paul Kirchoff, "The Principles of Clanship in Human Society," 370-381–Distinguishes and compares two kinds of kinship groupings with one another in terms of their nature and cultural consequences.

Harumi Befu and Leonard Plotnicov, "Types of Corporate Unilineal Descent Groups," 382-397–Sets forth a classification of unilineal descent groups and contrasts them structurally and in terms of the kinds of cultural activities they tend to be associated with.

William E. Mitchell, "Theoretical Problems in the Concept of Kindred," 398-408–Explores the nature of the bilateral grouping sometimes known as the kindred and suggests its presence in all kinds of cultures.

Marc J. Swartz, "Political Anthropology," 409-446–Summarizes current trends in the anthropological study of political mechanisms.

E. Adamson Hoebel, "Law and Anthropology," 447-461–Explores the nature and functions of law in folk and civilized cultures.

Morton H. Fried, "On the Evolution of Social Stratification and the State," 462-478–Offers a trial theory.

May Edel, "African Tribalism," 518-531–Explores the relationship of tribal political organization to the government of modern Uganda.

Conrad M. Arensberg, "American Communities," 532-551–Distinguishes among several types of American communities and explores their places in the total culture.

GOLDSCHMIDT

Ralph Linton, "The Essentials of Family Life," 227-233–Reviews the various kinds of family organization which man has devised.

Bronislaw Malinowski, "A Woman-centered Family System," 233-239–Explores family life in the Trobriand Islands, where each individual is regarded as descended from his mother and not from his father.

Martin Yang, "The Chinese Family Pattern," 239-246–Describes the extended family organization of a rural Chinese village and explores some of its implications.

John R. Seeley, R. Alexander Sim, Elizabeth W. Loosley, "The Suburban Family Pattern," 246-261–Describes the life of an upper middle class suburban family in modern North America.

Walter Goldschmidt, "Groups in Human Society," 271-280–Sets forth the universal characteristics of human groups and indicates their range and variety.

Charles Horton Cooley, "The Primary Group," 280-283–Describes the nature of the family and other groups important in the early socialization process.

Harvey W. Zorbaugh, "The Absence of Group Affiliations," 283-290–Discusses the effects of the absence of meaningful social ties among residents of a large American city.

Kalervo Oberg, "Group Solidarity among the Tlingit," 290-295–Shows the effectiveness of the Tlingit clan in commanding the loyalty of its members.

Edward A. Shils and Morris Janowitz, "Primary Group Loyalty in Military Action," 296-301–Shows the importance of small group loyalty to the fighting effectiveness of the German Army during World War II.

Ralph Linton, "The Nature of Status and Role," 323-332–Reviews the concepts of status and role.

Waldemar A. Nielson, "Situational Aspects of Social Role," 332-337–Describes a case in which a situational change deprived a leader of his effectiveness.

Lloyd A. Fallers, "Role Conflict of the African Chief," 337-346–Shows the predicament of the modern African chief, who is expected to fulfill one role by his European superordinates and another by his African subjects.

Alvin W. Gouldner, "Role Conflict among Union Leaders," 346-349–Describes the difficulties of the union leader, who is expected to play one kind of role by his labor colleagues and another by his business associates and his family.

John Fischer, "Status Symbols and Status Roles in America," 349-356–Illustrates changing symbols of prestige in American culture.

H. G. Barnett, "Status Symbols and Power Roles in New Guinea," 357-364–Illustrates changing prestige symbols in a New Guinea tribe.

Robert M. MacIver, "The Essentials of Law and Order," 373-381–Sets forth the idea that political systems are built on the model of the family.

Lewis Henry Morgan, "Iroquois Governance," 381-390–Describes the governmental system of the Iroquois league.

K. N. Llewellyn and E. Adamson Hoebel, "Emergence of Law on the Plains," 391-395–Outlines the governmental functions of the military societies of the Plains Cheyenne.

William Foote Whyte, "Leadership and Authority in Informal Groups," 395-408–Describes the leadership structure of a street corner gang in an American city.

Alexander Hamilton, "The Problem of Authority in Formulating the American Constitution," 408-415–A prominent founder of the American government discusses the problem of allocating authority.

HAMMOND

David G. Mandelbaum, "Social Groupings," 146-163–Distinguishes the major kinds of groups found among the world's peoples.

Lloyd A. Fallers and Marion J. Levy, Jr., "The Family: Some Comparative Considerations," 163-166–Attempts to define the family in terms of its functions and notes the various kinds of units which perform such functions.

E. Kathleen Gough, "The Nayars and the Definition of Marriage," 167-180–Describes the marriage system of the Nayar caste of Central Kerala, India and notes its implications for defining marriage.

Marshall D. Sahlins, "The Segmentary Lineage: An Organization of Predatory Expansion," 181-200–Describes the segmentary lineage systems of the Tiv and the Nuer of tribal Africa and notes their linkages.

Kenneth Little, "The Role of Voluntary Associations in West African Urbanization," 201-215–Explores the nature of West African voluntary associations and how they helped the people adjust to the effects of urban-industrial influences.

Gerald D. Berreman, "Caste in India and the United States," 215-222–Defines caste and notes the similarities of caste in India and race relations in the United States.

Lucy Mair, "Primitive Government," 224-231–Investigates the problem of defining government.

Lauriston Sharp, "People Without Politics: The Yir Yoront," 231-239–Sets forth the system of social order of the Yir Yoront of Australia and suggests that they lack political organization.

Kenneth E. Read, "Leadership and Consensus in a New Guinea Society," 239-249–Analyzes the characteristics of political leaders in the General Asaro Valley of New Guinea and concludes that certain personality characteristics are associated with the type of political system which prevails there.

Jan Vansina, "A Comparison of African Kingdoms," 249-258–Describes and compares the several kinds of highly centralized governments prevailing in much of Negro Africa.

E. Adamson Hoebel, "Ifugao Law," 258-274–Describes legal procedure among the Ifugao of interior Luzon in reference to the nature and functions of law.

Lloyd A. Fallers, "Nationalism in Uganda," 274-282–Explores the cultural history and traditional ideology of the Baganda as a basis for understanding Uganda nationalism.

George P. Murdock, "Changing Emphases in the Study of Social Structure,"

444-450–Reviews the trends toward the study of processes in social organizations and asks that the foundational contributions of the structural approach not be forgotten.

JENNINGS AND HOEBEL

Felix M. Keesing, "Bontok Social Organization," 189-200–Describes the household, village, marriage, the family, kinship terms, age and generation, sibling seniority, and rank among the Bontok of the northern Philippines.

A. M. Hocart, "Kinship Systems," 200-203–Illustrates the pitfalls of letting preconceived notions derived from Euroamerican culture govern our understanding of alien systems of kinship terminology.

Bronislaw Malinowski, "Brother-Sister Avoidance among the Trobriand Islanders," 203-205–Describes proscriptions of intimacies between brothers and sisters in a Melanesian group.

Crashing Thunder, "The Teachings of My Father," 205-210–Instructions of a Winnebago Indian father to his son.

Philip Drucker, "Rank, Wealth, and Kinship in Northwest Coast Society," 211-216–Description of relationships among kinship, rank, and wealth among the Indians of the Northwest coast of North America.

Clellan S. Ford, "The Role of a Fijian Chief," 216-221–Describes the responsibilities and behaviors of a Fijian chief.

Charles K. Meek, "Ibo Law," 221-231–Describes the legal concepts of a Nigerian tribe.

Max Gluckman, "Gossip and Scandal," 332-337–Examines the social and cultural functions of gossiping.

SHAPIRO

Claude Levi-Strauss, "The Family," 261-285–A general cross cultural and functional view.

David G. Mandelbaum, "Social Groupings," 286-309–A review of the major kinds of social groupings found among the world's cultures.

Chapter II

DUNDES

Clifford Geertz, "Ethos, World-View and the Analysis of Sacred Symbols," 301-315–Analyzes some Javanese values and their symbolization in the shadow-puppet play.

FRIED, VOL. II.

M. J. Ruel, "Religion and Society among the Kuria of East Africa," 636-650–Deals largely with the place of ritual in the religion and social organization of the Kuria, especially the passage rites.

Robin Horton, "Ritual Man in Africa," 651-673–Examines contrasting approaches to interpreting African religious ritual and proposes an alternative line of inquiry.

Eric R. Wolf, "The Virgin of Guadalupe: A Mexican National Symbol," 700-706–Indicates how the Guadalupe symbol links various aspects of Mexican culture, Indian and national.

HAMMOND

Clifford Geertz, "The Slametan, a Javanese Ritual," 308-311–Describes a Javanese ceremony and explores its meanings.

Nur Yalman, "The Ascetic Buddhist Monks of Ceylon," 312-321–Sets forth the organization, doctrine, ritual and functions of a Buddhist religious group.

JENNINGS AND HOEBEL

Alfred Metraux, "Tupinamba—War and Cannibalism," 177-180–Explores the functions of war and associated cannibalistic rites in a South American tribe.

Horace Miner, "Body Ritual among the Nacirema, 255-258–An ironic exploration of some of the ritual-magical implications of American behavior.

Chapter 12

DUNDES

James George Frazer, "The Roots of Magic," 79-119–A classic analysis of magic.

Franz Boas, "The Concept of Soul Among the Vandau," 137-143–Describes the soul concept in a tribe of Portuguese Southeast Africa.

Jaime de Angulo, "Singing For *Damaagomes* Among the Pit River Indians," 143-149–Describes how a field worker learned about guardian spirits among the Achomawi Indians of northern California.

Paul Fejos, "Magic, Witchcraft and Medical Theory in Primitive Cultures," 275-288–Reviews some major questions of medical anthropology in relation to native supernaturalism.

FRIED, VOL. II

Charles Wagley, "Tapirapé Shamanism," 617-635–Describes shamanism and its functions within the culture of a Brazilian jungle tribe.

GOLDSCHMIDT

Bronislaw Malinowski, "Primitive Man and His Religion," 483-487–Summarizes the various religious beliefs and practices of nonliterate cultures.

A. P. Elkin, "Religion of the Australian Aborigines," 488-493–Describes the main beliefs and rituals of the Australian aborigines.

Walter Goldschmidt, "Religious Participation and Social Position," 494-507–Shows how the denominations in an American community tend to differ in social class.

Clyde Kluckhohn and Dorothea Leighton, "The Religious World of the Navaho," 508-520–Summarizes Navaho religious beliefs and practices.

HAMMOND

Mischa Titiev, "A Fresh Approach to the Problem of Magic and Religion," 284-298–Evaluates the traditional distinction between magic and religion and proposes a superior dichotomy of religious practices.

Michael J. Harner, "Jívaro Souls," 299-308–Analyzes the beliefs of the Jívaro of Ecuador concerning souls and shows their linkages to warfare.

John Middleton, "Bewitching in Lugbara," 322-329–Describes witchcraft among the Lugbara of East Africa.

Donald C. Simmons, "Efik Divination, Ordeals, and Omens," 330-334–Describes some religious practices of a Nigerian group.

JENNINGS AND HOEBEL

George A. Pettitt, "The Vision Quest and the Guardian Spirit," 237-243–Relates the American Indian guardian spirit quest to education. Includes a description of the vision quest of the Thompson Indians of western Canada.

Robert F. Heizer, "The Hopi Snake Dance, Fact and Fancy," 243-245–Briefly describes the Hopi snake dance and considers how the rattlesnakes are handled without harm to the dancers.

Max Gluckman, "The Logic of African Science and Witchcraft," 246-253–Explores the meanings and functions of African witchcraft as a basis for showing that African logic is basically like that of Euroamerican logic.

SHAPIRO

R. Godfrey Lienhardt, "Religion," 310-329–Reviews the major forms of religious beliefs and practices.

Chapter 13

FRIED, VOL. II

Clyde Kluckhohn, "The Philosophy of the Navajo Indians," 674-699–Explores the basic assumptions of the Navaho world view.

GOLDSCHMIDT

Alfred L. Kroeber, "The Scientific Study of Values," 426-428–Advocates the study of values as a legitimate scientific inquiry.

Walter Goldschmidt, "The Comparative Study of Values," 428-433–Indicates the diversity of culturally defined values.

Edith Hamilton, "Athenian Values," 434-443–Presents upper class values in ancient Athens.

J. J. Maquet, "Ruanda Values," 443-450–Contrasts the values of the three social classes of the Ruanda of East Africa and indicates the principles underlying interclass relations.

Monica Wilson, "Nyakyusa Values," 450-458–Describes the values of an East African culture which emphasizes equality, friendliness, and sociability.

Robin M. Williams, Jr., "Generic American Values," 459-472–Surveys the main values of American culture.

Ralph Linton, "Universal Ethical Principles," 534-544–Indicates what the ethical systems of all cultures have in common.

Walter Goldschmidt, "The Ethical Prescriptions of Yurok Society," 544-553–Description of the ethical system of a California tribe, which is somewhat similar to the American system.

Richard B. Brandt, "Hopi Ethics," 554-556–The ethical system of the Hopi Indians.

Paul Radin, "Winnebago Ethical Attitudes," 556-560–Ethics of the Winnebago Indians.

Max Weber, "The Ethical Basis of Modern Capitalism," 560-572–A classic statement of the role played by Protestant values in the rise of modern capitalism.

David W. Maurer, "The Operation of Ethics in the Underworld," 572-577–Deals with the ethical attitudes of pickpockets.

HAMMOND

W. E. H. Stanner, "The Dreaming, an Australian World View," 288-298–Describes the world view of the Arunta tribe.

Chapter 14

DUNDES

Kenelm O. L. Burridge, "A Tangu Game," 315-318–Describes a game played by a New Guinea group.

Alan Merriam, "Purposes of Ethnomusicology: An Anthropological View," 343-352–A review of the contributions of ethnomusicology to the study of human behavior.

Ralph Linton, "Primitive Art," 352-364–General review of the nature and functions of art in nonliterate cultures.

"A Kipsigis Tale, Death and an Old Woman" 467-468–A short story from the culture of the Kipsigis of East Africa.

FRIED, VOL. II

Morton H. Levine, "Prehistoric Art and Ideology," 708-724–Compares the art of Upper Palaeolithic cultures with that of the Australian aborigines as a basis for inferences about the linkages between art and ideology.

James W. Fernandez, "Principles of Opposition and Vitality in Fang Aesthetics," 725-737–Analyzes contradictory elements in a culture of equatorial Africa, especially as manifested in wooden ancestor figures.

Paul Bohannan, "Artist and Critic in an African Society," 738-745–Suggests that studying art in its cultural context requires consideration of how the natives themselves evaluate the art of their fellows. Illustrated from the Tiv culture of West Africa.

Dennison Nash, "The Role of the Composer," 746-778–A cross-cultural comparison of the social roles of music composers.

Alan P. Merriam, "The Purposes of Ethnomusicology: An Anthropological View,"

779-788–A review of the contributions of ethnomusicology to the study of human behavior.

GOLDSCHMIDT

E. R. Leach, "Art in Its Social Context," 588-596–Defines art and shows its functions within a culture.

Ruth L. Bunzel, "The Primitive Artist at Work," 596-602–An exploration of the attitudes of Pueblo Indian potters toward their work.

Miguel Covarrubias, "Art and Artist in Bali," 602-607–Sets forth the content and functions of Balinese art.

Alan Lomax, "Cultural Context of Folk Songs," 607-619–Analyzes folk songs in relation to their cultural backgrounds.

R. Richard Wohl, "The Function of Myth in Modern Society," 619-626–Shows how the Horatio Alger stories were a function of certain aspects of American ideology.

Franz Boas, "The Esthetic Experience," 626-630–Stresses the universality of the aesthetic experience.

HAMMOND

E. R. Leach, "Art in Cultural Context," 344-350–Defines art and shows its functions within a culture.

David P. McAllester, "Enemy Way Music," 350-361–Shows how the music of the Enemy Way ceremony expresses Navaho cultural values.

Melville J. Herskovits, "The Study of African Oral Literature," 361-367–Reviews some of the problems and principles of studying African folklore.

Chapter 15

DUNDES

Ruth Benedict, "Child Rearing in Certain European Countries," 292-301–Explores the significance of swaddling in several European groups.

Don C. Talayesva, "Twins Twisted Into One," 440-448–A Hopi Indian tells of his infanthood.

FRIED, VOL. II

Ruth Benedict, "Anthropology and the Abnormal," 791-808–Explores how the personality traits thought normal in one society may be culturally defined as mental illness in another.

Anthony F. C. Wallace, "The Cultural Distribution of Personality Characteristics," 809-831–Explores the variation of personality characteristics within a culture and reviews and evaluates important concepts in ethnopsychology.

Margaret Mead, "The Implications of Culture Change for Personality Development," 832-844–Indicates the effects of acculturation on personality organization.

GOLDSCHMIDT

Clyde Kluckhohn, "The Educational Process," 179-187–Reviews the main features of education.

Laura Thompson and Alice Joseph, "The Education of the Hopi Child," 187-194–Describes the child training practices of the Hopi Indians.

James West, "Childhood Education in Rural America," 194-208–Describes the child training practices of an Ozark community.

Margaret Mead, "Cultural Transmission of Parental Anxiety," 209-215–Indicates how modes of parent-child interaction in the American middle class produce anxieties.

George A. Pettitt, "Educational Practices of the North American Indian," 215-218–Generalizes about the ways in which American Indian groups trained their children.

HAMMOND

A. Irving Hallowell, "Culture and Personality," 451-465–Reviews the principles underlying the study of the relationships between culture and personality.

Jennings and Hoebel

Jules Henry, "A Cross-cultural Outline of Education," 442-450–Sets forth a detailed outline for comparing the educational aspects of the world's cultures and indicates some of its implications.

Robert F. Spencer, "Some Relations of School and Family in American Culture," 451-459–Applies anthropological principles to understanding the role of the school in American culture.

Chapter 16

Dundes

Camara Laye, "A Malinké Remembers His Mother," 448-454–A highly Western-ized Malinke of West Africa tells of his childhood. Illustrates the effects of change on the individual.

William W. Stein, "The Case of the Hungry Calves," 487-499–An anthropologist reports on the failure of a suggested change due to lack of knowledge of the indigenous culture.

Anacleto Apodaca, "Corn and Custom: The Introduction of Hybrid Corn to Spanish American Farmers in New Mexico," 449-504–Explores the reasons for the rejection of hybrid corn.

Don Adams, "The Monkey and the Fish: Cultural Pitfalls of an Educational Adviser," 504-510–Analyzes the difficulties in bringing about educational changes in Korea.

Margaret Mead, "The Application of Anthropological Techniques to Cross-National Communication," 518-536–Analyzes the bases for misunderstanding between Americans and the British.

Fried, Vol. ii

Charles J. Erasmus, "An Anthropologist Looks at Technical Assistance," 565-582–Uses data from Latin America in evaluating technical assistance programs.

Alexander Lesser, "The Right Not to Assimilate: The Case of the American Indian," 583-593–Reviews the problems and the implications of assimilating the American Indian.

Laura Thompson, "Applied Anthropology and the Development of a Science of Man," 594-614–Examines the relationships between applied anthropology and anthropological science.

Goldschmidt

Lauriston Sharp, "Technology and Social Institutions: Australia," 157-166–Reviews the cultural repercussions of the introduction of steel axes to the Yir Yoront.

W. F. Cottrell, "Technology and Social Institutions: America," 166-169–Traces the disruptive effects on an American community of a change from steam to diesel trains.

Hammond

Lauriston Sharp, "Technological Innovation and Culture Change: An Australian Case," 84-94–Reviews the cultural repercussions of the introduction of steel axes to the Yir Yoront.

George E. Simpson and David F. Aberle, "Cultural Deprivation and Millenial Movements: A Discussion," 334-342–An analysis of a back-to-Africa cult in Jamaica in terms of relative deprivation theory.

Melville J. Herskovits, "For the Historical Approach in Anthropology: A Critical Case," 436-443–States the case for the study of cultural history as a basis for understanding the cultural present.

Jennings and Hoebel

Erik K. Reed, "Diffusionism and Darwinism," 317-319–Argues that extreme diffusionism is much more akin to biological evolution than unilinear cultural evolutionism is.

Fred Eggan, "Some Aspects of Culture Change in the Northern Philippines," 322-326—Suggests that change in a given culture can be understood better within the context of larger changes occurring in a region containing several groups in varying degrees of contact with civilization.

Ralph Linton, "The Social Consequences of a Change in Subsistence Economy," 327-331—Explores the cultural consequences of a shift from dry rice cultivation to wet rice production among the Tanala of Madagascar.

Edward M. Bruner, "Cultural Transmission and Cultural Change," 338-342—Sets forth a hypothesis to explain why some elements of culture are more resistant to change from contact than others. Utilizes data on the Mandan and Hidatsa Indians.

Lauriston Sharp, "Steel Axes for Stone Age Australians," 342-348—Reviews the cultural repercussions of the introduction of steel axes to the Yir Yoront.

A. Irving Hallowell, "The Backwash of the Frontier: The Impact of the Indian on American Culture," 348-361—Describes the continuing effects of American Indian cultures on the culture of the United States.

Kenneth E. Boulding, "Where Are We Going If Anywhere? A Look at Post-civilization," 362-368—Speculates as to the nature of the world culture of the future.

Eliot D. Chapple, "Anthropological Engineering: Its Use to Administrators," 422-426—Reviews the major ways in which anthropology has been applied to solve administrative problems.

H. G. Barnett, "Anthropology as an Applied Science," 426-430—Considers certain problems attending the application of anthropology to human affairs.

Lisa R. Peattie, "Interventionism and Applied Science in Anthropolgy," 430-436—Reviews the problem of whether or not or how applied anthropologists permit values to affect their work.

Allan R. Holmberg, "The Research and Development Approach to the Study of Change," 436-442—An anthropologist explores the implications of his unsought action role in changing the culture of a Peruvian Indian group.

Lyle Saunders, "Healing Ways," 459-468—Describes the folk medicine of the Spanish-speaking peoples of the Southwest United States and analyzes their reaction to scientific medicine.

SHAPIRO

Ruth Benedict (edited by Margaret Mead), "The Growth of Culture," 182-195—Briefly reviews the nature of cultural change.

Appendix C

CULTURAL ANTHROPOLOGY BOOKS

The following highly selected sample may prove useful to those who wish to consult full length works on cultural anthropology and its major specialties.

ANTHROPOLOGY

CLIFTON, JAMES A., ed., 1968. *Introduction to Cultural Anthropology.* A valuable collection of up-to-date statements on the specialties of cultural anthropology. Strongly emphasizes approaches and major problems of each.

HAYS, HOFFMAN R., 1958. *From Ape to Angel.* Summarizes the contributions of many anthropologists, both early and recent, to the development of the field.

HERSKOVITS, MELVILLE J., 1947. *Man and His Works.* Though too old to include the latest anthropological findings, one of the best comprehensive presentations of the field.

HOEBEL, E. ADAMSON, 1966. *Anthropology: The Study of Man.* 3rd edition. Both comprehensive and up-to-date.

HONIGMANN, JOHN J., 1959. *The World of Man.* Very comprehensive. Superior explication of many concepts.

KLUCKHOLN, CLYDE, 1949. *Mirror For Man.* A good popular summary of anthropology.

TAX, SOL, ed., 1964. *Horizons of Anthropology.* Young anthropologists indicate significant developments in the various specialties.

CULTURE

BENEDICT, RUTH, 1934. *Patterns of Culture.* A classic explication of the significance of cultural variability.

KROEBER, A. L. AND CLYDE KLUCKHOHN, 1952. *Culture: A Critical Review of Concepts and Definitions.* The most comprehensive examination of how anthropologists define and use the culture concept.

FIELD METHODS

BEATTIE, JOHN, 1965. *Understanding an African Kingdom.* An autobiographical account of Beattie's work among the Nyoro.

ROYAL ANTHROPOLOGICAL INSTITUTE, 1951. *Notes and Queries on Anthropology,* 6th edition. Detailed instructions as to what to look for in studying a culture, and suggestions as to method.

WILLIAMS, THOMAS RHYS, 1967. *Field Methods in the Study of Culture.* A systematic treatment of the major phases and problems of ethnographic work.

LANGUAGE AND CULTURE

GLEASON, H. A., JR., 1961. *An Introduction to Descriptive Linguistics,* rev. ed. Sound and well balanced, and not too difficult.

HALL, ROBERT A. JR., 1960. *Linguistics and Your Language,* 2nd revised edition. A brief, popular treatment of linguistics stressing a relativistic approach to language.

HYMES, DELL, ed., 1964. *Language in Culture and Society.* A comprehensive treatment of ethnolinguistic problems. A book of readings integrated by text written by author.

TECHNOLOGY

SAYCE, R. U., 1963. *Primitive Arts and Crafts.* A review of the technology of nonliterate groups.

SINGER, CHARLES and others, eds., 1954. *A History of Technology.* Volume I is of greatest relevance to nonliterate technology.

ECONOMIC ORGANIZATION

MELVILLE J. HERSKOVITS, 1952. *Economic Anthropology.* The best general work on economic anthropology.

POLANYI, KARL, CONRAD M. ARENSBERG AND HARRY W. PEARSON, eds. 1957. *Trade and Market in the Early Empires.* A book of readings which incorporates the contributions of the economist Karl Polanyi to the reorientation of the field of economic anthropology.

SOCIAL ORGANIZATION

BOHANNAN, PAUL, 1963. *Social Anthropology.* A perceptive statement of the range and variety of social arrangements.

HOEBEL, E. ADAMSON, 1954. *The Law of Primitive Man: A Study in Comparative Legal Dynamics.* Defines law and its functions and indicates the range and variety of nonliterate legal customs.

LOWIE, ROBERT H., 1948. *Social Organization.* A general treatment of social arrangements.

MAIR, LUCY, 1962. *Primitive Government*. A general treatment, but emphasizes Africa.

MURDOCK, GEORGE P., 1949. *Social Structure*. An important detailed analysis of kinship arrangements.

SCHAPERA, I., 1956. *Government and Politics in Tribal Societies*. Compares three African political systems. Good on nature of political organization.

SCHUSKY, ERNEST L., 1965. *Manual of Kinship Analysis*. Brief and effective explication of kinship arrangements.

RELIGION AND RITUAL

HOWELLS, WILLIAM W., 1948. *The Heathens*. An easy reading account of the range and variety of nonliterate religious beliefs and practices.

NORBECK, EDWARD, 1961. *Religion in Primitive Society*. A good general statement on religion as an aspect of culture.

IDEOLOGY

EDEL, MAY AND ABRAHAM EDEL, 1959. *Anthropology and Ethics*. Analyzes the range and variety of ethical principles and explores their implications.

FORDE, C. DARYLL, ed., 1954. *African Worlds: Studies in the Cosmological Ideas and Social Values of African Peoples*. Presents the world views of nine African groups.

RADIN, PAUL, 1955. *Primitive Man as Philosopher*, rev. ed. A sound presentation of the modes and content of nonliterate thought.

THE ARTS

ADAM, LEONHARD, 1949. *Primitive Art*. One of the best general introductions to the subject.

DUNDES, ALAN, 1965. *The Study of Folklore*. A book of readings.

MERRIAM, ALAN P., 1964. *The Anthropology of Music*. Explores the problems and findings of ethnomusicology. Emphasizes linkages between music and other aspects of culture.

NETTL, BRUNO, 1956. *Music in Primitive Culture*. Explores the range and variety of musical forms.

SMITH, MARIAN W., 1961. *The Artist in Tribal Society*. A symposium on the functions of art within culture.

THOMPSON, STITH, 1951. *The Folktale*. Explores the range and variety of folktales as well as approaches to their study.

THE LIFE CYCLE (INCLUDING CULTURE AND PERSONALITY)

BARNOUW, VICTOR, 1963. *Culture and Personality*. A general review of the field.

FORD, CLELLAN S., 1945. *A Comparative Study of Human Reproduction*. Explores the range and variety of customs concerning menstruation, coitus, conception, pregnancy, childbirth, and infanthood.

GOODY, JOHN R., 1962. *Death, Property and the Ancestors.* Deals with the range and variety of death customs and their functions within cultures.

CULTURAL DYNAMICS

BARNETT, H. G., 1953. *Innovation: The Basis of Cultural Change.* Detailed analysis of the processes by which cultures change.

FOSTER, GEORGE, 1962. *Traditional Cultures: And the Impact of Technological Change.* Explores barriers and stimulants to change as well as approaches to planned change.

HERSKOVITS, MELVILLE, 1964. *Cultural Dynamics.* A general review of the field.

SPICER, EDWARD H., 1952. *Human Problems in Technological Change.* Case studies on introduced change with analysis in terms of basic principles of change.

BIBLIOGRAPHY

ADAM, LEONHARD, 1947. "Virilocal and Uxorilocal," *American Anthropologist*, 49, No. 4, Part 1, 678.

ADAM, LEONHARD, 1949. *Primitive Art*, rev. Harmondsworth, Middlesex: Penguin Books.

BARNETT, H. G., 1953. *Innovation: The Basis of Cultural Change*. New York: McGraw-Hill Book Company.

BARNETT, H. G., 1960. *Being A Palauan*. New York: Holt, Rinehart and Winston.

BARNOUW, VICTOR, 1963. *Culture and Personality*. Homewood, Illinois: The Dorsey Press.

BASCOM, WILLIAM R., 1948. "Ponapean Prestige Economy," *Southwestern Journal of Anthropology*, 4, No. 2, 211-221.

BASCOM, WILLIAM R., 1955. "Urbanization Among the Yoruba," *American Journal of Sociology*, 60, No. 5, 446-454.

BEALS, ALAN R., 1962. *Gopalpur: A South Indian Village*. New York: Holt, Rinehart and Winston.

BEALS, RALPH L. AND HARRY HOIJER, 1965. *An Introduction to Anthropology*. New York: The Macmillan Company.

BEATTIE, JOHN, 1960. *Bunyoro: An African Kingdom*. New York: Holt, Rinehart and Winston.

BEATTIE, JOHN, 1965. *Understanding an African Kingdom*. New York: Holt, Rinehart and Winston.

BENEDICT, RUTH, 1934. *Patterns of Culture*. New York: Houghton Mifflin Company.

BENNETT, WENDELL C., AND R. M. ZINGG, 1935. *The Tarahumara, An Inland Tribe of Northern Mexico*. Chicago: University of Chicago Press.

BIDNEY, DAVID, 1953. *Theoretical Anthropology*. New York: Columbia University Press.

BIRKET-SMITH, KAJ AND FREDERICA DE LAGUNA, 1938. *The Eyak Indians of the Copper River Delta, Alaska*. København: Levin & Munksgaard.

BOAS, FRANZ, 1895. "The Social Organization and the Secret Societies of the Kwakiutl Indians," *Report of the U. S. National Museum for the Year Ending June 30, 1895*. 331-738.

BOAS, FRANZ, 1907. *The Eskimo of Baffin Land and Hudson Bay*. Bulletin of the American Museum of Natural History, No. 15. Washington: Government Printing Office.

BOAS, FRANZ, 1964. *The Central Eskimo.* Lincoln: University of Nebraska Press.

BOHANNAN, PAUL, 1963. *Social Anthropology.* New York: Holt, Rinehart and Winston.

BROCA, M. PAUL, 1872. "History of the Transactions of the Anthropological Society of Paris from 1865-1867," trans. by C. A. Alexander, in *Annual Report of the Board of Regents of the Smithsonian Institution, 1868.* 376-391.

BURLING, ROBBINS, 1962. "Maximization Theories and the Study of Economic Anthropology," *American Anthropologist,* 64, No. 4, 802-821.

CHANCE, NORMAN A., 1966. *The Eskimo of North Alaska.* New York: Holt, Rinehart and Winston.

CHAPPLE, ELIOT D. AND CARLETON S. COON, 1942. *Principles of Anthropology.* New York: Henry Holt and Company.

CHOMSKY, NOAM, 1957. *Syntactic Structures.* The Hague, The Netherlands: Mouton & Co.

CLIFTON, JAMES A., ed., 1968. *Introduction to Cultural Anthropology.* Boston: Houghton Mifflin Company.

CODERE, HELEN, 1950. *Fighting With Property.* American Ethnological Society, Monograph 18. Seattle: University of Washington Press.

COHEN, RONALD, 1967. *The Kanuri of Bornu.* New York: Holt, Rinehart and Winston.

CULWICK, A. T. AND G. M. CULWICK, 1935. *Ubena of the Rivers.* London: George Allen and Unwin.

DALTON, GEORGE, 1961. "Economic Theory and Primitive Society," *American Anthropologist,* 63, No. 1, 1-23.

DALTON, GEORGE, 1965. "Primitive Money," *American Anthropologist,* 67, No. 1, 44-65.

DANIEL, GLYN E., 1950. *A Hundred Years of Archaeology.* London: Gerald Duckworth and Co.

DOWNS, JAMES F., 1966. *The Two Worlds of the Washo.* New York: Holt, Rinehart and Winston.

DOZIER, EDWARD P., 1966. *Hano: A Tewa Indian Community in Arizona.* New York: Holt, Rinehart and Winston.

DOZIER, EDWARD P., 1967. *The Kalinga of Northern Luzon, Philippines.* New York: Holt, Rinehart and Winston.

DRIVER, HAROLD E., 1961. *Indians of North America.* Chicago: University of Chicago Press.

DRUCKER, PHILIP, 1965. *Cultures of the North Pacific Coast.* San Francisco: Chandler Publishing Co.

DUBOIS, CORA, 1944. *The People of Alor,* Vol. 1. Minneapolis: University of Minnesota Press.

DUBOIS, CORA, 1955. "The Dominant Value Profile of American Culture," *American Anthropologist,* 57, No. 6, Part 1, 1232-1239.

DUNDES, ALAN, 1965. *The Study of Folklore.* Englewood Cliffs, New Jersey: Prentice-Hall.

DUNDES, ALAN, ed., 1968. *Every Man His Way.* Englewood Cliffs, New Jersey: Prentice-Hall.

DUNN, STEPHEN P. AND ETHEL DUNN, 1967. *The Peasants of Central Russia.* New York: Holt, Rinehart and Winston.

EDEL, MAY AND ABRAHAM EDEL, 1959. *Anthropology and Ethics.* Springfield, Illinois: Charles C. Thomas, Publishers.

EGGAN, FRED, 1950. *Social Organization of the Western Pueblos.* Chicago: The University of Chicago Press.

EVANS-PRITCHARD, E. E., 1937. *Witchcraft, Oracles, and Magic Among the Azande.* London: Oxford University Press.

FIRTH, RAYMOND, 1951. *Elements of Social Organization.* London: Watts and Co.

FORD, CLELLAN S., 1945. *A Comparative Study of Human Reproduction.* Yale University Publications in Anthropology, No. 32. New Haven: Yale University Press.

FORDE, C. DARYLL, ed., 1954. *African Worlds: Studies in the Cosmological Ideas and Social Values of African Peoples.* London: Oxford University Press.

FORDE, C. DARYLL (in collaboration with Mary Douglas), 1956. "Primitive Economics," in *Man, Culture, and Society,* ed. Harry L. Shapiro. New York: Oxford University Press.

FORTES, M., R. W. STEEL AND P. ADY, 1947. "Ashanti Survey, 1945-46: An Experiment in Social Research," *The Geographical Journal,* 110, Nos. 4-6, 149-179.

FOSTER, GEORGE, 1162. *Traditional Cultures: And the Impact of Technological Change.* New York: Harper and Brothers, Publishers.

FOSTER, GEORGE, 1967. "Introduction: What is a Peasant?" in *Peasant Society: A Reader* by Jack M. Potter, May N. Diaz and George M. Foster, eds. Boston: Little, Brown and Company.

FRASER, THOMAS M., JR., 1966. *Fishermen of South Thailand: The Malay Villagers.* New York: Holt, Rinehart and Winston.

FRIED, MORTON H., ed., 1968. *Readings in Anthropology,* 2d ed., Vol. I. New York: Thomas Y. Crowell Company.

FRIED, MORTON H., ed., 1968. *Readings in Anthropology,* 2nd ed., Vol. II. New York: Thomas Y. Crowell Company.

FRIEDL, ERNESTINE, 1962. *Vasilika: A Village in Modern Greece.* New York: Holt, Rinehart and Winston.

GLEASON, H. A., JR., 1961. *An Introduction to Descriptive Linguistics,* rev. New York: Holt, Rinehart and Winston.

GLUCKMAN, MAX, 1955. *Custom and Conflict in Africa.* Glencoe, Illinois: Free Press.

GOLDSCHMIDT, WALTER, ed., 1960. *Exploring the Ways of Mankind.* New York: Holt, Rinehart and Winston.

GOODENOUGH, WARD H., 1955. "A Problem in Malayo-Polynesian Social Organization," *American Anthropologist,* 57, No. 1, Part 1, 71-83.

GOODY, JOHN R., 1962. *Death, Property and the Ancestors.* Stanford: Stanford University Press.

GORDON, C. WAYNE AND NICHOLAS BABCHUK, 1959. "A Typology of Voluntary Associations," *American Sociological Review,* 24, No. 1, 22-29.

GOUGH, KATHLEEN, 1961. "Nayar: Central Kerala," in *Matrilineal Kinship.* eds. David M. Schneider and Kathleen Gough. Berkeley and Los Angeles: University of California Press.

GREGORY, T. E., 1933. "Money," *Encyclopedia of the Social Sciences,* Vol. X. ed. Edwin R. A. Seligman. New York: The Macmillan Company.

HALL, ROBERT A., JR., 1960. *Linguistics and Your Language,* 2nd ed. Garden City, New York: Doubleday and Company.

HAMMOND, PETER B., ed., 1964, *Cultural and Social Anthropology: Selected Readings.* New York: The Macmillan Company.

HART, C. W. M., AND ARNOLD R. PILLING, 1960. *The Tiwi of North Australia.* New York: Holt, Rinehart and Winston.

HAYS, HOFFMAN R., 1958. *From Ape to Angel.* New York: Alfred A. Knopf.

HENRY, JULES, 1964. *Jungle People: A Kaingang Tribe of the Highlands of Brazil.* New York: Alfred A. Knopf and Random House.

HERSKOVITS, MELVILLE J., 1937. "African Gods and Catholic Saints in New World Negro Belief," *American Anthropologist.* 39, No. 4, Part 1, 635-643.

HERSKOVITS, MELVILLE J., 1938. *Dahomey, An Ancient West African Kingdom.* New York: J. J. Augustin.

HERSKOVITS, MELVILLE J., 1948. *Man and His Works.* New York: Alfred A. Knopf.

HERSKOVITS, MELVILLE J., 1952. *Economic Anthropology.* New York: Alfred A. Knopf.

HERSKOVITS, MELVILLE J. ,1964. *Cultural Dynamics.* New York: Alfred A. Knopf.

HITCHCOCK, JOHN T., 1966. *The Magars of Banyan Hill.* New York: Holt, Rinehart and Winston.

HOEBEL, E. ADAMSON, 1954. *The Law of Primitive Man.* Cambridge: Harvard University Press.

HOEBEL, E. ADAMSON, 1960. *The Cheyennes: Indians of the Great Plains.* New York: Holt, Rinehart and Winston.

HOEBEL, E. ADAMSON, 1966. *Anthropology: The Study of Man.* New York: The McGraw-Hill Book Company.

HOGBIN, IAN, 1964. *A Guadalcanal Society: The Kaoka Speakers.* New York: Holt, Rinehart and Winston.

HONIGMANN, JOHN J., 1959. *The World of Man.* New York: Harper and Brothers, Publishers.

HONIGMANN, JOHN J., 1963. *Understanding Culture.* New York: Harper and Row, Publishers.

HORIWITZ, MICHAEL M., 1967. *Morne-Paysan: Peasant Village in Martinique.* New York: Holt, Rinehart and Winston.

HOWELLS, WILLIAM W., 1948. *The Heathens.* Garden City, N. Y.: Doubleday and Company.

HYMES, DELL, 1962. "The Ethnography of Speaking," in *Anthropology and Human Behavior,* eds. Thomas Gladwin and William C. Sturtevant. Washington: Anthropological Society of Washington.

HYMES, DELL, ed., 1964. *Language in Culture and Society.* New York: Harper and Row, Publishers.

JENNINGS, JESSE D., AND E. ADAMSON HOEBEL, eds., 1966. *Readings in Anthropology,* 2nd edition. New York: McGraw-Hill Book Company.

JONES, WILLIAM, 1939. *Ethnography of the Fox Indians,* Bureau of American Ethnology, Bulletin 125. Washington: Government Printing Office.

KLUCKHOHN, CLYDE, 1948. "As An Anthropologist Views It," in *Sex Habits of American Men,* ed. Albert Deutsch. New York: Prentice-Hall.

KLUCKHOHN, CLYDE, 1949. *Mirror For Man.* New York: McGraw-Hill Book Company.

KRIGE, ÉILEEN JENSEN, 1936. *The Social Systems of the Zulus.* Pietermaritzburg: Shuter and Shooter.

KROEBER, ALFRED L., 1902. "The Arapaho," *Bulletin of the American Museum of Natural History,* 18, Parts 1 & 2, 1-129.

KROEBER, ALFRED L., 1917. "The Superorganic," *American Anthropologist,* 19, No. 2, 116-123.

KROEBER, ALFRED L., 1948. *Anthropology,* new ed. New York: Harcourt, Brace and Company.

KROEBER, ALFRED L., 1962. "California Basketry and the Pomo," in *The California Indians,* ed. R. F. Heizer and M. A. Whipple. Berkeley and Los Angeles: University of California Press.

KROEBER, ALFRED L. AND CLYDE KLUCKHOHN, 1952. *Culture: A Critical Review of Concepts and Definitions.* New York: Alfred A. Knopf and Random House.

KUPER, HILDA, 1963. *The Swazi: A South African Kingdom.* New York: Holt, Rinehart and Winston.

LAYARD, JOHN, 1942. *Stone Men of Malekula.* London: Chatto and Windus.

LEACH, E. R., 1954. "Primitive Time-Reckoning," in *A History of Technology,* Vol. I. eds. Charles Singer, E. J. Holmyard and A. R. Hall. London: Oxford University Press.

LEE, DOROTHY, 1949. "Being and Value in Primitive Culture," *Journal of Philosophy,* 46, No. 13, 401-415.

LESSA, WILLIAM A., 1966. *Ulithi: A Micronesian Design for Living.* New York: Holt, Rinehart and Winston.

LEVINE, ROBERT A. AND BARBARA B. LEVINE, 1966. *Nyansongo: A Gusii Community in Kenya.* New York: John Wiley and Sons.

LEVI-STRAUSS, CLAUDE, 1956. "The Family," in *Man, Culture, and Society,* ed. Harry L. Shapiro. New York: Oxford University Press.

LEWIS, OSCAR, 1951. *Life in a Mexican Village.* Urbana: University of Illinois Press.

LEWIS, OSCAR, 1960. *Tepoztlan: Village in Mexico.* New York: Holt, Rinehart and Winston.

LINTON, RALPH, 1936. *The Study of Man.* New York: Appleton-Century-Crofts.

LINTON, RALPH, 1939. "The Tanala of Madagascar," in *The Individual and His Society* by Abram Kardiner. New York: Columbia University Press.

LINTON, RALPH, 1943. "Nativistic Movements," *American Anthropologist*, 45, No. 2, 230-240.

LINTON, RALPH, 1952, "Universal Ethical Principles: An Anthropological View," in *Moral Principles of Action*, ed. Ruth Nanda Anshen. New York: Harper and Brothers, Publishers.

LINTON, RALPH, 1955. *The Tree of Culture.* New York: Alfred A. Knopf.

LITCHFIELD, EDWARD H., 1956. "Notes on a General Theory of Administration," *Administrative Science Quarterly*, 1, No. 1, 3-29.

LOWIE, ROBERT H., 1913. "Societies of the Crow, Hidatsa and Mandan Indians," *Anthropological Papers of the American Museum of Natural History*, 11, Part 3. 145-358.

LOWIE, ROBERT H., 1920. Primitive Society. New York: Boni and Liveright.

LOWIE, ROBERT H., 1935. *The Crow Indians.* New York: Rinehart and Company.

LOWIE, ROBERT H., 1940. *Introduction to Cultural Anthropology*, new ed. New York: Rinehart and Company.

LOWIE, ROBERT H., 1948. *Social Organization.* New York: Holt, Rinehart and Winston.

LOWIE, ROBERT H., 1954. *Indians of the Plains.* New York: McGraw-Hill Book Company.

MADSEN, WILLIAM, 1960. *The Virgin's Children.* Austin: University of Texas Press.

MADSEN, WILLIAM, 1964. *Mexican-Americans of South Texas.* New York: Holt, Rinehart and Winston.

MAIR, LUCY, 1962. *Primitive Government.* Harmondsworth, Middlesex: Penguin Books.

MALINOWSKI, BRONISLAW, 1935. *Coral Gardens and Their Magic*, Vol. 1. New York: American Book Company.

MALINOWSKI, BRONISLAW, 1937. *Sex and Repression in Savage Society.* New York: Harcourt, Brace and Company.

MALINOWSKI, BRONISLAW, 1944. *A Scientific Theory of Culture and Other Essays.* Chapel Hill: University of North Carolina Press.

MALINOWSKI, BRONISLAW, 1953. *Argonauts of the Western Pacific.* New York: E. P. Dutton and Co.

MANDELBAUM, DAVID G., 1940. "The Plains Cree," *Anthropological Papers of the American Museum of Natural History*, 37, Part 2. 155-316.

MANDELBAUM, DAVID G., 1956. "Social Groupings," in *Man, Culture, and Society*, ed. Harry L. Shapiro. New York: Oxford University Press.

MAQUET, J. J., 1954. "The Kingdom of Ruanda," in *African Worlds: Studies in the Cosmological Ideas and Social Values of African Peoples.* London: Oxford University Press.

MARETZKI, THOMAS W., AND HATSUMI MARETZKI, 1966. *Taira: An Okinawan Village.* New York: John Wiley and Sons.

MARRETT, R. R., 1912. *Anthropology.* New York: Henry Holt and Company.

MARSH, GORDON AND WILLIAM S. LAUGHLIN, 1956. "Human Anatomical Knowledge among the Aleutian Islanders," *Southwestern Journal of Anthropology*, 12, No. 1, 38-78.

MEAD, MARGARET, 1928. *Coming of Age in Samoa.* New York: William Morrow and Company.

MEAD, MARGARET, 1930. *Social Organization of Manua.* Bernice P. Bishop Museum, Bulletin 76. Honolulu: Bernice P. Bishop Museum.

MEAD, MARGARET, 1935. *Sex and Temperament in Three Primitive Societies.* New York: William Morrow and Company.

MEAD, MARGARET, 1961. "Anthropology Among the Sciences," *American Anthropologist*, 63, No. 3, 475-482.

MERRIAM, ALAN P., 1964. *The Anthropology of Music.* Evanston, Illinois: Northwestern University Press.

MIDDLETON, JOHN, 1965. *The Lugbara of Uganda.* New York: Holt, Rinehart and Winston.

MINTURN, LEIGH and JOHN T. HITCHCOCK, 1966. *The Rājpūts of Khalapur, India.* New York: John Wiley and Sons.

MURDOCK, GEORGE P., 1934. Our Primitive Contemporaries. New York: The Macmillan Company.

MURDOCK, GEORGE P., 1949. Social Structure. New York: The Macmillan Company.

NADEL, S. F., 1942. A Black Byzantium. London: Oxford University Press.

NETTL, BRUNO, 1956. Music in Primitive Culture. Cambridge: Harvard University Press.

NEWMAN, PHILIP L., 1965. Knowing the Gururumba. New York: Holt, Rinehart and Winston.

NIDA, EUGENE A., 1954. Customs and Cultures. New York: Harper and Brothers, Publishers.

NIDA, EUGENE A., 1957. Learning a Foreign Language, rev. New York: Friendship Press.

NORBECK, EDWARD, 1961. Religion in Primitive Society. New York: Harper and Brothers, Publishers.

NORBECK, EDWARD, 1965. Changing Japan. New York: Holt, Rinehart and Winston.

NYDEGGER, WILLIAM F. AND CORINNE NYDEGGER, 1966. Tarong: An Ilocos Barrio in the Philippines. New York: John Wiley and Sons.

OPLER, MORRIS EDWARD, 1945. "Themes as Dynamic Forces in Culture," American Journal of Sociology, 51, No. 3, 198-206.

OPLER, MORRIS EDWARD, 1946. "An Application of the Theory of Themes in Culture," Journal of the Washington Academy of Sciences, 36, No. 5, 136-166.

OSWALT, WENDELL H., 1966. This Land Was Theirs. New York: John Wiley and Sons.

PETRULLO, VINCENZO, 1939. The Yaruros of the Campanaro River, Venezuela. Anthropological Papers No. 11, Bureau of American Ethnology, Bulletin 123. Washington: Government Printing Office.

PIERCE, JOE E., 1964. Life in a Turkish Village. New York: Holt, Rinehart and Winston.

PITTMAN, DEAN, 1948. Practical Linguistics. Cleveland: Baptist Mid-Missions.

POLANYI, KARL, 1944. The Great Transformation. New York: Rinehart and Company.

POLANYI, KARL, 1966. Dahomey and the Slave Trade. American Ethnological Society, Monograph 42. Seattle: University of Washington Press.

POLANYI, KARL, CONRAD M. ARENSBERG, AND HARRY W. PEARSON, eds., 1957. Trade and Market in the Early Empires. Glencoe, Illinois: Free Press.

POSPISIL, LEOPOLD, 1963. The Kapauku Papuans of West New Guinea. New York: Holt, Rinehart and Winston.

PRINS, A. H. J., 1953. East African Age-Class Systems. Groningen, Djakarta: J. B. Wolters.

RADIN, PAUL, 1955. Primitive Man as Philosopher, rev. New York: Dover Publications.

REDFIELD, ROBERT, 1947. "The Folk Society," The American Journal of Sociology, 52, No. 4, 293-308.

REDFIELD, ROBERT AND ALFONSO VILLA ROJAS, 1962. Chan Kom: A Maya Village. Chicago: University of Chicago Press.

ROMNEY, KIMBALL AND ROMAINE ROMNEY, 1966. The Mixtecans of Juxtlahuaca, Mexico. New York: John Wiley and Sons.

ROWE, JOHN HOWLAND, 1946. "Inca Culture at the Time of the Spanish Conquest," in Handbook of South American Indians, Vol. 2, ed. Julian Steward, Bureau of American Ethnology, Bulletin 143. Washington: Government Printing Office.

ROYAL ANTHROPOLOGICAL INSTITUTE OF GREAT BRITAIN AND IRELAND, 1951. Notes and Queries on Anthropology, 6th ed. London: Routledge and Kegan Paul.

SAHLINS, MARSHALL D. AND ELMAN R. SERVICE, eds., 1960. Evolution and Culture. Ann Arbor: University of Michigan Press.

SAPIR, EDWARD, 1921. Language. New York: Harcourt, Brace, and Company.

SAYCE, R. U., 1963. Primitive Arts and Crafts. New York: Biblo and Tannen.

SCHAPERA, I., 1956. Government and Politics in Tribal Societies. London: C. A. Watts and Co.

SCHUSKY, ERNEST L., 1965. *Manual of Kinship Analysis*. New York: Holt, Rinehart and Winston.

SCHWEINFURTH, GEORG, 1874. *The Heart of Africa*, Vol. II. New York: Harper and Brothers, Publishers.

SERVICE, ELMAN R., 1958. *A Profile of Primitive Culture*. New York: Harper and Brothers, Publishers.

SHAPIRO, HARRY, ed. 1956. *Man, Culture, and Society*. New York: Oxford University Press.

SHARP, LAURISTON, 1952. "Steel Axes for Stone Age Australians," in *Human Problems in Technological Change*, ed. Edward H. Spicer. New York: Russell Sage Foundation.

SHARP, LAURISTON, 1958. "People Without Politics," in *Systems of Political Control and Bureaucracy*, ed. Verne F. Ray. Seattle: University of Washington Press.

SINGER, CHARLES, E. J. HOLMYARD AND A. R. HALL, eds., 1954. *A History of Technology*, Vol. I. London: Oxford University Press.

SMITH, MARIAN, 1961. *The Artist in Tribal Society*. New York: Free Press of Glencoe.

SMITH, RAYMOND T., 1956. *The Negro Family in British Guiana*. London: Routledge and Kegan Paul.

SPICER, EDWARD H., ed., 1952. *Human Problems in Technological Change*. New York: Russell Sage Foundation.

SPIER, LESLIE, 1928. "Havasupai Ethnography," *Anthropological Papers of the American Museum of Natural History*, 29, Part 3. 81-392.

SPOTT, ROBERT, AND A. L. KROEBER, 1943. "Yurok Narratives," *University of California Publications in American Archaeology*, 35, 143-256.

STEWARD, JULIAN H., 1937. "Linguistic Distributions and Political Groups of the Great Basin Shoshoneans," *American Anthropologist*, 39, No. 4, Part 1. 625-634.

STEWARD, JULIAN H., 1938. *Basin-Plateau Aboriginal Socio-political Groups*. Bureau of American Ethnology, Bulletin 120. Washington: Government Printing Office.

SWAN, JAMES G., 1870. "The Indians of Cape Flattery," *Smithsonian Contributions to Knowledge*, 16, 1-106.

SWIFT, LLOYD B., AND SELMAN AĞRALI, 1966. *Turkish: Basic Course Units 1-30*. Washington: U. S. Foreign Service Institute.

TAX SOL, ed., 1964. *Horizons in Anthropology*. Chicago: Aldine Publishing Company.

TAYLOR, ROBERT B., 1966. "Conservative Factors in the Changing Culture of a Zapotec Town," *Human Organization*, 25, No. 2, 116-121.

THOMAS, OWEN, 1962. "Generative Grammar: Toward Unification and Simplification," *The English Journal*, 51, No. 2, 94-99.

THOMPSON, STITH, 1946. *The Folktale*. New York: The Dryden Press.

TITIEV, MISCHA, 1963. *The Science of Man*, rev. New York: Holt, Rinehart and Winston.

TYLOR, EDWARD B., 1889. *Primitive Culture*, Vol. I. New York: Henry Holt and Company.

UCHENDU, VICTOR C., 1965. *The Igbo of Southeast Nigeria*. New York: Holt, Rinehart and Winston.

WALLACE, ANTHONY F. C., 1956. "Revitalization Movements: Some Theoretical Considerations for Their Comparative Study," *American Anthropologist*, 58, No. 2, 264-281.

WHORF, B. L., 1941. "The Relation of Habitual Thought and Behavior to Language," in *Language, Culture, and Personality*, eds. Leslie Spier, A. Irving Hallowell and Stanley S. Newman. Menasha, Wisconsin: Sapir Memorial Publication Fund.

WHORF, B. L., 1956. "Science and Linguistics," in *Language, Thought, and Reality*, ed. John B. Carroll. Cambridge: The M. I. T. Press.

WILLIAMS, THOMAS RHYS, 1965. *The Dusun: A North Borneo Society*. New York: Holt, Rinehart and Winston.

WILLIAMS, THOMAS RHYS, 1967. *Field Methods in the Study of Culture*. New York: Holt, Rinehart and Winston.

WILSON, GODFREY AND MONICA WILSON, 1945. *The Analysis of Social Change.* Cambridge: Cambridge University Press.

WILSON, MONICA, 1951. *Good Company: A Study of Nyakyusa Age-Villages.* New York: Oxford University Press.

WISSLER, CLARK, 1923. *Man and Culture.* New York: Thomas Y. Crowell Company.

YANG, M. K., 1966. *A Chinese Village: Taitou, Shantung Province.* New York: Columbia University Press.

INDEX